STUDIES IN IMPERIALISM

general editor John M. MacKenzie

When the 'Studies in Imperialism' series was founded more than twenty years ago, emphasis was laid upon the conviction that 'imperialism as a cultural phenomenon had as significant an effect on the dominant as on the subordinate societies'. With more than eighty books published, this remains the prime concern of the series. Cross-disciplinary work has indeed appeared covering the full spectrum of cultural phenomena, as well as examining aspects of gender and sex, frontiers and law, science and the environment, language and literature, migration and patriotic societies, and much else. Moreover, the series has always wished to present comparative work on European and American imperialism, and particularly welcomes the submission of books in these areas. The fascination with imperialism, in all its aspects, shows no sign of abating, and this series will continue to lead the way in encouraging the widest possible range of studies in the field. 'Studies in Imperialism' is fully organic in its development, always seeking to be at the cutting edge, responding to the latest interests of scholars and the needs of this ever-expanding area of scholarship.

European empires and the people

D1546044

MANCHESTER
1824

Manchester University Press

SELECTED TITLES AVAILABLE IN THE SERIES

European empires
and the people

POPULAR RESPONSES TO IMPERIALISM
IN FRANCE, BRITAIN, THE NETHERLANDS,
BELGIUM, GERMANY AND ITALY

John M. MacKenzie (Editor)
Giuseppe Finaldi
Bernhard Gissibl
Vincent Kuitenbrouwer
Berny Sèbe
Matthew Stanard

MANCHESTER UNIVERSITY PRESS
Manchester and New York

distributed exclusively in the USA by PALGRAVE

Published by MANCHESTER UNIVERSITY PRESS
OXFORD ROAD, MANCHESTER M13 9NR, UK
and ROOM 400, 175 FIFTH AVENUE, NEW YORK, NY 10010, USA
www.manchesteruniversitypress.co.uk

Distributed exclusively in the USA by
PALGRAVE MACMILLAN, 175 FIFTH AVENUE, NEW YORK, NY 10010, USA

Distributed exclusively in Canada by
UBC PRESS, UNIVERSITY OF BRITISH COLUMBIA,
2029 WEST MALL, VANCOUVER, BC, CANADA V6T 1Z2

British Library Cataloguing-in-Publication Data
A catalogue record for this book is available from the British Library

Library of Congress Cataloging-in-Publication Data applied for

ISBN   978 0 7190 7994 8   hardback
ISBN   978 0 7190 7995 5   paperback

First published 2011

The publisher has no responsibility for the persistence or accuracy of URLs for any external or third-party internet websites referred to in this book, and does not guaantee that any content on such websites is, or will remain, accurate or appropriate.

Typeset
by Helen Skelton, Brighton, UK
Printed in Great Britain
by TJ International Ltd, Padstow

CONTENTS

[v]

LIST OF ILLUSTRATIONS

CONTRIBUTORS

Giuseppe Finaldi is a lecturer in European History at the University of Western Australia. He has recently published *Mussolini and Italian Fascism* (2008) and *Italian National Identity in the Scramble for Africa: Italy's African Wars in the Era of Nation Building, 1870–1900* (2009). He is currently writing a history of Italian colonialism.

Bernhard Gissibl is a lecturer in Modern History at the University of Mannheim, Germany. He has just finished a PhD dissertation on 'The Nature of Colonialism: Hunting, Wildlife Conservation and the Politics of Game in the German Colonial Empire'. He has published several articles on the environmental history of German colonialism in East Africa and is currently co-editing a volume on the global transfer of the national park idea. Among his research interests are the political ecology of European imperialism, global history and environmental history.

Vincent Kuitenbrouwer is a lecturer at the Department of History of the University of Amsterdam and managing editor of the Dutch journal *Tijdschrift voor Geschiedenis*. He received his Master of Studies in imperial and commonwealth history at Oxford University (St Antony's College) and recently received his history doctorate at the University of Amsterdam. He has published on the metropolitan debate about the Scramble for Africa and is also interested in various aspects of Dutch imperial history.

John MacKenzie is Professor Emeritus of Imperial History at Lancaster University and is a Fellow of the Royal Society of Edinburgh. He has been editing the 'Studies in Imperialism' series of MUP for twenty-five years. His recent books include *Peoples, Nations and Cultures* (edited 2005), *The Scots in South Africa* (2007), and *Museums and Empire* (2009). He is currently editing *Scotland and the British Empire* for the Oxford University Press Companion Series to the History of the British Empire. He has long had a commitment to comparative approaches to imperial history.

Berny Sèbe is a lecturer in Colonial and Postcolonial Studies at the University of Birmingham (UK), with research interests in the cultural history of the French and British empires. He recently completed his doctoral thesis (DPhil, Oxon) on the making of British and French heroes who acted in Africa between 1870 and 1939, in which he analysed the ways in which explorers, missionaries, officers or administrators were promoted, manufactured and 'packaged' for home consumption in the context of the wave of 'New Imperialism'. He has published several articles and book chapters, is currently revising his thesis entitled 'Heroic imperialists' for publication and is co-editing a volume on the 'Echoes of Empire'.

Matthew G. Stanard is Assistant Professor in the Department of History at Berry College, where he teaches world history, modern European history, the history of Africa since 1800, as well as a course on imperialism, colonialism, and nationalism. He has published a number of essays on Belgian imperialism, expositions of empire, and colonial culture. His book on Belgian pro-empire propaganda is forthcoming from the University of Nebraska Press. Stanard received his PhD in modern European history from Indiana University-Bloomington where he worked with the late William B. Cohen.

INTRODUCTION BY JOHN MACKENZIE

This book is about the 'colonisation of consciousness'. This phrase was coined by the Comaroffs to describe the effects of missionary endeavour among the Tswana people in southern Africa,[1] but it is equally applicable to the domestic populations of the imperial powers, both actual and aspirant, in Europe. The European scramble for colonies in the nineteenth and early twentieth centuries was driven by rather more than the interests of an elite, aristocratic and bourgeois. It became something of a national endeavour necessarily embracing large segments of the peoples of several states, all of which were intent on securing a slice of the action in the almost unstoppable project of the Europeanisation of the globe. Some of these states had a track record, having been involved in imperial activity for several centuries. Others were new to the game and became convinced that involvement in these processes was a necessary test of their status as nations, of their participation in the modernist project of progress.

There is a second phrase that has been applied to the processes of imperial rule which is also ripe for conversion to the domestic setting. In a recent book, D.A. Low has laid out ways of characterising the different levels of imperialism. One of these is 'internalised imperialism', which he has defined as 'the permeation through the imperial power, and its colonial agents in particular, of an ingrained assurance of their inherent right to rule others'.[2] In this formulation, 'colonial agents' presumably refers to the politicians and civil servants, military forces and bureaucrats who actually conquered and ran the empire. But it is surely apparent that it can also apply to those who ran all those agencies without which that rule could not have taken place – the world-wide dimensions of post offices, for example, the various forms of necessary infrastructure in shipping, railways, public works, commercial houses, banks, the study of environmental resources and their exploitation, as well as civic organisations, educational bodies and much else. This was true in the case of all the empires considered here. We can also add medical institutions, particularly important in the Belgian Congo, for example. In other words 'colonial agents' must embrace all those involved in the operations of imperial states, both in the metropolis and in the colonies, in the latter case both those who considered themselves to be 'sojourners' or, in more modern parlance, 'expatriates', and those who migrated as settlers.

But 'internalised imperialism' and the metaphor of 'permeation' can surely go further yet. The development, existence and promotion of imperial rule must imply levels of consent, not least among the population of the dominant powers. It may be that such levels of consent, if in patchy and intermittent ways, were already in existence in the early centuries of European expansion, but by the second half of the nineteenth century, we have entered an era of more widespread availability of education – and hence of expanded levels of literacy – extensions of the franchise (initially mainly among males), and therefore of mass politics.[3] All of this was accompanied by a burgeoning print culture, as well as forces of the mass market accompanied by extensive advertising, more readily consumable forms of entertainment, and other means by which extensive permeation could be achieved. Even if the final effects may be disputed, many of the cultural agencies were in place which had the potential to create internalised imperialism. And such forces had the capacity to promote that colonisation of consciousness which ensured that the imperial project was a national endeavour. The contributors to this book will argue that, in variable ways, there was some degree of success. Indeed, it can be said that the very existence of critics of empire and often strident anti-imperial polemics help testify to the reality and pervasiveness of imperial ideas and their popular expression.

In any case, these various catalysts to permeation did not exist in some kind of vacuum. People lived in a real world of work or the lack of it. While it is readily acknowledged that the economics of empire is a highly fraught area of discussion, that the actual commercial significance of colonial possessions was often much less significant than the protagonists of empire hoped, still there were, in each European state, significant sectors which were dependent upon the imperial relationship. This was not necessarily a national connection since this could often involve the colonies of other powers. Finance houses, shipping firms, commercial companies, and industrial concerns utilising colonial products existed (in different forms and of varying significance) in each of the European countries examined in this book. In the twentieth century, this was also true of airlines. The development of SABENA, for example, was aided by its important connections with the Congo, and something of a new scramble for air routes took place.[4] Moreover, these identifiable connections could also apply to examples of 'informal imperialism', that is areas of the globe, such as Latin America and China, where there was no direct imperial rule, but where economic relationships were based on obvious disparities of power between the trading partners. In all of these ways, the influence of unequal power relations upon the working population of the metropolitan power could well be greater than the raw statistics of the economic relationship actually suggest.

The historian E.P. Thompson used his celebrated phrase 'the enormous condescension of posterity' for the various English craftspeople whom he was rescuing from obscurity.[5] But it is a phrase which equally well applies to the industrial and commercial workers who were caught up in webs of imperial and quasi-imperial economic relationships. Such workers were very much aware of the manner in which their employment – albeit jobs in which they were invariably exploited and inadequately paid – were dependent upon colonial connections. This would be true, for example, of those who laboured in jute and cotton mills or in munitions production across Europe, though such forms of employment were by no means universal. It would also be a central factor in the lives of various members of the armed forces in each European state that became caught up in the colonial enterprise. Such people were also aware – and advertisers constantly reminded them of the fact – that some key foodstuffs were similarly sourced, notably the tea or coffee that they drank, the sugar and chocolate that provided energy, the grain from North America (much of it, it is true, from the United States), the tinned and frozen meats (the latter from the 1880s) which reduced the price of these products (often to the detriment of metropolitan agriculture). To these we can add the palm-oil-based soap with which they washed, the rubber that rendered the bicycle a new and viable means of locomotion in the later nineteenth and twentieth centuries, the copper that was crucial to electricity and various industrial processes, all of them also important in employment. Finally, gold, diamonds and other minerals had produced both a surge in colonial economies, and therefore in migration, and also speculative ambitions that more might be found. Such opportunities for migration, for a privileged and free movement across the world, also heightened awareness of these global forces (the balance of American and colonial migration will be considered below). All of these connections, well understood and often taught in schools, were perfectly apparent to the people caught up in them. To suggest otherwise would indeed be condescending.

This leads to the necessary discussion of a definition of the terms contained in the title of this book and of the various key words which act as its constant refrain. Imperialism can be defined as the imposition of power by one people over another, arising from the inequalities in relations represented by technological advances in systems of communications, transportation and warfare, together establishing highly unequal means of trade and exchange. The word thus embraces all forces and activities involved in the establishment and maintenance of transcolonial empires and implies that the imperial authority can re-form aspects of the international system in its own image. It has long been recognised that these inequalities were as evident in 'informal' imperial relations (where direct rule was not necessarily established) as in 'formal' (where it was). Imperial powers therefore set out to reframe global geo-politics to their own advantage. They were, however, subject to debilitating rivalries and to the classic mix of success and failure. In this book, these fundamental ideas are taken further: they are applied to the generalised sense of European superiority which was unquestionably a characteristic of our period (from the nineteenth century to decolonisation in the twentieth). This awareness of inequalities in power relationships, underpinned by ideological notions such as those of race difference, climatic determinism, social Darwinism and alleged stages of progress, spawned that sense of 'inherent right to rule' or at least to dominate, even when it was not fully translated into formal empire. To deal with another supposed distinction, imperialism is often used to refer to the generalised forms of these phenomena, including the imposition of authority over indigenous peoples, while colonialism relates to the establishment of territories of settlement by whites. However, this distinction is often hard to sustain, not least because so many territories reflect aspects of both. Thus, the peoples of Europe, through a range of social classes from aristocracies through the bourgeoisie to many labouring sectors (perhaps only excepting those at the very poorest end of the spectrum), were well aware of this complex of ideologies, of the ways in which their lives were affected by new forms of globalisation. It became increasingly impossible for European populations, even many people in rural areas, to imagine that their lives were based only on local circumstances.

'European Empires and the People' could imply two different approaches. One might be a severely social imperial one, reflecting concerns with the social effects of the economic dimensions of imperialism, with politicians' overt objectives in attempting to create class conciliation through these phenomena, partly by the expedient of relieving internal tensions by releasing them into external adventure. This thesis has been particularly controversial in German history, but in some respects may work well in the Italian case. In a different form it has also been applied to Britain, where some significant politicians and writers, notably Joseph Chamberlain, set out to establish a direct connection between imperialism and working-class welfare. Another is the study of the cultural and propagandist characteristics of the national imperial thrust, of the manner in which so many cultural institutions (and these can include educational, publishing, entertainment, advertising and much else) adopted imperial content within their cultural frameworks. The centre of gravity of this book lies somewhat to the second of these, but the first is sufficiently important that it is also taken into account. Moreover, seeking consent for the imperial adventure is not necessarily equivalent to a conscious attempt to divert social stresses outwards. Such an interpretation implies a highly refined degree of instrumentality, one that was carefully calculated and promoted to very specific ends.

Politicians seldom plan with such precision and infrequently achieve such satisfactory outcomes. The reality is probably more messy. Imperialism was a dominant idea and force of the age. In some respects, forms of consent were achieved almost in spite of the ambitions of an elite (one that was in any case always fractured). Various forms of social imperialism and their cultural expressions were represented in this period and they are difficult to separate in pursuing the themes of the colonisation of consciousness and the permeation of empire through internal imperialism.

Nevertheless, these phrases do perhaps imply a hegemonic process, even perhaps elements of social control. But the studies in this book recognise that there is a third way between a social imperial and a purely cultural approach. It may be suggested that the permeation of these ideas was never a purely top-down phenomenon. As the imperial experience became increasingly mixed up with elements of the adventure tradition in popular culture, with aspects of spectacular theatre (and later film), with military excitements, with a sense of the privilege of superiority and (in some respects) economic well-being, it became a prime location of the interaction of social classes. There is ample evidence that people were voluntarily involved, that they negotiated their reactions to these world-wide events in cross-class ways. In some respects, the cultural colonisation was self-induced, the permeation was facilitated by popular acceptance rather than resistance. The very strength of these cultural expressions was based upon willing compliance rather than hegemonic control. The world had become an oyster for Europeans generally, a place that could be accessed for migration and jobs, for adventures and tourism, depending on the social class of the participants.

This sense of the increasing significance of the global for both ordinary lives and the national well-being was projected by a whole range of agencies, sometimes (but perhaps infrequently until the inter-war years of the twentieth century) governments themselves, but principally by imperial and geographical, armed forces and commercial pressure groups, by advertisers, by educationalists and by the Christian churches now involved in ambitions for extensive proselytisation. It should be stressed that all these efforts were directed at men, women and children, with a great deal of material beamed at a new generation both inside and outside the classroom. Individual politicians and, in some cases, political parties were also caught up in these efforts to persuade populations of the benefits of imperial rule. All of this activity was reflected not only in the political debates of the age, but also in entertainment forms, in major shows of the era such as exhibitions and international expositions, in the vastly expanded networks of the press and of publications of all sorts. It was also promoted by apparently new fascinations (though often with some historical precedents), such as the creation of national heroes, iconic figures regarded as touchstones of patriotic endeavour, by statuary, memorials, place-name commemorations, ceremonies, eulogistic speech-making and sermons. All these characteristics of the age charted the shift from a generalised sense of a supposedly divinely inspired, if often latent, impe-rial authority towards the creation of formal colonies as a rite of passage of the modern state. This book offers six case studies, embracing France, Britain, the Netherlands, Belgium, Germany and Italy, providing evidence for such developments right across (mainly Western) Europe. It seeks to establish that imperialism involved key articulations of power which operated in multiple directions, directed at indigenous peoples and settlers on the one hand and at members of the domestic population on the other. The exercise of power in each case was, of course, very different, but both were vital to the continuing existence and extension of the imperial project.

Such a comparative approach to imperialism has been relatively rare, but is surely necessary for its full understanding. The central characteris-tics and dimensions of trans-national imperialism have been considered in pioneering works such as William Woodruff's *Impact of Western Man: a Study of Europe's Role in the World Economy 1750–1850* (1966), D.K. Fieldhouse's *The Colonial Empires, A Comparative Survey from the Eighteenth Century* (also 1966) and E.J. Hobsbawm's *The Age of Empire 1875–1914* (1987). More recently, there have been efforts to explain and compare historical examples of the imperial process, as in H.L. Wesseling's *Imperialism and Colonialism* (1997), in John Darwin's strik-ingly extensive *After Tamerlane: the Global History of Empire* (2007), in Robert Aldrich's edited work *Age of Empires* (2007), offering parallel surveys of no fewer than thirteen empires and Dominic Lieven's rather more focused *Empire* (2002), which compares the Russian empire with various rivals. But this is the first time that any work has attempted to survey the centripetal or reflexive aspects of empire and imperialism upon domestic populations in Europe. By far the majority of works in the field have dealt with the British Empire, but there is now an extensive and very important historiography relating to each of the empires consid-ered here. Questions of the influence of colonialism and related phenomena to the social, cultural and political histories of the metropol-itan European states have often proved to be highly controversial. This work sets out to present key evidence for the notion that the European empires were not, and could not be, divorced from developments in the home states.

Empires and others

The imperial ambitions of the European powers in the nineteenth century have been depicted as a high point of the fiercely nationalistic, and ultimately self-destructive, character of the period. There is, perhaps, much truth in this, and it may be that it was these essentially chauvinistic phenomena which were projected to domestic populations. Yet we need to note that imperialism was never a purely national phenomenon, never merely a set of compartmentalised and competitive events. Among European powers it aroused cooperation as well as conflict. European empires (and their imitators such as the United States and Japan) learned from and copied each other. Nationals of one state worked in the empires of others: clear examples lie in forestry, in the pursuit of aspects of scientific and technical developments, in medicine and in developing institutions such as museums, botanical gardens and zoos. Thus, all were involved in environmental and scientific, technical and medical developments which were emblematic of the onward march of the very modernism that seemed to define and justify their dominant status. There were other key parallels in the imperial experience. If the European imperial powers 'othered each other' in multi-lateral and complex ways, their approach to indigenous others was essentially similar, equally domineering and often violently aggressive. All constructed race and related natural historical and climatic studies in similar ways. All became involved in new disciplines, such as geo-politics or microbiology, and recognised their significance in respect of both dominance of the globe and rivalries and dangers within those patterns of dominance. To these we may add colonial studies, with components like anthropology, which served in all empires to train colonial officials and others. Various institutes and university departments were founded (though not universally) to promote new disciplines, reflecting a degree of academic support for imperial power. Moreover, the gathering pace of the extension of imperial authority also produced striking parallels in the ways in which imperial ambitions were projected to the people. It also involved reacting to 'others' in a whole variety of ways.

For example, all were involved in the impulse towards the propagation of Christian missions. All the Protestant denominations and the Roman Catholic orders founded the manifold numbers of missionary societies which emerged in the nineteenth and twentieth centuries. These societies intriguingly brought together the need to re-evangelise populations at home as well as the imperative, as Christians interpreted it, to spread the word of a Christian God abroad. Sometimes this was done on a co-operative basis, with Protestant societies penetrating the colonies of Catholic states and vice versa. But often this was also seen in competitive ways, with something of a scramble for denominational territory taking place. Just as the Portuguese, to mention an empire not dealt with here, were never wholly reconciled to Protestant missionary activity in their African territories, so too did Leopold II pressurise Catholic orders to develop Congolese missions and help to restrict the influence of their Protestant counterparts. Such 'alien' influences might also be identified in border regions, where cross-border economic activity was accompanied by cultural and religious influences. Katanga, the southern Congolese province, would be a good example. Sometimes, however, imperial administrators, anxious about causing cultural and consequently political disturbance, forbade the presence of missionaries, as the British did in Northern Nigeria. Sometimes, Christian rivalries led to major conflicts, as in Uganda. But in all cases, the missionary societies had two major requirements: one was inevitably for recruits, both clerical and lay; another was for the raising of funds which would finance the many mission stations and churches founded throughout the world, both in formal and informal imperial regions.

Such demands for funds resulted in parallel developments in all the states dealt with in this book, namely the appearance of missionaries on leave acting as agents for their missions and speaking in the churches and halls of many cities, towns and villages in the metropolitan state. Many mission journals were founded to spread the news of missionary activities, often dressed up in heroic guise. Missionary exhibitions and meetings were held to create popular and attractive ways in which the message could be disseminated. Local newspapers highlighted the role of missionaries from specific localities in promoting the evangelisation of the globe. Moreover, missionaries were major disseminators of constructions of indigenous peoples, through visual images, through exhibitions, through the bringing of the 'natives' of empire to the metropolis for education and sometimes ordination. They were also significant promoters of the gendered relationships of the age. If these activities were sometimes 'liberal' in terms of some of the more rigid racial attitudes of the day, they nonetheless sought to emphasise difference, for it was only through alleged cultural and spiritual differences that the necessity of their work overseas could best be promoted and funded. The precise relationship between this missionary impulse and imperialism has been much debated,[6] but it cannot be denied that the Christian churches, clergymen and missionaries were major promoters of the world view, albeit in complex and nuanced ways, which underpinned the entire imperial thrust, even if they were at times highly critical of specific actions of the imperial powers. Sometimes such criticism was directed at rival powers, sometimes at their own metropolitan state or at imperial officials and their actions at the periphery.

Missionaries were also important, in all of these states, in creating an arena for women's involvement in imperialism. A rich historiography has developed around aspects of gender and imperialism, but less work has been done on the reactions of women 'at home'.[7] In each of the colonial empires, women arrived on frontiers and lived among indigenous peoples, initially as wives of missionaries, later as independent workers on mission stations, where they were active as nurses and teachers, and by the end of the century as doctors, gaining access to the women's world of 'native' peoples in ways that men never could. In the Catholic empires, nuns also became very significant on the missionary frontiers. In the case of the Belgian Congo, to use one example, this was the one area where women played a major role. By 1934, there were more female missionaries than male counterparts working in the colony.[8] The significance of this for the home populations is that women became just as effective, if not more so, as propagandists for missionary activities throughout the formal and informal imperial worlds. They too became speakers, writers, contributors to missionary magazines when home on leave. It may even be the case that such women helped to develop the role of women in the voluntary activities of the 'home' churches.[9] There was also a tendency to see women as having a special role as guardians of morality, of patriotism and of race purity.[10]

Missionaries certainly saw the 'others' of empire as being constituted by indigenous peoples, the supposedly racially distinct populations who were depicted as offering, in some respects, both the justification and the rationale for proselytisation and for aspects of imperial rule. Imperialism was based on the concept of difference, racial differences which were expressed through stages on an evolutionary ladder of progress, symbolised by notions of political and legal organisation, technological gaps and a range of social criteria including the presentation of the body, the treatment of women and cultural constructs of the environment.

But this process of 'othering' also involved both rival and friendly imperial powers. If empire was predicated on the 'othering' of black and brown peoples across the world, so was it also influenced by white 'others'. This happened in a whole range of different ways. The imperial urge was increasingly promoted by fear of the activities of dominant imperial others. In terms of available territory, the world was a finite place, some of which was largely out of bounds. If territory was finite, resources worth having were even more so. The activities of geologists, botanists, surveyors and agricultural theorists (sometimes before the imposition of imperial rule, but often only afterwards) tended to wind up a sense of a scramble for the distribution of available resources. In some cases, territories were acquired in speculative hope rather than in confident expectation. But in every case there was a sense that if one state did not move, then others might, to the detriment of future opportunities for settlement or exploitation. This operated in multilateral as well as bilateral ways. A good example is Leopold II's acquisition of the Congo, which virtually happened by default. Leopold neither 'conquered' the Congo in the conventional sense (only perhaps in the so-called 'pacification' moves after formal recognition of control) nor did he fight other European powers for it. What he did do was cleverly play off the mutual fears of Britain, France and Germany, none of which wished to see any of their rivals securing such a vast and potentially rich territory. Leopold was able to achieve his ends through the medium of international conferences and protestations of free trade. Of course it is also true that many politicians were highly sceptical of passions that often seemed more presumptuous than practical. Yet it is significant how far apparently reluctant politicians were sucked into the whole process. Two good examples would be Bismarck in Germany and both Gladstone and Salisbury in Britain. Yet they were caught up in the anxious 'othering' that was such a characteristic of the period.

For example, opinion formers in some of the empires considered here (notably Britain, Germany and Italy, less so in the case of France, Belgium and the Netherlands) were constantly exercised by the 'loss' of their fellow countrymen through migration to the United States. One of the several fantasies of empire was that such a drain of people could be averted by the foundation of colonies through which migrating citizens could be contained within an imperial Greater Britain, La Plus Grande France and the other notions of the extension of nationalities overseas. Apart from in the British and French cases, the first with its extensive colonies of settlement, the second with its North African and other possessions, this generally proved to be illusory. Migratory movements within the four other empires, the Dutch, Belgian, German and Italian, were relatively slight. But in the history of imperialism illusion has invariably been more influential than reality. *Ex post facto* arguments about the actual results of the establishment of imperial rule are irrelevant in the discussion of the imperial passions which often fuelled expansion. It is the inflated ambitions of empire and their projection to the citizens of European states that most need to be considered. Moreover, once the Americans, particularly after the Spanish-American War of 1898 and the growth of the US navy (under the influence of Alfred Thayer Mahan), began to flex their global muscles, they became increasingly significant as potential rivals to European authority. At the same time, the imperial baton was passing to the ambitiously modernising and imitative state, Japan, while the Russian authoritarian tsarist empire in both Europe and Asia was transformed into its even more rigidly controlled Soviet counterpart.

Within this context of the wider manifestation of imperial ambitions, the six empires considered here were involved in complex webs of 'othering' in relation to each other. The British and French were traditional rivals and, in some respects, continued to be so until the later nineteenth century.[11] The forging of the British state and national identity has been ascribed to the influence of the French as 'others' in the late eighteenth century and certainly the iconography of the British Empire in that century and the Napoleonic era was largely framed out of Anglo-French rivalries.[12] This was of course a two-way process, with the extended French empire of the nineteenth century being at least partially built upon the sense of resentment against the British. This contest may well have had a significant effect on the formation of a French national identity.[13] The Dutch also regarded the British as a prominent rival which had helped to diminish their own power, not least in the loss of Ceylon (Sri Lanka) and the Cape. This particular rivalry had a potent expression in the powerful sense of injustice which the Dutch brought to bear upon the South African Wars between the British and the Afrikaners, particularly the second and major war of 1899–1902. Nevertheless, the Dutch also had some regard for Britain, as a Protestant and democratic power. Apart from the case of South Africa – where Dutch residual influence was informal rather than formal – Dutch and British imperial interests were seldom in direct conflict after the Dutch losses of the Napoleonic wars.

Many opinion formers in Germany saw their national destiny as lying in the formation of a set of global power relations to rival those of Britain and France. The size of the newly unified German state in the heart of Europe, the scale and modernising speed of its economy, the significance of its rapid urbanisation and the advanced character of its infrastructures and its armed forces (not to mention the glories of its literary and musical cultures) all seemed to dictate the need for an enlarged position 'in the sun'. The British journalist and politician, Leopold Amery, during a stint as correspondent of *The Times* in Berlin, identified German jealousies of the British, whom they saw as sprawling across the world in wholly unjustifiable ways, as being one of the most significant energisers of Wilhelmine Germany.[14] For the Germans, there can be little doubt that the British, with whom Wilhelm II was well acquainted through his dynastic relations, were the primary 'other'. The British seemed over-privileged and over-endowed, particularly as they appeared to be a state already in decline, where political, social and above all economic institutions seemed to compare very poorly with their German equivalents. On the British side, anxiety about German expansiveness led to a sense of desperately attempting to maintain a more comforting status quo that had been established during the era of British dominance in the mid to late nineteenth century. In other respects, all this was also true of the Franco-German relationship. For Germany, France seemed to be a somewhat weak neighbour, yet France, despite its defeat in 1871, seemed more successful in colonial terms. Meanwhile France, having turned to empire at least partially as a substitute for the loss of Alsace and Lorraine, continued to fear German territorial ambitions in Europe.

On the other hand, Germany was itself to become one of the most threatening of all these 'others'. On a wider front, we should note the extensive manifestations of European anxieties. The translation of German ambitions into territorial acquisitions in the Pacific in the 1880s caused considerable political alarm in Australia and New Zealand, prompting the creation in those British territories of settlement of some of the defensive cultural institutions (such as propagandist and polemical geographical societies) which had already appeared in Europe.[15] Australian and New Zealand fear of the German 'other' would only be assuaged with their acquisition of League of Nations mandates in the Pacific after the Versailles settlement. Meanwhile, in Europe in the twentieth century, three of the imperial powers considered here saw their metropolitan states occupied, in whole or in part, by Germany. The Dutch, the Belgians and the French inevitably saw the German Empire, both in its European and in its attempted global guises, as the major threat to their existence. Each of them appealed to empire to supply the wherewithal to resist and, indeed, to provide evidence of the continuity of independent statehood, displaced from Europe into their Asian or African possessions. In each case, free Netherlands, free Belgium and free France were seen as residing within the colonial empires, a safe haven (in some instances) from European aggression. If Japan's imperial ambitions had already been expressed in the 1890s and the early years of the twentieth century, its yearning for empire was perhaps developed during the First World War, when its anti-German stance ensured that it capitalised on the removal of German influence from the Far East. In the 1930s and the Second World War, Japan, its Western allegiances now reversed, duly became a highly threatening imperial other, all the more terrifying because so patently based upon the governing concepts of the European empires, including their economic theories and their expressions of power through effective armed forces. Japan occupied parts of American, Chinese, French, Dutch and British empires, helping indeed to bring the whole imperial structure, at least in its essentially nineteenth-century form, crashing down by the thorough discrediting of these crude expressions of power. As is well known, the Japanese role in the decolonisation of the European empires was considerable.

In the case of the Italians, there was a highly complex process of reacting to others. The British constituted a major case of apparent success through the possession of empire. The French showed what could be done in creating zones of influence and power across the Mediterranean. The Germans reflected the manner in which a newly unified state apparently required colonies to assert in full its nationhood, its aspirations for economic advancement and its maintenance and development of a national project for both state and people. Italy was also influenced by its ancient history, by the immensity of the historic power of Rome, its centre now necessarily transformed into a modern imperial capital.[16] In many ways, Italy came to represent the manner in which European empires, and their projection to their own populations, emerged from anxieties about rivalries, from constant references to exemplars, from the contagion of illusions and fantasies (mainly rooted in ideas about economics and migrations) and from convictions about the supposed relationship of imperialism to full maturity as a modern state.

Empires and the people in the inter-war years of the twentieth century

What has been described as processes of rival and fearful 'othering' in some respects reached their peak in the years between the First and Second World Wars of the twentieth century. This was a period when it used to be said that imperialism had been thoroughly discredited. The First World War had demonstrated how destructive the national and imperial rivalries of the late nineteenth and early twentieth centuries could be. Nationalist bourgeoisies were beginning to emerge in Asia and, at an earlier stage of development, in Africa and the Caribbean. European powers were transparently weakened and their capacity to exert their authority was gravely reduced. While the older and bloated empires of the British and the French seemed to grow to their fullest extent with the adoption of the mandated former German and Ottoman territories in the Middle East and Africa (with the Italians securing some crumbs from the imperial table), this seemed to be merely a prelude to decline, symbolised by rapid developments in Egypt and, later, in Iraq. Civil disturbances, riots and strikes, became relatively endemic in colonial territories in the 1930s as the effects of the world economic crisis came to bear upon colonial territories. Moreover, intellectual and cultural forces also seemed to be moving against the imperial zeitgeist of the pre-war era.

Yet there is a great paradox in all of this. As the several chapters in this book demonstrate, those same inter-war years saw the stepping up of imperial propaganda throughout the surviving imperial powers. In Germany, the polemics of colonial revanchism were common. These were based on the concept of *Koloniale Schuldlüge* or colonial guilt lie, the allegedly false accusation that the Germans were incapable of civilised rule, and such revisionism aroused the fears of the other states. Thus, continuing rivalries were undoubtedly a part of this, but the main reason was the severe cyclical instabilities of the world economy. These were already apparent in the years immediately following the 1914–18 war and in some cases were reflected in the considerable growth in migration which occurred in this period. Given that the Americans were beginning to raise quota barriers, these migrant flows, particularly from Britain and Italy, to a much lesser extent France,[17] were now more closely focused on imperial possessions. But such flows were also unstable, for they were often followed by high levels of return migration, particularly as the effects of the 'Great Depression' set in during the years after 1929. That Depression also caused some imperial powers to retreat from policies of free trade, particularly as other European powers, notably Germany, had long been protectionist. The idea took hold that empires might offer individual national solutions to world recession. At any rate, the colonial economic nexus, the dream and the fantasy of the nineteenth century, could now, perhaps, be made to work. Metropolitan imperial powers might be saved by colonial resources, imperial exports and intra- rather than inter-empire commerce.

It is striking that these inter-war years saw the peak of the organisation of imperial exhibitions, notably in Britain, France and Belgium (with Germany as an active exhibitor), now more focused on empires than ever before. It is also the period when governments began to play a more extensive role in imperial propaganda, when modern cultural phenomena, such as poster campaigns and other forms of advertising, were directed towards the consumption of empire products. It was also an era when entertainment forms, now supplemented in a major way by the ever-burgeoning cinema, continued to be focused upon imperial subjects, as were publications, advertising and some educational activities. All of these are dealt with in the various chapters below. In the Italian case, this movement led to a fresh burst of imperial aggression in Abyssinia. This was domestically successful in the short term, but it stimulated the anxieties of other powers, even if they were exposed as willing to compromise and appease. The Italian invasion of this iconic African state also created a tremendous fillip for anti-imperial nationalists across the globe.

Yet, to return to an earlier theme, while the rivalries of European empires are easy to document, the fact is that all of these empires continued to indulge in imitation, transfers and borrowing. European imperial institutions and methodologies were often strikingly similar –

and were indeed transferred to Japan in the twentieth century. And all were ultimately based upon violence and on dominant racial and racist ideas. For the indigenous peoples of empire, there may have been some differences in the ways Europeans treated them, perhaps particularly at the level of 'native' elites, but ultimately it mattered little to the general population which power was in charge. So far as the peoples of Europe were concerned, the imperial experience helped, paradoxically, to further 'Eurocentrism', to instal the naturalisation of Europeanness as 'whiteness', a concept highly significant in recent cultural, social and political controversies relating to the immigration of black and Asian peoples. And this despite the fact that European imperial powers had used troops from their empires in their great wars (which through imperialism became global) of the twentieth century. Domestic populations were often less aware of this, for such forces received little publicity. There are contemporary dimensions to the theme of European Empires and the People which should never be forgotten.

Rationale and acknowledgments

For reasons of space, it has been necessary to omit Spain and Portugal from this book. In many respects this is regrettable, and it is to be hoped that a future volume will repair this loss. There is, however, some case for it. It has generally been thought that the Spanish Empire was in steep decline during the period covered here. The decolonisation of Latin America had effectively taken place in the 1820s (even if this had led to the imposition of informal imperial structures). While it is true that the survival of major parts of the Spanish Empire in the nineteenth century was remarkable and carried that long-standing imperial power into the modern world, still by the end of that century, particularly after the war with the USA, Spanish colonies, with a few small exceptions, had disappeared. The Portuguese Empire was also an older empire dating from the earliest years of European expansionism, but it did experience something of a territorial, political and cultural renaissance in the later nineteenth century. This was partly in reaction to the turbulence set up by the scramble for Africa by other powers. After the establishment of the Portuguese Republic in 1910, it was widely thought that Portugal would lose the stomach for empire, with the British and the Germans working on agreements for the carving up of the Portuguese territories, particularly in southern Africa. But the new quasi-fascist state from the 1920s conflated imperial rule with Portuguese history and national endeavour. Portugal was portrayed as an African as well as a European territory. The African colonies were to be treated as part of metropolitan Portugal. In modern times, work has been done on aspects of Portuguese African exploration, partially involving resentment at inflated British claims, and also on the winding up of Portuguese public opinion in relation to the aggression of Britain in the scramble for Africa. Still research on the projection of empire to the Portuguese people more generally remains to be accomplished – or at least to be disseminated more widely. Hence, Portugal was also, regrettably, left out of this study.

Portugal would also be exceptionally important in any discussion of the end of empires, and that reflects another omission, namely that the contributions to this book do not span the decolonisation period. Most chapters briefly comment on the (formal at least) decolonising of these empires, but, again for reasons of space, there is no attempt to deal with the post-colonial period, with issues of neo-colonialism, or with post-colonial theory. The literature relating to these is now immense and would require a separate book. There is no intention to convey that these historical and scholarly phenomena are in any way less important than the cultural and imperial issues, together with the associated and extensive historiographical material, covered here.

As the title page implies, this is a co-authored book rather than a collection of essays. All the authors have made significant input into each other's chapters and this introduction has been, in some respects, a collaborative effort. To facilitate this, five of them (the exception was Giuseppe Finaldi who was unable to overcome the 'tyranny of distance' between Australia and Europe to be able to attend) met in a symposium at the editor's home in Perthshire, Scotland. In the agreeable surroundings of Old Bank House and its gardens in Alyth, four lively, hard-hitting and immensely stimulating seminars took place in early July 2009. Discussions were continued through our mealtimes. Each of the authors wishes to offer their profound thanks to all the others for their valuable insights. All would also wish to express their gratitude to Nigel Dalziel for handling so much of the social side of this event. It was also enlivened by the presence at dinner of Irene Robertson and Georgina Whitmore. Moreover, we are grateful to Emma Brennan, Kim Walker and the team at Manchester University Press for recognising at an early stage the significance of this book and for doing so much to bring it to publication. The supportive, but also critically constructive, reports of two anonymous readers were greatly appreciated. The editor would like to thank his physician, Dr. Graham Johnston, the surgeon Michael Lavelle Jones, the oncologist Professor Munro, the pharmacist Kay Duff and all the medical services at Ninewells Hospital, Dundee, for bringing him through a recent serious illness. He would also express his pride in the fact that this book brings the number of titles in the 'Studies in Imperialism' series close to ninety, a very considerable tribute to a large number of authors and editors who have contributed works, as well as to Manchester University Press. Individual acknowledgments appear at the end of each chapter.

Notes

1 J. and J. Comaroff, *Of Revelation and Revolution: Christianity, Colonialism and Consciousness in South Africa*, 2 vols (Chicago 1991, 1997).
2 D.A. Low, *Fabrication of Empire* (Cambridge 2009), p. 22.
3 Compulsory education acts were passed in Britain in 1870 and 1872 and the franchise was extended in 1884, 1918 and 1928 (universal male and female over 21 from the latter date); in unified Germany, the male franchise was extended in 1871 while literacy rates were already high because the provision of primary education had been widespread throughout the German states; in France primary education was provided under acts of 1833 and 1881 and universal male suffrage dated from 1848; in Belgium, the key dates were 1879 (education) and 1894 (male franchise); in the Netherlands the equivalent dates are 1900 (education), 1917 (male franchise) and 1919 (female); in unified Italy, three-year compulsory education (ages 6–9) dated from 1877, rising to 11 a few years later and to 14 in 1922–23; from 1882, the franchise was enjoyed by 10–20% of males over 21 (with tax preconditions), was extended to literate males over 21 in 1913 and to non-literates and army veterans over 30, with universal male suffrage in 1919. After the fascist era, male and female suffrage was introduced in 1945.
4 Gordon Pirie, *Air Empire* (Manchester 2009).
5 E.P. Thompson, *The Making of the English Working Class* (Harmondsworth 1968), p. 13.
6 Compare Brian Stanley, *The Bible and the Flag* (Leicester 1990) and Andrew Porter, *Religion Versus Empire?* (Manchester 2004).
7 See, for example, Clare Midgley (ed.), *Gender and Imperialism* (Manchester 1998); Nupur Chaudhuri amd Margaret Strobel (eds), *Western Women and Imperialism: Complicity and Resistance* (Bloomington IN 1992); Anne McClintock, *Imperial Leather: Race, Gender, Sexuality in the Colonial Contest* (London 1995); Philippa Levine (ed.), *Gender and Empire* (Oxford 2004); Philippa Levine and Susan R. Grayzel (eds), *Gender, Labour, War and Empire* (Basingstoke 2009).
8 Jean Pirotte, 'Les Armes d'une mobilisation. La Littérature missionaire de la fin du XIXe siècle à 1940' in Marc Quaghebeur and Emile Van Balberghe (eds), *Papier blanc, encre noire: cent anes du culture francophone en Anfrique Centrale* (Brussels 1992), p. 73., There were also many women working as teachers, nannies and nurses in the Netherlands Indies by the twentieth century.
9 For the example of Scotland, see Lesley A. Orr Macdonald, *A Unique and Glorious Mission: Women and Presbyterianism in Scotland 1830–1930* (Edinburgh 2000).
10 For pioneering work in this field, see Anna Davin, 'Imperialism and motherhood', *History Workshop Journal*, 5 (1978), pp. 9–65.
11 This was symbolised by what may be described as competitive hero-worship: the French elevation of Colonel Marchand into an imperial hero matched the British response to Kitchener after their confrontation at Fashoda on the upper Nile in 1898. B. Sebe, 'Celebrating British and French Imperialism: The Making of Colonial Heroes Acting in Africa, 1870–1939', D.Phil thesis, University of Oxford, 2007.
12 Linda Colley, *Britons: Forging the Nation 1707–1837* (London 1996).
13 Robert and Isabelle Tombs, *That Sweet Enemy: the French and the British from the Sun King to the Present* (New York 2007).
14 L.S. Amery, *The German Colonial Claim* (London 1939), pp. 9–11 and John M. MacKenzie, '"Mutual goodwill and admiration" or "jealous ill-will"?' in Dominik Geppert and Robert Gerwarth (eds), *Wilhelmine Germany and Edwardian Britain* (Oxford 2008), pp. 91–114.
15 Morag Bell, Robin Butlin and Michael Hefernan (eds), *Geography and Imperialism*

1820–1940 (Manchester 1995) contains references to these Australian and New Zealand developments, *passim*.

16 David Atkinson, Dennis Cosgrove and Anna Notaro, 'Empire in modern Rome: shaping and remembering an imperial city, 1870–1911', in Felix Driver and David Gilbert (eds), *Imperial Cities* (Manchester 1999), pp. 40–63, and other chapters in the same volume.

17 France experienced a smaller population growth than other European countries and her North African territories were able to absorb any emigrant outflow.

CHAPTER 1

Exalting imperial grandeur: the French Empire and its metropolitan public

Berny Sèbe

The long shadow of the lost 'first' empire

By 1919, the French had assembled one of the largest empires in the world, second only to the British. It encompassed vast swathes of territories in North, West and Central Africa (all interconnected), as well as the Indochinese peninsula and large tracts of Oceania, conquered in their majority between 1830 and 1912. Following the Treaty of Versailles, the lion's share of the formerly German colonies of Cameroon and Togoland, as well as Lebanon and Syria, previously under Ottoman control, joined France's possessions to cover 12.3 million square kilometres in total, around twenty-three times the size of the metropole. In the 1930s, this country of just over forty million people ruled over 110 million inhabitants. Such successful expansion for a nation which feared above all the spectre of decline following the Franco-Prussian war, may suggest that the empire would have been regarded with particular fondness by the French public. In reality, French popular reactions to overseas action have been more complicated than the retrospective success of colonial policy might lead us to believe.

Nineteenth-century imperial expansion, which started in 1830 and really took off in the late nineteenth century, suffered from the long shadow cast by the loss of the 'first' French Empire in the Americas following the Seven Years War (1756–63) and the Treaty of Paris. It was also hampered by the political instability of the country, which saw no fewer than seven different régimes between 1830 and 1962 and remained prone to governmental instability during most of the period. Unable to pursue long-term policies, the country seemed ill-equipped to regain its leading colonial role. The scarce outbursts of popular enthusiasm for the colonies were often linked to other factors, and imperial questions rarely featured prominently in the metropolitan political life. Arguably, the empire did not play a key role for the French economy,[1] contrary to what happened in Britain.

Yet, at the same time, other clues tend to indicate that awareness of the wider world, which was both a prerequisite to and a consequence of imperial expansion, had been a feature of French cultural life since at least the seventeenth century. Narratives of exploration in Oceania by Bougainville and La Pérouse were much publicised in pre-revolutionary France. Not only did books such as *Le Voyage de Bougainville* flatter nationalist feelings, but they also 'stimulated the popular imagination, much the way news of the moon shots would do two hundred years later'.[2]

Is this enough to conclude that the metropolitan public was predisposed to take an interest in France's imperial destiny, if it ever did so? First, real or fantasised narratives of discovery could lend themselves to a variety of readings, sometimes even anti-imperial.[3] Second, the variety of phenomena to take account of in order to answer this question has meant that the impact and even the existence of a form of 'popular imperialism' in France has been a long-running matter of academic debate since the publication of Raoul Girardet's seminal study of the 'colonial idea in France from 1871 to 1962'.[4] Looking at the composition and impact of the 'Colonial Party',[5] historians long argued that the French 'colonial party' enjoyed limited popular outreach and failed to turn France into a colonial country.[6] Inspired by the directions of research pioneered by John MacKenzie, specialists of the French Empire started to combine methodologies from social and cultural history[7] to revise our perception of French popular imperialism. While in the mid-1980s Pierre Nora still limited in his *Lieux de mémoire* (*Realms of Memory*) France's colonial past to the 1931 Vincennes colonial exhibition, interest in the cultural expression of French imperialism at home had become clearly visible less than a decade later.[8] By the early 2000s, the concept of 'French popular imperialism' no longer appeared as an oxymoron[9] and it was even tested on the *longue durée*[10] or in a specific period of French history.[11] In the meantime, extensive edited volumes of old literary or other artistic works about France's colonies catered to an ever-growing public.[12]

Contrary to most of the other countries dealt with in this book (apart from Great Britain), French popular imperialism has attracted much scholarly attention in the last two decades. The primary purpose of this chapter will be to offer a broad historiographical overview of this rich field, as part of our analysis of 'European Empires and the People', whilst also suggesting some new interpretations. It will summarise works undertaken about a variety of aspects of French culture such as the press, artistic production (literature, paintings, music, plays, cinema, photography), trade (advertisements, colonial committees), religion, political activities (electoral strategies, role of the Colonial Group, propaganda), scientific research (especially medical and social sciences and the humanities), entertainment (museums, exhibitions and 'human zoos') and culinary customs. The various ways in which the cultures of colonial territories influenced the metropolis will also be considered – an aspect which until recently has remained neglected.[13]

Although it took a long time for overseas and imperial activities to occupy a noticeable place in French culture, a slow but regular process of familiarisation combined with changing international status ensured that 'popular imperialism' has gradually become a salient feature of French cultural production and *Weltanschauung*, even leading to forms of acculturation in post-colonial France. The chapter follows a long process of maturation over more than a century and a half. Major domestic political changes and international events of unprecedented magnitude have defined relatively clear phases in the development, consolidation, retraction and metamorphosis of imperial sentiment in France, which will shape the structure of the present chapter. A chronological approach seems desirable as popular imperialism was inevitably linked to the actual expansion of French overseas possessions: popular interest in a region could be a prelude to, or more often a consequence of, designs of conquest. This methodological choice calls for two preliminary clarifications. First, all key chronological turning points are merely indicative of a process of change which usually occurs over more than a single year: beyond the inevitable periods of gestation between production and commercialisation of popular material, mindsets tend to evolve slowly and there are always precursors and latecomers in any cultural trend. Second, this timeline should not make the reader lose sight of the fact that some underlying themes were a feature of the period as a whole.

While imperial expansion was rarely linear, some cultural expressions linked to imperialism were prone to continuity over the *'longue durée'*. French interest in 'oriental' themes and subjects dated back at least to the 1798 expedition to Egypt (in itself a form of imperialism)[14] and was kept alive through a variety of cultural productions[15] which prospered even under the Restoration, when France seemed to have given up imperial ambitions. The power of attraction of the exotic 'Orient' which prevailed in France throughout the nineteenth century and even beyond, for good or bad, interacted throughout the period with imperial sentiment, in a more complex and dialectic manner than has often been argued.[16] Increased sensibility to exoticism and later forms of 'escapism' often mixed with imperial pride, while the gradual valorisation of the concept of 'adventure' mirrored and fostered imperial expansion.[17] The 'exotic' could take a variety of forms, ranging from smells, sunlight or landscapes to the lascivious appeal of Oriental women in their harem, first popularised by Orientalist paintings but later disseminated on a larger scale through postcards.[18] This complex interplay between the discovery of difference, curiosity and patriotic appropriation, blending in varying proportions Orientalism, exoticism and nationalism, represents the backbone of the relationship between the French and their empire throughout the period. It also poses the question as to whether popular taste for the exotic necessarily went hand in hand with imperial backing. In certain cases, the wish to avoid the acculturation or exploitation of local populations led to forms of anti-colonialism,[19] but it is indisputable that improved overseas communication due to imperial links increased awareness of non-European worlds.

The influence of the empire on French cultural production could often be very direct. Under the Third Republic, history teaching in schools systematically justified imperialism, undoubtedly making a durable impact on generations of Frenchmen and women.[20] Books about the Orient (usually Algeria, Morocco or Tunisia) were given away as school prizes.[21] In the meantime, newspapers, illustrated magazines, an increasingly available imagery and a variety of colonial paraphernalia brought 'Greater France' into French homes.[22] 'Popular imperialism' was not as marginal as has sometimes been argued. It was related to the ever-evolving sense of French identity and was, to a certain extent, linked to the profound changes in the make-up of the French population which the country witnessed in the twentieth century.[23] Religious feelings and proselytism also played a role (at least temporarily) in promoting colonial expansion, even after the state became secular in 1905.[24] The cosmopolitanism of Paris as a European capital city, which had been evident throughout the nineteenth century, was reinforced when it also became a major imperial centre: this appears clearly, for instance, in the history of Arab influence in Paris.[25] Although the hegemony of the capital in this domain was uncontested, awareness of the empire was also evident in the provinces.[26] For instance, the French state endowed museums in the provinces with works about North Africa.[27] Soldiers or officers returning from the colonies disseminated personal knowledge of the colonies at various levels of society, both in Paris and the province.

The empire was at the core of debates about territorial and socio-cultural identity. Algeria was, at least administratively, fully integrated into French national territory, while the dividing lines between 'mainstream/traditional' Frenchness and 'imperial/exotic' features were constantly subject to discussion and negotiation,[28] especially because conceptions of French identity remained caught between republican universalism and persistent racial prejudices.[29]

In terms of national development, colonial conquests fostered medical and technical advancements which benefited the metropolitan populations,[30] and were often widely publicised in an attempt to valorise the country's achievements (see the *Institut Pasteur*[31]). Discoveries linked to colonial development were swiftly included in the curricula of schools of medicine and universities (especially those of Paris, Bordeaux and Marseilles), while the fields of history, anthropology and sociology expanded both theoretically and geographically.[32] Although scientific research and military activity did not always work hand in hand, several areas of investigation were heavily influenced by imperial activity, be it the development of new fields (for example, knowledge of the African continent[33]) or the appearance of objects of study serving colonial purposes (e.g. the *Kabyle myth*[34]).

For the sake of concision, this chapter will look only at metropolitan France, although popular imperialism was particularly strong among European populations in the colonies themselves, where it strengthened the links with the 'mother-country', which some settlers had never personally visited. This was especially true in Algeria, where conceptions of Frenchness and interpretations of the colonial universe were closely intertwined in *pied-noir* popular culture.[35] This was all the more important as Algeria was the *pièce de résistance* of the French Empire.

Coincidental popular imperialism: the early conquest of Algeria, Oceanian islands and along the Senegal River (1830–70)

Although France regained some of her colonies after the Napoleonic Wars, French colonial expansion did not resume in earnest until the conquest of Algiers in June 1830. Militarily, it proved to be a success, but it was a failure in terms of internal politics: Charles X's initiative clearly lacked popular support, and the expedition to Algiers did not manage to prevent the occurrence of a régime change.[36] In the following forty years, France would see three further political régimes, one of which (the Second Empire) advocated close Franco-Arab co-operation. Although it is too early to speak of 'popular imperialism' for this period (some would even argue that 'popular *anti*-imperialism' was rife[37]), these are formative decades during which colonial questions gradually acquired importance in French political and intellectual life. It was also the first instance of what would become a pattern of French public opinion: that of opposing any new overseas conquest (on budgetary grounds or otherwise), but then of equally opposing any withdrawal once the conquest has been carried out.[38]

While the conquest of Algeria beyond Algiers was initially conducted with much hesitation, French expansion took place in the Pacific and

Oceania in the 1840s,[39] and along the Senegal River in the 1850s and 60s under the impulse of Governor Faidherbe. French adventurers and conquerors vied with German and British explorers in both the Far East and West Africa. The question of the emancipation of slaves in the French colonies attracted moderate publicity in the 1840s due to the action of the *Société française pour l'abolition de l'esclavage*, until all slaves were freed in 1848.[40] Influenced by enduring negative stereotypes, the French public showed little interest in Africa or in black people in general.[41] Against this backdrop of mostly uncoordinated activity encompassing various continents, these three decades saw a slow but nonetheless steady development of interest in exotic, remote places, with a predilection for Algeria and Indochina: this laid the groundwork for future interest in French overseas territories.

Indochina made a promising start, with Khmer art, impressively embodied in Angkor Vat, gaining prominence as more visitors followed in the footsteps of the European who had first publicised the site, Father Charles-Emile Bouillevaux. The public marveled at the architecture and sculpture of the abandoned site which had just been 'rediscovered' by the French, therefore enhancing national self-esteem.[42] The appearance of Henri Mouhot's drawings of Angkor in *Le Tour du monde* in 1863 and the posthumous publication of his travel diaries in the *Bibliothèque rose illustrée*[43] also did much to inspire interest in the 'pearl of the Far East' which France was adding to her possessions. The publicity surrounding other expeditions to the area, such as those by Ernest Doudart de Lagrée, Louis Delaporte and Francis Garnier in search of the source of the Mekong (1866–88) popularised the cultural richness of the territory they proposed to turn into a 'French Far East'.[44] The cultures of French Indochina (especially that of the Khmers) subsequently sparked sustained interest from explorers, scientists (archaeologists, historians, linguists) and writers, whose findings were shared with the metropolitan public through books and articles.[45]

In spite of it being an almost accidental conquest, Algeria retained, more than any other colony, the attention of all those who held expansionist views for France. Although the French conquest did not suffice to turn Algeria into a major destination for European travellers, a few notable artists and intellectuals did visit it, such as Delacroix as early as 1832 and Louis Veuillot and Tocqueville in the 1840s, whose writings in the press supported French colonial designs.[46] The policy of limited colonisation gradually disappeared as grand designs were made for an Algeria under French control, giving rise to optimistic pleadings by the Saint-Simonians in favour of an enlightened, technocratic imperialism, as exemplified by Ismael Urbain[47] or Prosper Enfantin, author in 1852 of *La Colonisation de l'Algérie*. This ideal directly inspired the construction of the Suez Canal and its dependencies under the leadership of Ferdinand de Lesseps, in the 1860s.[48]

France's newest colony (and its southern limits) became the object of sustained literary, artistic and scientific interest. The encyclopedic *Exploration scientifique de l'Algérie* appeared between the 1840s and the 1860s.[49] Eminent writers started to head south: Théophile Gautier, an influential supporter of the Orientalist movement,[50] found in Algeria the inspiration for *Loin de Paris* (1865) and Flaubert visited Algeria and Tunisia in 1858 as a prelude to the writing of *Salammbô* (1862). Artists such as Delacroix or Eugène Fromentin found in the pure North African sunlight a source of inspiration for their paintings – sometimes, also for their writings, such as Fromentin's *Un été dans le Sahara* (1854) and *Une année dans le Sahel* (1858). Painters often triumphantly celebrated the French conquest, as was the case of the *Prise de la Smala d'Abd-el-Kader* or the *Bataille d'Isly* by Horace Vernet (the official painter of the Algerian campaigns under Louis-Philippe) and many other works by Théodore Gudin, Félix-Henri Philippoteaux or Augustin Régis. Some artists were simply inspired by Algerian landscapes, such as Théodore Frère, Théodore Chassériau or Adrien Dauzats,[51] while others intended to denounce more or less directly the excesses of French colonisation in Algeria. Arguably, Delacroix's *Femmes d'Alger*,[52] described as 'the most beautiful painting in the world' by the leading art dealer Ambroise Vollard,[53] was one such denunciation. Algeria also started to feature regularly in popular songs such as *La Casquette du Père Bugeaud* (which appeared ca. 1845) and several others produced after the surrender of Abd-el-Qader in 1847.[54] Algeria appeared for the first time in French educational books: the 'almost official' reading book of the Second Empire and a common Catholic school textbook under the Third Republic, Charles Jeannel's *Petit-Jean* (1846), dedicated two complete chapters to the seizure of Algiers.[55] Colonial Algeria appeared for the first time on the occasion of the French National Exhibition of 1849 and the 1851 London universal exhibition. The universal exhibitions of 1855 and 1867 in Paris allowed an increasing amount of space to France's colonial territories.[56] The wealthy could judge for themselves and some of them started to winter in Algeria, where tourism developed at the same time as an increasing number of guidebooks about the region appeared.[57]

As territories under French control expanded, the Sahara opened new perspectives, whetting the appetite of the educated French public for exploration: Félicien David composed *Le Désert* in 1844, General Daumas published his pioneering *Le Grand Désert* in 1849 and Fromentin went as far south as Laghouat and Aïn Mahdi in the early 1850s. The explorer Henri Duveyrier published in 1864 his *Touareg du Nord* which founded an enduring myth around the Tuaregs, often presented as 'modern knights'.[58] The Paris Geographical Society (founded in 1821) promoted interest in the African interior, a task which was made easier as French possessions expanded south. Supporters of southward expansion gladly recalled the precedent of René Caillié who, unlike Gordon Laing, had managed to come back alive from Timbuktu to describe this mythic city.[59]

This period was a foundational moment in the relationship between the French public and the country's colonies. These decades were the starting point of a phenomenon which would have a durable impact on French collective memory in a variety of guises.[60] It is also at this moment that historical reference to the Roman presence in North Africa started to be used to justify colonial conquest on the grounds that France was a 'New Rome'.[61] The liberal poet Victor Hugo declared of the conquest of Algeria that 'it is civilization marching against barbarity. It is an enlightened people [the French] which finds a people in the night [the native populations of Algeria]. We are the Greeks of the world; it is our duty to illuminate the world.'[62] Undertaken without an overall plan, French expansionism unwittingly placed these newly acquired territories on the imaginary map of the French psyche, with hardly any other asset than their mysterious and exotic appeal.

'Two daughters or twenty servants?' The dilemma of the early Third Republic and its echoes in public debate (1870–98)

The fall of the Second Empire brought six decades of institutional stability, contrasting starkly with quasi-perpetual governmental instability. The defeat by Prussia quickly placed the relevance of overseas expansion in question: while undeniably the ultimate goal was the reconquest of the *'blue line of the Vosges'*, were new colonies an asset or a burden? Popular perceptions of imperialism are inseparable from this dilemma which divided politicians at least until the Fashoda crisis, against the backdrop of persisting rivalry with Great Britain, especially in the carve-up of Africa. Internationally, colonial expansion was likely to alienate Britain, and it is not a coincidence that many imperialists were also Anglophobes. By contrast, the Germanophobes favoured a revival of a form of cross-Channel *Entente*, and consequently opposed imperial development, which they believed was an obstacle to such rapprochement.[63] This hesitation was perceptible in the cultural production related to the empire.

One of the most emblematic episodes of this period of apparent colonial uncertainty, which spilled far beyond the corridors of power, was the clash between the imperialist advocate Jules Ferry and the Radical Georges Clemenceau, who opposed colonialism on moral and strategic grounds. Other major anti-colonial figures included the nationalist *député* Paul Déroulède, who famously exclaimed: 'I had two daughters [Alsace and Lorraine] and you are offering me twenty servants [the colonies].' In spite of this opposition,[64] Ferry succeeded in securing the French protectorate over Tunisia and the conquest of Tonkin, but he was voted out of power after the defeat of Lang-Son, in March 1885. The memorable debate at the Chambers between pro- and anti-expansionists shows that colonial questions could become a major issue on the political scene and give rise to a variety of cultural productions, from articles in the press to popular songs celebrating expansion (e.g. *La Tonkinoise*, 1883) or ridiculing Ferry (e.g. *La Fin du Tonquinois*, 1886).[65] Ferry himself delivered passionate nationalist calls for expansion in *Le Tonkin et la mère-patrie* (1890).[66] Although colonial questions never again rose to such political prominence as in March 1885 (apart from during the Fashoda crisis), the work carried out behind the parliamentary scenes by the so-called 'Colonial Group',[67] under the leadership of Eugène Etienne, combined with the entrepreneurship of French officers on the spot,[68] ensured that France conquered during that period most of her possessions in West and North Africa, as well as in Indochina, in spite of frequent hesitations.

As the French Empire took shape against a backdrop of uncertainty, the French public was not unaware of overseas activity. The development of the popular penny press, combined with improved literacy rates and increased political awareness, allowed the French public to widen its horizons. Illustrated supplements to major newspapers (such as *Le Petit Journal* from 1884 onwards and *Le Petit Parisien* from 1889) often featured on their front cover an evocative colour engraving depicting scenes of colonial conquest. Mass-circulation titles as well as general interest newspapers such as *Le Temps* regularly featured African topics, and some of them (especially *Le Petit Journal*) developed an openly pro-colonial stance. With circulation figures sometimes above the million mark, their views enjoyed a wide readership. Illustrated magazines such as *L'Illustration* or *Le Tour du monde* eagerly relayed to their readers stories of exploration, conquest or future opportunities for development in the colonies.[69] Eager to vulgarise geographical knowledge through a variety of social activities (lectures, school prizes, etc.), geographical societies in Paris and the provinces actively promoted a better awareness of the empire, a task which made them popular, judging from membership figures.[70] The geographical movement remained overwhelmingly imperialist and heartily promoted the cause of French overseas expansion.[71] Colonial advocates, whether politicians, writers or journalists, made extensive use of the concept of the 'civilising mission' to justify their expansionist agenda, which gradually became part and parcel of the ideals of the Third Republic.[72] Some authors of children's books such as Alfred Assollant or Paul d'Ivoi eagerly shared their imperial enthusiasm with younger generations, especially through adventure fiction intended to inculcate positive feelings about the colonies (sometimes at the price of blatant Anglophobia).[73] Intellectuals such as the economist Paul Leroy-Beaulieu in *De la colonisation chez les peuples modernes* (1874), the historian and geographer (and vice-president of the Marseilles geographical society) Paul Gaffarel in *Les Colonies françaises* (1880), or the geographer Onésime Reclus in *France, Algérie et colonies* (1886), all theorised their belief in the need for France to expand her rule and culture overseas, a task which the *Alliance française* (established in 1883) also aimed to undertake. Eminent religious figures such as the Archbishop of Algiers, Mgr Lavigerie, issued loud calls for emigration from Alsace and Lorraine to Algeria after the Prussian annexation, and promoted missionary effort through the founding of the *Œuvre des écoles d'Orient* and the order of the White Fathers.[74] Through his famous *Toast of Algiers* (1890), Lavigerie reconciled the Republic with the French episcopacy, allowing for closer co-operation between Church and state on overseas questions.[75] Explorers or officers were at the centre of (or themselves orchestrated) public relations campaigns which brought the imperial question to the attention of the public. When Pierre Savorgnan de Brazza came back from the Congo in 1882, public enthusiasm forced the French government to ratify the treaty he had concluded with the Congolese king Makoko.[76] Ambitious colonial projects, such as the Trans-Saharan railway, got widespread publicity celebrating their potential and their beneficial impact on France's international image (although the slaughter of the Flatters mission ultimately struck the Trans-Saharan project a fatal blow).[77]

As the years went on, the public was exposed to a variety of cultural material related to the empire, which familiarised the population with it. Representations of non-Western worlds became commonplace on the occasion of *Expositions universelles* (especially the 1867, 1878, 1889 and 1900 Paris exhibitions), while a specifically colonial exhibition took place for the first time in Lyons in 1894.[78] At the 1889 Paris Universal exhibition, African populations from the colonies appeared in a variety of roles which attracted the public's attention, and the 'Senegalese Village' on the Champ-de-Mars proved to be 'a very popular attraction'.[79] Imperial locations increasingly became sources of inspiration in the visual arts, and Algeria appealed to some of the most prominent French artists.[80] Gustave Guillaumet, often presented as the 'Millet of North Africa', who also produced a travelogue entitled *Tableaux algériens* (1888), ventured

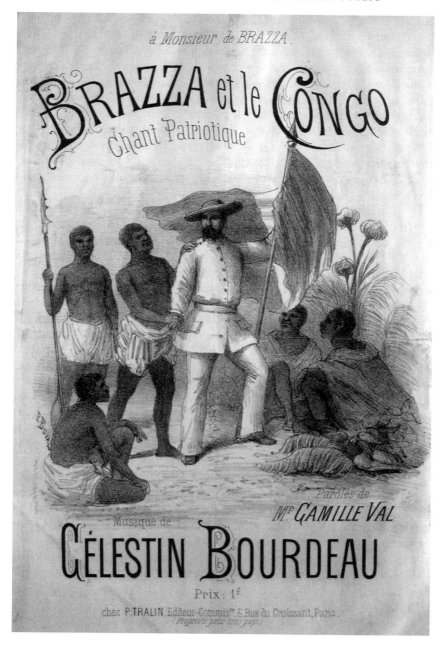

1.1 Song sheet cover 'Brazza and the Congo, patriotic song' (music by Célestin Bourdreau, lyrics by Camille Val), undated (c. 1880s). (Courtesy Berny Sèbe)

south to Biskra, Laghouat and the Sahara. The oasis of Bou Saâda became the second fatherland of the prolific Orientalist painter Etienne Dinet. Following his admiration for Delacroix's work, Auguste Renoir spent three months in Algiers in the early 1880s, finding the material to produce around thirty paintings directly referring to scenes in the colony. In Polynesia, Paul Gauguin produced some of his most famous paintings, although their impact was not immediate. His posthumous celebrity much publicised Tahiti and the Tahitian way of life. Photographic art allowed its practitioners to depict vividly and valorise the territories that now formed the empire, as exemplified by Jean Geiser who provided a rich ethnographic and historical inventory of Algeria in the second half of the century.[81]

By and large, it was essentially in the written world that the empire acquired a notable place during this period, inspiring major writers such as Guy de Maupassant[82] or Alphonse Daudet, who featured Algeria in both *Tartarin de Tarascon* (1872) and *Lettres de mon moulin* (1878). Indochina inspired the works of Jules Boissière (*Dans la forêt*, 1896) and Albert de Pouvourville (*L'Annam sanglant*, 1890). Throughout the period, accounts of exploration appeared at a swift pace (especially through the bulletins of geographical societies) and their results were disseminated (at times, after being enhanced for popular consumption) by opportunist writers or were included in the output of armchair travellers, arousing public interest in new explorations and recent territorial acquisitions.[83] Books by the officer, explorer and hermit Charles de Foucauld, the Navy officer Pierre Loti,[84] or the writer and colonial administrator Paul Bonnetain, brought lively descriptions of North and West Africa and Indochina to a wide audience enthused by the imperial mindset which influenced their descriptions.[85] Critical appraisals of colonialism remained marginal.[86]

These decades, which presented a contrasting situation, appear as a period of transition. Whereas public opinion was not systematically enthusiastic about new imperial acquisitions, the progress of exploration, the organisation of a missionary effort of an unprecedented scale, and the steady expansion of overseas possessions resulted in an increasing influence of the colonies upon a notable amount of cultural producers – especially painters, writers and thinkers. In the next decades, pro-imperial feelings would gradually filter down to the rest of the population.

The Belle Époque *and the reinforcement of imperial feelings (1898–14)*

A major political turning point, the 1898 Fashoda incident could not remain without effect on French cultural life. Paradoxically, the climb-down before the British government paved the way for the 1904 *Entente Cordiale*, ultimately giving a free hand to France in Morocco. Under this new international system of alliances, colonial possessions seemed unquestionably more an asset on the international stage than a drain on national resources, and Germany appeared as France's major threat while Britain was France's potential ally. Although Anglophobia still remained rife in certain circles, such as the Navy and colonial supporters, public opinion in general favoured a peaceful settlement of the Fashoda question and relatively quickly forgot France's humiliation.[87] Politically, this change in international politics meant that the Radicals (who had been so adamantly opposed to colonial expansion in earlier decades) chose to keep and even extend France's colonial possessions when they were in power, from 1898 onwards. It also meant that two distinct types of nationalism finally converged: those who traditionally rejected imperialism in order to favour European action, and those who believed that France's prestige could only be restored through colonial expansion. The former, who had opposed colonial expansion on the grounds that exotic campaigns weakened, rather than strengthened, the French army, now saw overseas territories as a possible source of strength.[89] This was the climax of a process which started in the 1890s and lasted until the inter-war period, and which both mirrored and shaped changing popular attitudes.[90]

More frequent 'colonial exhibitions' in the metropolitan territory (1906 in Marseilles 1907 in Paris) and the swift succession of seven 'colonial congresses' in the first years of the century (following the precedent of the first such congress in 1889) testify to these changing attitudes towards France's empire, especially as the colonial lobby managed to keep its momentum. Following an early initiative in Marseilles in 1893, Chambers of Commerce contributed to the promotion of the empire through the *instituts coloniaux* set up in Bordeaux (1901) and Nancy (1902) and the launching of specifically colonial teaching in Lyons and Nantes, respectively from 1899 and 1902 onwards.[91] Academically, the colonies became more visible in a variety of higher education institutions beyond the limits of geographical or colonial circles. The *Ecole coloniale*, founded in 1895, offered a clear administrative path to colonial service (although somewhat less prestigious than other metropolitan careers). The *Société d'histoire des colonies françaises*, founded in 1912 under the impulse of Alfred Martineau, intended to provide greater recognition to

1.2 The crowds gathering every day in front of the pavilion of the Journal des Colonies, Colonial Exhibition Marseilles 1906. (postcard, courtesy Berny Sèbe)

France's colonial past. Following some early initiatives of the 1880s,[92] ambitious historical books undertook to tell the story of France's colonial epic,[93] while the colonies gained full status in history and geography schoolbooks. In 1902, a geography textbook for the penultimate year before the baccalaureate dedicated 130 pages (out of 650) to 'colonial France'.[94]

As the colonial question left the realm of controversy to enter that of consensus, the public recognised the virtue of famous empire-builders. The readers of *Le Petit Parisien* ranked Brazza in twelfth position among the most important Frenchmen of the nineteenth century.[95] The long-lasting celebrity of Major Marchand as a result of Fashoda,[96] and the successful public-relations campaigns of leading military figures such as Gallieni or Lyautey in favour of imperial expansion,[97] helped to push colonial questions up on the agenda. Even when they were not successful, imperial heroes could be potent vectors of enthusiasm for the empire, as was the case of a plethora of books on Marchand. The serialised editions of Michel Morphy's twenty-eight volumes blending patriotism and imperial exaltation in their description of *Le Commandant Marchand et ses compagnons d'armes à travers l'Afrique* met with popular acclaim: 75,000 copies were dispatched to bookshops in less than a year. Marchand was certainly one of the most celebrated national heroes of his time, due not only to his achievements (which were even praised by his British competitors) but also to the domestic and international context (the Dreyfus Affair, nationalist agitation, short-lived but palpable Franco-British tension and Anglophobia). However, other heroes who were less in the limelight, such as Gallieni or Monteil, still managed to attract their share of buyers, a fact that reveals a long-term trend.[98]

The literary interest in the colonies further developed, as new authors found inspiration in imperial themes, centered on the two poles of Indochina[99] and Algeria.[100] Algeria inspired its most eccentric 'trans-cultural' writer, Isabelle Eberhardt, an admirer of Muslim life and customs and perhaps, with Emile Masqueray, one of its first and most vocal defenders against colonial rule. Her work was given a wider echo by her friend and fellow journalist at *Al-Akhbar* in Algiers, Victor Barrucand.[101] Themes linked to the empire received formal literary recognition through the Goncourt Prize, awarded in 1905 to Claude Farrère for *Les Civilisés* (which criticised colonial life in Indochina[102]), while the Tharaud brothers obtained the same prize the following year for *Dingley, l'Illustre Ecrivain*, a severe indictment of Rudyard Kipling and British imperialism.[103] This period also saw the birth of a Francophone type of literature attached to, and emanating from, the colonies. Louis Bertrand, a secondary school teacher in Algiers from 1891 to 1899, praised the colonial epic unfolding in Algeria[104] and initiated the *'algérianiste'* literary movement, which would flourish especially in the inter-war years with authors such as Robert Randau, Charles Coutin and Jean Vignaud.[105] His initiative proved so successful that the following years saw attempts at theorising the colonial novel.[106]

Beyond the written world, the colonies penetrated the national psyche through various means. Popular songs often reflected consensus about imperialism; pieces celebrating the indigenous troops who had contributed to the conquest appeared in swift succession.[107] Imperial links made it easier to travel to the colonies, and this at least partly accounts for the increasing influence of African art on new artistic schools, such as Cubism, or for the fascination with North Africa felt by artists such as Henri Matisse.[108] The submission of the Tuaregs of the Hoggar in 1902, following the battle of Tit, paved the way for widespread celebration of the 'Blue Men' or 'the Men of the Veil', from now on allies of the French in their conquest of the Sahara.

The First World War, the call to the empire and its repercussions on popular perceptions (1914–18)

Confronted with the bloodiest conflict of its history, France found key allies in Great Britain and the USA, but also in the form of soldiers from the colonies. As early as 1910, the eminent colonial officer Mangin had advocated in his best-seller *La Force noire* the use of black troops in order to compensate for the ailing birthrates of the motherland.[109] Some 607,000 soldiers from the colonies took part in the fighting.[110] Campaigns of official propaganda or spontaneous celebrations in the popular press and through postcards, praising the contribution of the Africans in an attempt to strengthen morale, as well as (on a more limited scale) everyday contact between the French populations and 'Senegalese' riflemen (especially during 'wintering' in Southern France), gave a vivid illustration of the participation of the empire in the war effort. Children's magazines such as *Les Belles Images* or *La Jeunesse illustrée* regularly featured colonial troops in their illustrated stories.[111] The illustrated weekly *A la baïonnette* celebrated inter-allied fraternisation between the Muslim *tirailleur* and the Hindu fighter in the British army,[112] Maurice Delafosse celebrated the 'ferocity' of the 'black soldier' in *La Dépêche coloniale*, and popular newspapers such as *Lectures pour tous* sometimes featured scenes from the everyday lives of African soldiers in France.[113] Although it seems shockingly paternalistic by today's standards, this perception of the African soldier as a 'grown-up child' who was faithful to his adoptive motherland and who could savagely repel Teutonic attacks increased awareness of, and sympathy for, the colonies and their indigenous inhabitants.[114] Evocative descriptions of the experience of African soldiers in France were swiftly published in book form,[115] and the figure of the Senegalese *tirailleur* appeared as early as 1915 in the popular comic series *Bécassine*.[116] In 1915, adverts and tins produced by the firm Banania started to feature an apparently simple-minded but friendly African *tirailleur* savouring a bowl of the chocolate powder drink and smiling a triumphant *'Y'a bon'* ('Great Stuff') in pidgin French (interestingly also known as *'français tirailleur'*). The long-lasting success of this marketing strategy until the 1960s testifies to the unique place of the African *tirailleurs* (who epitomised the empire) in the French psyche following the Great War.[117]

Beyond the case of the *tirailleurs*, other wartime situations enhanced the role of the colonies in national life. Indochinese workers and soldiers were occasionally celebrated in the press, giving rise to the project of a *Force jaune*,[118] and the empire was regularly described as a provider of useful raw materials. Some major colonial figures also came to prominence during, or as a result of, the Great War: Marshal Hubert Lyautey as

Minister of War in 1916, General Marchand as the leader of the Tenth Division of Colonial Infantry, also called *'Division Marchand'*, Captain Baratier, who died on the front in Champagne, and above all Ernest Psichari, the grandson of Ernest Renan. His death on the Western front was given an epic meaning by Maurice Barrès, consequently bringing to light his career as a desert officer in Mauritania.[119] By showing the usefulness of the empire in circumstances which threatened the future of France, the Great War contributed to increase awareness of, and pride in, the colonies.

The inter-war years and the climax of self-confident popular imperialism (1918–39)

Profoundly shaken by the unprecedented scale of the Great War, the French public was more likely than ever to exalt imperial grandeur, especially as the French empire further expanded in Africa and the Middle East through the trusteeship system of the League of Nations.[120] The desirability of imperial territories now being a given, debates focused on the best ways of administering overseas possessions and making them profitable for France in an increasingly competitive and uncertain world. These decades saw the empire come to play a key role in the national psyche and start to influence French world views significantly beyond colonial circles. The repetition of the imperial theme in a wide variety of cultural products ensured it got through to the widest audiences it had ever been able to reach.[121] Official celebrations set the tone: overseas troops paraded on Bastille Day 1919, the Senegalese deputy Blaise Diagne received the *Légion d'honneur*, and a monument to the black heroes of the Great War was erected in Reims in 1924.

Constantly oscillating between repression and hesitant liberalisation, but fundamentally in agreement about the need to retain the colonies, the argument between Left and Right was limited to the *modus operandi* of imperial France. Consequently, colonial questions rarely reached the top of the political agenda in France, except at three moments which represent almost exactly the beginning, the middle and the end of the period considered here: the aftermath of victory over Germany, the early 1930s with the centenary of the conquest of Algeria (1930) and the Vincennes colonial exhibition (1931), and the anxiety-filled years between Munich and the Fall of France. The rest of the time, Parliament did not show much enthusiasm for discussing questions related to 'Greater France'.[122] This did not mean – far from it – that the empire was absent from French cultural and intellectual life between these peaks of imperial fever. As we shall see, awareness of the empire increased sharply over the period, as a result of converging evolutions: propaganda campaigns from the *coloniaux*, better integration between the metropole and the empire, and the unprecedented cultural appeal of the colonies as a subject of literary and artistic works.

During these two decades, the French imperialist movement relentlessly 'waged a systematic propaganda campaign at home and overseas',[123] against a backdrop of initially limited popular interest in the colonies or even parliamentary hostility towards costly overseas possessions.[124] The scaling up of the activities of the *Agence générale des colonies* in the 1920s led to the production of an exceptionally varied arsenal of propaganda tools, ranging from postcards and stamps to gramophone records, books and movies, but also calendars, medals, pennants and toys.[125] Their pro-imperial message was still relayed at local level through the *instituts coloniaux*, which opened new branches in Nice, Le Havre, Montpellier and finally Paris (in 1920).[126] Faithful to the heritage of the generation of Eugène Etienne, propagandists intervened much more directly and officially in the press than at the time of the 'Colonial party'. Subsidies from the Ministry of the Colonies from the 1920s onwards amounted to 'sponsorship of the mass press': a wide variety of daily newspapers of diverse political persuasions (except the Socialists and the Communists) received ministerial subsidies in view of promoting the empire to their readers – reaching an overall amount of 342,000 francs for the year 1937 alone.[127] From 1927 onwards, the *Journal des débats* often included a section entitled *Revue coloniale* and, from 1931, *Le Temps* started to publish a weekly supplement, *Le Temps colonial*, while the illustrated periodical *Le Monde illustré* regularly featured a colonial supplement and *Les Echos* published biannual special issues on the colonies. Colonial sections also blossomed in provincial newspapers, in addition to the occasional exotic illustration on the front cover of *Le Petit Journal* or *Le Petit Parisien*. Over seventy colonial newspapers and periodicals appeared regularly in the late 1920s, some of them heavily subsidised by the Ministry of the Colonies.[128] In 1929–30, the *Comité de propagande du centenaire de l'Algérie*, which brought together journalists, academics, politicians and officers in order to emulate 'a durable movement of opinion in metropolitan France in favour of Algerian France', claimed to be putting all the weight of its publicists and their networks into a propaganda campaign promoting French Algeria in the metropolitan press,[129] in addition to the 1,200,000 copies of the *Cahiers du centenaire de l'Algérie* distributed in 1930. Towards the end of the 1920s, Radio-Paris broadcast numerous programmes on colonial topics.[130] The press and the radio duly exalted imperial grandeur.

Young people were increasingly exposed to 'Greater France'. The Ministry of Education expanded the share of colonial history and geography in official curricula.[131] Various youth associations, such as the *Ligue maritime et coloniale*, the *Fédération des jeunesses coloniales* and the *Fondation Lyautey*, publicised imperial achievements and fostered colonial vocations. Children could learn about the empire through comics such as *Zig et Puce* or even Hergé's *Tintin au Congo* (1931) which, although it referred to the Belgian Congo, conveyed a particularly obvious imperial message, as was the case later with *Le Crabe aux pinces d'or* (1940). In 1934, following on the highly successful stories about the young colonised African *Bonhomme Bana* and *Bamboula* (a *tirailleur* who had come back to Senegal to become a banana planter for Banania), Banania presented to children *L'Histoire du joyeux Y'a bon* which stressed the benefits of a closer partnership between France and her colonies. More rigorous data was also made available in an effort to educate new generations in imperial matters. Several hundred thousand copies of an overview of the colonies by J. Léotard, the general secretary of Marseilles' geographical society and the editor of the newspaper *Les Colonies*, were distributed, in particular during the 'colonial weeks'.[132] The abovementioned '*Comité du centenaire*' undertook large-scale information campaigns in primary and secondary schools in both the metropole and the colonies, and awarded around 170 travel grants to teachers and lecturers wishing to visit Algeria, in the hope that their experiences would reach at least 20,000 pupils.[133]

At university level, the need to study the empire and disseminate scientific knowledge about it became increasingly evident in academic circles. Following earlier successes in Cairo and Hanoi in the nineteenth century, the Dakar *Institut français d'Afrique noire* and the *Institut d'études arabes de Damas* gave to the colonies a prominent place in a variety of disciplines, such as archaeology, anthropology, biology, botany, ethnology, prehistory and paleo-anthropology. French scientists vied for pre-eminence overseas in a variety of domains, replicating in the academic domain geo-political struggles.[134] The time for self-reflection had already come, with a monumental six-volume *Histoire des colonies françaises et de l'expansion de la France dans le monde*, edited between 1929 and 1934 by the former minister of the Colonies Gabriel Hanotaux and the *Collège de France* professor Alfred Martineau. A *Bibliographie d'histoire coloniale* (1900–32), published in 1932, testified to the dynamism of the field.

The impact of all these initiatives in the press, and in education and research, was multiplied by the practical consequences which the possession of an empire had for metropolitan France. Colonial exhibitions provided the illusion of a 'tour of the colonies', highly charged with exoticism, national pride and self-congratulation, as happened in Marseilles (1922), in Strasbourg (1924) and above all in Vincennes (1931), coming hot on the heels of the centenary of the conquest of Algeria. The apotheosis of 'Greater France', Vincennes was by far the most successful of all colonial exhibitions, with eight million visitors, generating between thirty and thirty-five million francs profit.[135] It succeeded in integrating the empire into French culture[136] and its impact outlasted the exhibition, especially in the form of the Musée colonial, later baptised *Musée de la France d'outre-mer*. In December 1935, the *Salon de la France d'outre-mer* took place at the prestigious *Grand Palais* in Paris. The Paris Universal exhibition of 1937 presented the French colonies on the *Ile aux Cygnes*, a strategic location a stone's throw from the Eiffel Tower and the *Palais de Chaillot*. This pride in the achievements of overseas France coincided with increased curiosity about extra-European worlds and customs,[137] especially from Black Africa.[138] Growing interaction between the metropole and the colonies, facilitated by improved maritime links, also familiarised the French with overseas populations, sometimes giving rise to anxieties[139] but also highlighting the benefits of such imperial cosmopolitanism[140] beyond the appeal of exoticism which explained the unrelenting success of 'human zoos'.[141] Lastly, the development of tourism during the period relied heavily on publicity campaigns which evocatively described in words and in widely distributed images the 'desirable difference' of the colonies.[142] These decades saw representations of the empire multiply in the metropole, making it an inescapable feature of French national culture.

The empire was also popularised because it appeared clearly as the fertile terrain where technical prowess, moral merit or religious devotion could blossom and demonstrate France's greatness. The aeronautical prowess of Mermoz and St Exupéry in the *Aéropostale* are a case in point. The mechanical feats of the Trans-Saharan automobile crossing (1921), the *Croisière noire* (1924–25), and the *Croisière jaune* (1931–32) proved to be long-lasting publicity coups for both the car manufacturer Citroën and the empire: highly successful books by the expeditions' leader, Louis Audouin-Dubreuil,[143] appeared in conjunction with much-publicised movies produced by Gaumont.[144] These initiatives aimed to open up the Sahara to tourism, in an effort to promote the appeal of the colonies in the metropole.[145] In the religious domain, missionaries eagerly promoted their achievements to the communities of believers through a variety of publications which fostered a paternalistic but sincerely generous interest in the colonies, their populations and their religious standing.[146]

Beyond the obvious role of the colonies as the backdrop for French achievements, their intrinsic drawing power grew over the period even if, retrospectively, it appears marred by a tendency to exoticism and cliché. The artistic and literary potential unfolded by imperial territories was diligently exploited by a variety of cultural producers – songwriters, writers, artists or film-makers. Musical production celebrated colonial territories, rather than merely lionising their conquest.[147] Highly evocative Banania posters playing on the appeal of the colonial epic and reaching an unprecedented audience, campaigns of recruitment for colonial troops celebrating France's colonial mission ('Engagez-vous dans les troupes coloniales'), adverts from the tourist offices of Cochinchina or Algeria or railway companies such as Chemins de fer algériens de l'Etat or Paris-Lyon-Méditerranée, all familiarised the public with these far-flung territories which had become so accessible and desirable after the Great War. This fever was not limited to wall-size images; even collectables increasingly featured imperial themes. Hundreds of chromolithographies Liebig, chocolate cards from Suchard or Cémoi, and children's promotional albums, depicted the French colonies. All these came in addition to film posters, art prints, photographs which were widely distributed in illustrated newspapers, magazines, books, prints, adverts or postcards. The latter were a particularly efficient vector of colonial propaganda and strengthened awareness of the empire in the metropole.[148] This rich iconographical production has been subject to scrutiny in recent scholarship,[149] but the sheer quantity of material available and still to be identified makes it an almost inexhaustible source of documentation on popular perceptions of the empire, which demonstrates the extent of its impact on the public.

Inter-war painters inspired by the colonies could count on governmental support, giving imperial topics more visibility on the national scene and bringing more recognition to what amounted to a modern form of Orientalism. The Grand Prix artistique de l'Algérie encouraged creative work on Algeria. The Ministry of the Colonies awarded no fewer than seventeen artistic prizes, while awards by governor-generals everywhere in the empire allowed French artists to draw inspiration from the colonies and share their enthusiasm for them with the metropolitan public. The Villa Abd-el-Tif in Algiers, founded in 1907 on the model of the Villa Medicis in Rome, reached maturity in the inter-war years and contributed to the development of a rich artistic life in Algiers, closely knitted with that of Paris and exporting to France a romantic and desirable image of the colony with the help of artistic unions which were well-connected with artistic circles in the metropole.[150] Exhibitions allowed the works of earlier Orientalists such as Etienne Dinet to reach wider audiences, while events such as the Salon de la France d'outre-mer and the classical Salon des peintres orientalistes français and Salon de la société coloniale des artistes français displayed only works inspired by the colonies.[151] The inter-war years were a particularly rich period of artistic production about the empire,[152] and had maximal metropolitan impact as a result of the close cultural links between the metropole and its overseas territories (particularly Algeria).

Writers and publishers found in the colonies countless opportunities to make their trade blossom. There was of course a market for state-sponsored celebratory publications coinciding with imperial celebrations, as well ad hoc books such as Marius Leblond's *L'Empire de la France*, published in the year of the Vincennes exhibition. Some post-war accounts of the Great War showed the wartime usefulness of the colonies.[153] Other authors used the still-popular heroic vein, with titles such as Jean d'Esme's *Les Défricheurs d'empires* (1937), or the *Lyautey* published in 1939 by the Academician André Maurois. Publishing houses diligently catered for (and contributed to) public interest in imperial topics and colonial heroism. The publisher Plon marked the celebrations of Vincennes with the launch of a series entitled *Les Grandes Figures coloniales*, which included biographies of great imperial heroes.

Apart from a few notable exceptions,[154] the majority of these works did not break with the canons of colonial literature, blending exoticism with a romanticised apology of the civilising mission. The Parisian literary establishment recognised the growing influence of this trend, with the award of the 1921 Goncourt prize to the Antillean René Maran for his novel set in Black Africa, *Batouala*. The sheer variety of new topics which the empire offered was a literary bonanza for many. Indochina inspired in that period at least a dozen authors, the most significant of whom were Roland Dorgelès and André Malraux. Dorgelès' *Sur la route mandarine* was first published in 1925 and sold 23,000 copies in its first year of publication, reaching a print run of 31,000 by 1931.[155] André Malraux found in the French Far East the material for three of his most famous novels, *Les Conquérants* (1928), *La Voie royale* (1930) and *La Condition humaine*, which was awarded the 1933 Goncourt prize. Due to geographical and political proximity, North Africa remained by far the most important provider of exotic inspiration. In Morocco, Marshal Lyautey acted as patron of numerous writers whom he invited to visit the Protectorate, about which André Chevrillon and the brothers Jérôme and Jean Tharaud[156] produced memorable literary pieces. In Algeria, a century of colonial presence allowed for the maturation of 'Algerianist' novelists,[157] such as the prolific Robert Randau who praised the imperial cause but also described with sympathy Muslim societies and pleaded for a future Franco-Muslim Algeria. The journalist, writer and one-time president of the *Société des Gens de Lettres*, Jean Vignaud found in North Africa the inspiration for two of his most successful novels, *La Maison du Maltais* (set in Sfax 1926) and *Sarati le terrible* (set in Algiers). In the inter-war years alone, the latter was turned into a film and a lyrical drama, while the former inspired no fewer than two films. In the 1930s, the members of the so-called *Ecole d'Alger* (the term was a posthumous invention) reacted against earlier claims for the neo-latinisation and re-Christianisation of Algeria and instead defended the idea of a Mediterranean, 'multicultural' North Africa. Among its members were Gabriel Audisio (author in 1926 of *Trois hommes et un minaret*, which was awarded the *Grand Prix de l'Algérie*), the historian Jules Roy and the future Nobel Prize winner Albert Camus, who made clear references to Algeria in *Noces* (1938).

These years also saw the culmination of a long period of romanticisation of the Sahara and its inhabitants, a peculiarity of the French popular taste I have termed 'Saharomania'.[158] The posthumous success of the works of Isabelle Eberhardt and Ernest Psichari and the visual appeal of the desert[159] facilitated the development of popular fascination with the wilderness of the Sahara, for the way of life of its most famous inhabitants, the Tuaregs, and for the Frenchmen who had conquered this territory.[160] Books retelling the story of the military conquest of, or spiritual elevation brought about by, the Sahara were undoubtedly successful in the inter-war years. *Le Général Laperrine, grand Saharien*, by the novelist, journalist and historian José Germain, had already reached its twenty-third edition by 1923, just one year after its launch,[161] while René Bazin's *Charles de Foucauld, explorateur du Maroc, ermite au Sahara* reached a print-run of 44,000 copies in a year.[162] The figure of Father de Foucauld, 'the *marabout* of the Hoggar, a man of God and a great Frenchman',[163] exerted a durable appeal for the French public, as did that of Ernest Psichari, about whom eight biographies were published in the inter-war years. Beyond biographies, works of fiction strengthened the position of the Saharan theme in cultural life: novelists such as Pierre Benoit,[164] Joseph Peyré, Antoine de Saint-Exupéry or the young Roger Frison-Roche found in 'the Great Desert' an inexhaustible source of inspiration which had a romantic, military and ethnological appeal. The life and death of Michel Vieuchange in his attempt to reach the forbidden city of Smara in Western Sahara captivated popular imagination.[165] In the scientific realm, a generation of scholars who would make decisive contributions to the knowledge and popularisation of Africa among the French public appeared in this period.[166]

Popular imagination was susceptible to the almost magical power of moving images, especially when they brought remote and exotic locations into the confines of a cinema. It made this medium a particularly powerful vehicle for imperial sentiment,[167] and film directors quickly realised how much they could benefit from bringing the colonies into the cities: even contemporaries theorized the appeal of movies which took place in colonial locations.[168] About ninety French films were shot in the Maghreb in the inter-war years.[169] Featuring eminent actors such as Jean

Gabin, Raimu or Josephine Baker, some of them became the blockbusters of the time, such as J. Feyder's *L'Atlantide* (until G. W. Pabst produced his more Expressionist version in 1932) and *Le Grand Jeu*, Julien Duvivier's *Pépé le Moko*, and Léon Poirier's *L'Appel du silence*, on the life of Charles de Foucauld. Described by Georges Sadoul as the 'representative of official cinema under the Third Republic',[170] Poirier wanted to 'spread throughout the world the fame of France and the quality of her élite'[171] and the hermit Foucauld appears in his film as 'a soldier of the faith',[172] but the appeal of colonial adventure and imperial settings also largely contributed to its resounding success.[173] It was seen by ten million cinema-goers in its first eight months, was awarded the *Grand Prix du cinéma français*[174] and attracted considerable interest (at least 81,000 copies of the book based on the film were printed in the first year). A few years later, as the clouds of the Second World War loomed, a few influential official propaganda films exploited the reassuring presence of the empire.[175]

Weakened and divided, yet more popular than ever: French imperialism during the Second World War (1940–45)

As France faced the growing peril of an inevitable war, the government increasingly relied upon the existence of the empire to reassure its citizens, to forget 'France's impotence',[176] and to compensate for the country's many weaknesses compared with Germany.[177] In the press, both in the capital and the provinces,[178] the colonies were regularly invoked as potential saviours for the French nation. In the middle of the 'phoney war', Georges Mandel, the Minister of the Colonies, praised the 'unanimous fervour' of colonial populations who fought with France a 'holy war for freedom and dignity', in a newsreel which reminded audiences that 'France is an empire with one hundred and ten million inhabitants' and claimed 'we will win because we are the strongest'.[179] This optimistic promise did not pass the test of arms. Outdated, hardly changed since the Great War, the 'call to Africa' did not avert the fall of France.[180] Ironically, a *Quinzaine impériale française* was taking place (2–19 May 1940) at the very moment Guderian's *Panzerdivisionen* broke through the Ardennes.

The empire looked like the last card on which France could gamble her survival. Neither the Vichy government nor the Free French were unaware of this reality, and they fought bitterly for the control of this key asset: as a result, French political divisions struck the colonies acutely, and the Second World War literally 'quartered' the empire, to use Paul-Marie de la Gorce's term.[181] This was even more the case after the

Provisional Government of the French Republic was established in Algiers in 1943.

The fact that French Equatorial Africa (AEF) was the first territory to rally to the Free French was frequently used in the propaganda produced by the British and the Gaullists. The image of the Guyanese-born AEF governor, Félix Eboué, featured prominently in Allied propaganda targeting the empire: for instance, small posters showed an image of de Gaulle and Félix Eboué illustrating the slogan 'L'Empire se lève pour faire la guerre'. The promise not to lay down arms until the French flag flew on the cathedral of Strasbourg, made by Colonel Leclerc de Hauteclocque after the capture of Koufra from the Italians, was idealised and used extensively to boost morale and lend credibility to the Free French.[182] The press of the Free French in Africa regularly featured imperial contributions to the war effort.

However, apart from BBC programmes broadcast from London, only a limited amount of Gaullist material about the empire reached the bulk of the metropolitan public. Until the Liberation, it was more likely to be subject to Vichy propaganda, which also presented the empire as a remedy to France's misfortunes. Policy-makers in the Vichy government placed the empire at the centre of their 'National Revolution'.[183] The *Agence économique des colonies*, set up in 1941 to replace and centralise earlier institutions inherited from the Third Republic, undertook sustained propaganda campaigns in various media: in the press and on the airwaves (*Radio-Vichy* and *Radio-Paris*), exhibitions, posters, films, 'imperial fortnights', children's games and books, imperial contests, stamps ... The explicit aim was to celebrate the empire, remind the population of its existence and usefulness to the French nation, and finally to encourage new vocations among the youth (especially those of the élite).[184] The new authorities not only welcomed the 'traditional' propaganda activities of the *Ligue maritime et coloniale française*, but they also took direct initiatives: on the occasion of the *Semaine de la France d'outre-mer* (15–22 July 1941), French people were actively reminded that they had an empire ('*Français, vous avez un empire*'). In partnership with the national railway company SNCF, five state-sponsored carriages forming the *train-exposition des colonies* toured around France between 1941 and the summer 1944, stopping in dozens of major cities in both the occupied and free zones and attracting around 486,000 visitors.[185] Colonial propagandists could count on right-wing newspapers such as *Je suis partout* or *Le Flambeau* to develop a pro-imperial stance. News about events in the empire appeared in the national press, especially when they could stir up Anglophobia and support for Marshal Pétain. Features about the empire also regularly appeared in the press, in an attempt to boost faltering morale. Films about the empire were not as important as in the inter-war years (especially as the gradual loss of control of the colonies by Vichy meant that they could no longer be shot there), but some still celebrated France's overseas destiny.[186] Documentary films (sometimes based on pre-war footage) were also shown regularly in cinemas, praising the empire or fostering both colonial enthusiasm and Anglophobia.

In spite of paper shortages, the period saw new books featuring the empire coming out, such as Albert Camus' *L'Etranger* (1942), which was largely set in Algiers. The empire also appeared in numerous reprints of works which were thought to be edifying in the context of the 'National Revolution' and the regeneration of the country's forces. Material likely to whip up anti-British feeling was diligently fed into the market. In an effort to revive the memory of the humiliation of Fashoda, books about the Marchand mission were reprinted, and past colonial rivalries between France and Britain were also regularly revisited. Confronted with a bleak present and an uncertain future, the French under Vichy were prone to believe in the virtues of *Historia Magistra Vitae*. Biographies on colonial figures (re-)appeared at an unusually swift pace. No fewer than fifteen titles (new or re-printed) on Charles de Foucauld were registered at the French National Library between 1940 and 1945, five on Henry de Bournazel and eight on Lyautey.[187] The Saharan saga, with Joseph Peyré its leading exponent, was still bearing fruit. The Occupation slowed the rhythm of the appearance of new publications promoting the imperial idea, but was far from stopping it completely. A range of official publications were produced on the occasion of the colonial fortnights, such as *L'Empire, notre meilleure chance* or *Français, vous avez un empire* (1942), the latter being distributed at 100,000 copies. Several authors produced *ad hoc* works detailing the key role the empire had to play for the 'new France' which would emerge in a German-dominated world, where they hoped France would have a key role as the leader of a new 'Euro-African' area.

The empire seemed to be the place where the future of France would be played out as the country was living the darkest years of its history. Both Vichy and the Free French realised it, and played the 'imperial card': in reaction against the British Empire for the former, in support of it for the latter. Popular imperialism ran high at a time when France's morale ran abysmally low. The steep rise in the number of candidates presenting the competitive examination for the *Ecole coloniale*, showed clearly that the empire had become a much sought-after professional option.[188]

The Swan Song: pride in a vanishing empire (1945–62)

Paradoxically, it was at the moment when France most needed her empire for consolation and resources that serious cracks appeared in the colonial edifice, especially as returning colonial soldiers found that their contribution to the war effort was not given due recognition.[189] With riots and subsequent bloody repression in Algeria in May 1945, a seriously compromised position in Indochina from the end of the Second World War until 1954, and a general uprising in Madagascar in 1947, the empire seemed more in crisis than ever. This was precisely the point when imperial awareness was undeniably a reality: in 1949, an opinion poll found that 85 per cent of secondary school pupils felt that France could be proud of its activities overseas.[190]

Unwilling to yield to the growingly vocal discontent among the colonized, political reformers aimed to tie the empire more closely to the metropole, through the new constitutional principle of the French Union. The Fourth Republic, born out of the ruins of the war, granted a key strategic role to the colonies, as a way of reasserting the status and prestige lost by France during the war.[191] Consensus on the need to keep the empire was almost total: apart from the Communists (France's most popular political party at that time), all other political forces supported what was now called 'Overseas France' in an attempt to tone down its colonial nature. François Mitterrand famously claimed that 'Algeria is France',[192] and it was under the premiership of the Socialist Guy Mollet that the violence of the Algerian conflict escalated. This almost unanimous political agreement in Paris explains why seventeen years of almost uninterrupted uprisings and a regime change were necessary for France to complete the decolonisation of her empire through Algerian independence, and left her no choice but to replace imperial grandeur with the European project.[193]

Such radical changes and their associated traumas (civil and military losses, repatriation of the majority of the settlers, political divisions at home) could not leave popular perceptions of the empire untouched. At worst, empire now meant war and conscription – an aspect anti-colonial and/or Communist activists never failed to stress. At best, a new imperial consensus had to be found to justify the permanence of an order which seemed condemned everywhere. This new doctrine was articulated around a paternalistic ideology of development for Africa[194] and the illusion of complete integration for Algeria, well exemplified by the enthusiasm generated by North African sportsmen, all lionised for their contribution to French teams.[195] Orchestrated by the *Agence de la France d'outre-mer* (which was simply a re-branding of the organisation inherited from Vichy), official propaganda stressed more than ever developmental activities undertaken under the aegis of the French Union: medical programmes, construction of infrastructure and affordable housing (such as Fernand Pouillon's *Diar el-Mahçoul* in Algiers), education, and welfare. Similar messages were spread through a variety of private and semi-official publicity, while in schools the French Union was enthusiastically promoted in the curricula for geography and history, in textbooks, on maps and on a variety of supporting material designed to inculcate pride in 'Greater France' among the younger generations. Comic strips blended celebrations of France's modernising role with old clichés combining exoticism with praise for European heroism.

Artists and writers took longer to adapt to the new circumstances. Educated and trained in the inter-war years, some of them simply used peacetime opportunities to carry on with their trade. In the world of the arts, the School of Algiers reached its full potential, making the most of the closer links woven between Paris and Algiers during the war and also the opportunities offered by the *Villa Abd-el-Tif* and the *Ecole des beaux-arts d'Alger*.[196] Among film-makers, the celebratory mood of the inter-war years remained prevalent, especially because some projects had been interrupted by the war and their production resumed unchanged after the conflict had ended. Eager to romanticise the bygone days of triumphant and secure imperial feeling,[197] these works avoided the discussion of contemporary problems of violence in Indochina and Algeria. Strict censorship ensured that this topic did not appear in French cinemas, in spite of the intentions of film-makers such as Alain Resnais or Jean-Luc Godard. In literature, traditional themes deriving from literary processes started in the inter-war years (often by the same authors) coexisted with the rise of new Francophone writing which aimed to reveal the voice of the colonised. Biographical works on great French conquering figures were emblematic of these traditional themes, which went hand-in-hand with the further popularisation of an idealised colonial environment. 'Overseas France' had at last won its spurs in the literary realm. Major writers of the period, such as the Academician Maurice Genevoix, set their fiction in the empire with so much success that one even collected the Goncourt prize (Romain Gary in 1956 with *Les Racines du ciel*). The *pied-noir* Albert Camus, who had made a name for himself before the war with *Noces*, openly claimed the influence of his Algerian background, making reference to Oran (*La Peste* 1947) and the Sahara desert (*L'Exil et le Royaume* 1957).[198] Awarded the Nobel Prize of Literature in 1957, he never managed to overcome in himself and in his work the colonial contradictions which finally made the survival of the empire impossible.[199] In the meantime, the Sahara enjoyed an ever-growing popularity, further reinforced in the late 1950s by the fact that it was spared the violence of the Algerian conflict[200] and appeared to be endowed with substantial oil reserves. Henri Lhote's exhibition at the Pavillon de Marsan in 1958 on the rock art painting of the Tassili of the Ajjers was described by André Malraux as 'one of the most memorable of the last half-century'.[201] The discovery of oil fields turned the Sahara into a cornerstone of French *imperial grandeur* in the 1950s. Books and even films advocated the implementation of ambitious plans of development under French rule, which were unrealistic given the likely outcome of the Algerian war.

Alongside these traditional voices, inherited from an earlier period, the metropolitan public had access to an increasing number of writings developing the views of the educated élites of the colonised populations: these decades saw the appearance of what would later be called 'postcolonial literature'.[202] Starting with Aimé Césaire and Léopold Sédar Senghor whose *négritude* movement had gained momentum since its inception in the 1930s, and enjoying the support of major French figures such as Jean-Paul Sartre, these new voices reached full maturity as the rift between French Republican ideals and practices became more obvious. The Algerian war proved to be a watershed, inspiring most of the works of Frantz Fanon and Albert Memmi, who vehemently denounced the foundations of the imperial system. Sometimes forbidden by the French censor, and judged incompatible with the patriotic feelings of significant sections of the French population, the most radical of these works took some time to reach large audiences: their constituency was initially limited to the most progressive left-wing intellectuals. Moderate authors established themselves more easily in the French literary landscape, although they exalted their traditions and customs and could not hide their discomfort, to say the least, with 'imperial France'. Political activity and literary creation reminded the French public that the time had come to turn the page of 'Greater France'. The winds of change had blown the empire away, yet France was left with a cultural heritage that is still patent today.

French popular imperialism: an indisputable phenomenon?

France has long been seen as a country too deeply attached to its metropolitan territory and traditional agrarian values to care about any overseas possessions. The body of evidence used to produce this chapter, only the tip of an immense iceberg of material, demonstrates the contrary. The increasing visibility of the colonial theme in the metropole over the period studied in this book represents an unquestionable evolution in French popular culture

Limited to a relatively small and educated constituency in the first half of the nineteenth century, material about the colonies became more widely available as better means of communication transformed French society from the 1870s onwards. Following the trauma of the Great War, the apparent consolidation of the colonial edifice, and the need to exalt the increasingly threatened 'grandeur' of the nation, the inter-war years saw the triumph of a self-confident imperial mindset. Weakened and humiliated during the Second World War, France inscribed the empire in her constitution at the very moment she was starting to lose control of it. Imperial sentiment was running at an all-time high among a distressed, often traumatised, population, but it soon became undermined by the prospect of indigenous insurgencies and the accompanying threat of the use of conscripts to crush them. Herein lies the great irony and the paradox of the story of popular imperialism in France: in the 1950s, when at last the empire had entered fully into the national imagination, it was as a cause of concern rather than enthusiasm.

The author would like to thank Michaël Abecassis, Jennifer Birkett, Raphaëlle Branche, Martyn Cornick, John Darwin, Jacques Frémeaux, Roger Little, Wm. Roger Louis, Brian Melican, Alexander Morrison, Steffen Prauser and Martin Thomas for their useful comments on the draft. All errors are his own.

Notes

(Unless otherwise stated, titles in French are published in Paris and those in English, in London.)

1 J. Marseille, *Empire colonial et capitalisme français: histoire d'un divorce* (1984).
2 L.D. Hammond, 'Introduction' to an English translation of Bougainville's *News from New Cythera* (Minneapolis 1970), 3. See also M. Thiéry, *Bougainville, Soldier and Sailor* (1932), 257.
3 R. Phillips, *Mapping Men and Empire* (1997), pp. 113–42.
4 R. Girardet, *L'idée coloniale en France de 1871 à 1962* (1972), 'avant-propos'.
5 C.M. Andrew, A.S. Kanya-Forstner, 'The French "Colonial Party": its composition, aims and influence, 1885–1914', *The Historical Journal (HJ)*, 14, 1 (March 1971), pp. 99–128, and 'The Groupe Colonial in the French Chamber of Deputies, 1892–1932', *HJ*, 17, 4 (Dec. 1974), pp. 837–66; M. Lagana, *Le Parti colonial français* (Quebec 1990); T. G. August, *The Selling of the Empire* (Westport CT 1985).
6 Ageron, *France coloniale ou parti colonial?* (1978).
7 At a moment when the field blossomed with the works of Pascal Ory, Dominique Kalifa, Jean-Yves Mollier, Jean-Pierre Rioux and Jean-François Sirinelli, among others.
8 In particular through the work of Jacques Marseille and of the ACHAC association (*Association connaissance de l'histoire de l'Afrique contemporaine*) and its *Images et colonies* research programme. See N. Bancel et al. (eds), *Images et colonies* (1993).
9 T. Chafer and A. Sackur (eds), *Promoting the Colonial Idea* (2002).
10 See in particular R. Aldrich, *Vestiges of the Colonial Empire in France* (Basingstoke 2005).
11 M. Thomas, *The French Empire Between the Wars* (Manchester 1995), pp. 185–208.
12 Among numerous examples: J. Marseille, *L'Age d'or de la France coloniale* (1986); A. Ruscio, *Que la France était belle au temps des colonies* (2000), and *Amours coloniales* (Brussels-Paris 1999); G. Dugas (ed.), *Algérie, un rêve de fraternité* (2003); A. Quella-Villéger, *Indochine: un rêve d'Asie* (1995).

13 Among the exceptions is M. Evans, *Empire and Culture: The French Experience, 1830–1940* (Basingstoke 2004).

14 A. Godlewska, 'Napoleon's geographers (1797–1815): imperialists and soldiers of modernity', in A. Godlewska and N. Smith (eds), *Geography and Empire* (Oxford 1994), pp. 31–54.

15 In particular, the publication of the results of the Expedition to Egypt, in nineteen volumes published between 1809 and 1822 under the title *Description de l'Egypte*.

16 See in particular E. Said, *Orientalism* (1978) and *Culture and Imperialism* (1993). For a discussion of Said's theories from an imperial historian's point of view, see J.M. MacKenzie, *Orientalism, History, Theory and the Arts* (Manchester 1995) and R. Irwin, *For Lust of Knowing* (2006).

17 S. Venayre, *La Gloire de l'Aventure* (1998).

18 This topic has attracted wide scholarly attention: see M. Alloula, *The Colonial Harem* (Minneapolis 1986), L. Sebbar, J.-M. Belorgey, *Femmes d'Afrique du Nord: cartes postales (1885–1930)* (Saint-Pourçain-sur-Sioule 2002); C. Taraud, *Mauresques: femmes orientales dans la photographie coloniale, 1860–1910* (2003); R.J. Deroo, 'Colonial collecting: women and Algerian cartes postales', *Parallax*, 4, 2 (1998), pp. 145–57.

19 See in particular J.-P. Biondi, *L'anticolonialisme en France de 1871 à 1914* (1973); C.-R. Ageron, *L'anticolonialisme en France de 1871 à 1914* (1973); C.-A. Julien, *Une pensée anticoloniale: positions 1914–1979* (1979) and C. Liauzu, *Histoire de l'anticolonialisme en France du XVIe siècle à nos jours* (2007).

20 E. Savarese, *L'ordre colonial et sa légitimation en France métropolitaine* (1998) and 'L'histoire officielle comme discours de légitimation. Le cas de l'histoire coloniale', *Politix*, 43 (1998), pp. 93–112.

21 L. Javion, 'L'Orient comme récompense', in J.-R. Henry and L. Martini (eds), *Littératures et temps colonial* (Aix-en-Provence 1999) pp. 205–8.

22 B. Sèbe, 'Celebrating' British and French Imperialism: The Making of Colonial Heroes Acting in Africa, 1870–1939, PhD thesis, University of Oxford, 2007, pp. 47–78.

23 On the question of immigration, see G. Noiriel, *Le Creuset français: histoire de l'immigration (19e–20e siècles)* (1988); M. Amar, P. Milza, *L'immigration en France au XXe siècle* (1990); R. Schor, *L'opinion française et les étrangers en France (1919–1939)* (1985), and *Histoire de l'immigration en France de la fin du XIXe siècle à nos jours* (1996). On the specific case of Algerian immigration to France, see B. Stora, *Ils venaient d'Algérie: l'immigration algérienne en France 1912–1992* (1992). On the question of race in the Republic, see C. Reynaud-Paligot, *La République raciale: paradigme racial et idéologie républicaine, 1860–1930* (2006) and *Races, racisme et antiracisme dans les années 1930* (2007).

24 On the relationship between France and Islam, see J. Frémeaux, *La France et l'Islam depuis 1789* (1991).

25 See for instance Ian Coller, 'Arab France: Mobility and Community in Early Nineteenth Century Paris and Marseille', *French Historical Studies* (*FHS*), Special Issue: 'Mobility in French History', 28 (2006), pp. 433–56 or, for an illustrated appraisal of Arab influence in Paris, P. Blanchard et al., *Le Paris arabe* (2003).

26 On this theme, see O. Georg, 'The French provinces and "Greater France"', in Chafer and Sackur (eds) *Promoting the Colonial Idea*, pp. 82–101; N. Bancel et al. (eds), *Lyon, capitale des outre-mers* (2007); P. Blanchard and G. Boëtsch, *Marseille, porte sud* (2005); R.-C. Grondin, 'L'Empire palimpseste: l'exemple des années trente dans le Limousin', *French Colonial History*, 7 (2006), pp. 165–80 and 'La colonie en province: diffusion et réception du fait colonial en Corrèze et en Haute-Vienne', doctoral thesis, University Paris 1 Panthéon-Sorbonne 2007.

27 E. Cazenave, *L'Afrique du Nord révélée par les musées de province* (2004).

28 E. Ezra, 'Colonialism exposed: Miss France d'Outre-Mer 1937', in S. Ungar and T. Conley (eds), *Identity Papers, Contested Nationhood in Twentieth Century France* (Minneapolis MN 1996), 50–65.

29 D.S. Hale, *Races on Display* (Bloomington IN 2008) and R.S. Fogarty, *Race and War in France: Colonial Subjects in the French Army 1914–1918* (Baltimore MD 2008).

30 See for instance W. B. Cohen, 'Malaria and French imperialism', *Journal of African History*, 24, 1 (1983), pp. 23–36.

31 For an appraisal of the link between medical research and imperialism in France, see A. Marcovich, 'French colonial medicine and colonial rule: Algeria and Indochina', in R. Macleod and M. Lewis (eds), *Disease, Medicine and Empire* (1988), pp. 103–17.

32 J. Rivallain, 'Introduction', *Société française d'histoire d'outre-mer: 90 ans de publications, tables bibliographiques (1913–2003)* (2003), pp. 3–12.

33 E. Sibeud, *Une science impériale pour l'Afrique ? La construction des savoirs africanistes en France (1878–1930)* (2002) and S. Dulucq, *Aux origines de l'histoire de l'Afrique: historiographie coloniale et réseaux de savoir en France et dans les colonies françaises d'Afrique subsaharienne (fin XIXe siècle–1960)* (forthcoming).

34 P.M.E. Lorcin, *Imperial Identities: Stereotyping, Prejudice and Race in Colonial Algeria* (London and New York 1995).

35 A.L. Smith, *Colonial Memory and Postcolonial Europe: Maltese Settlers in Algeria and France* (Bloomington and Indianapolis 2006), pp. 114–15.

36 J.-J. Jordi, 'La prise d'Alger', in J.-P. Rioux (ed.), *Dictionnaire de la France coloniale* (2007), pp. 27–32.

37 M.J. Heffernan, 'The Parisian poor and the colonization of Algeria during the Second Republic', *French History*, 3, 4 (1989), pp. 377–403, citing p. 380: M.R. Buheiry, Anti-Colonial Sentiment in France During the July Monarchy: The Algerian Case, PhD thesis, University of Princeton, 1974.

38 X. Yacono, *Histoire de l'Algérie* (1993), 78.

39 R. Aldrich, *The French Presence in the South Pacific, 1842–1940* (1990); H. Blais, *Voyages au grand océan: géographies du Pacifique et colonisation, 1815–1845* (2005).

40 L. Jennings, *French Anti-Slavery: The Movement for the Abolition of Slavery in France, 1802–1848* (Cambridge 2000).

41 W. B. Cohen, *The French Encounter with Africans: White Response to Blacks, 1530–1880* (Bloomington and London 1980).

42 For a discussion of the impact of Angkor Vat in the French media, see A. Barnett, 'Cambodia will never disappear', *New Left Review*, 180 (1990), pp. 101–25.

43 H. Mouhot, *Voyages dans les royaumes de Siam, de Cambodge et de Laos* (1868).

44 L. Delaporte, *Le Cambodge et les régions inexplorées de l'Indo-Chine centrale* (1875), *Une mission archéologique aux ruines khmers* (1877) and *Un temple khmer voué au nirvânâ* (1879).

45 J.-F. Klein, 'L'histoire de l'Indochine en situation coloniale', in O. Saaïdia and L. Zerbini, *La construction du discours colonial* (2009), pp. 89–123.

46 Tocqueville's texts on Algeria have been compiled and presented with an introduction by S. Luste Boulbina, *Sur l'Algérie* (2003).

47 M. Levallois, *Ismayl Urbain (1812–1884): l'autre conquête de l'Algérie* (2001).

48 P. Régnier and F.A. Amin, *Les Saint-Simoniens en Egypte* (Cairo 1989); S. Moussa and M. Levallois, *L'orientalisme des Saint-Simoniens* (2006).

49 On this encyclopedic work, see D. Nordman, 'Les sciences historiques et géographiques dans l'exploration scientifique de l'Algérie (vers 1840–vers 1860)', in H. Blais and I. Laboulais (eds), *Géographies plurielles* (2006), pp. 235–53.

50 D. Brahimi, *Théophile et Judith vont en Orient* (1990).

51 For an overview of the influence of Algeria on French painting, see M. Vidal-Bué, *Alger et ses peintres 1830–1960* (2002), *L'Algérie des peintres 1830–1960* (2002) and *L'Algérie du Sud et ses peintres, 1830–1960* (2003). For an illustrated overview of the Orientalist school, see L. Thornton, *Les Orientalistes: peintres voyageurs, 1828–1908* (1983).

52 M. Arama, *Eugène Delacroix, le cri d'Alger* (2008).

53 A. Vollard, *La vie et l'œuvre de Pierre-Auguste Renoir* (1919), quoted in S. Guégan, 'Le plus beau tableau du monde', v.a., *De Delacroix à Renoir: l'Algérie des peintres* (2003), pp. 34–7.

54 Ruscio, *Que la France était belle*, pp. 39–70.

55 G. Manceron, 'Ecole, pédagogie et colonies, 1870–1914', in P. Blanchard et al. (eds), *Culture coloniale en France* (2008), pp. 153–62.

56 S. Lemaire et al., 'Jalons d'une culture coloniale sous le Second Empire (1851–1870)', in Blanchard, *Culture coloniale*, pp. 96–100.

57 Such as C. Desprez, *L'hiver à Alger: le logement, le climat, la ville* (Meaux, 1861).

58 D. Casajus, *Henri Duveyrier, un Saint-Simonien au désert* (2007); P. Pandolfi, 'La construction du mythe touareg', *Ethnologies comparées*, 7 (2004), http://alor.univ-montp3.fr/cerce/r7/pl.p.htm (accessed 30 March 2009).

59 A. Quella-Villéger, *René Caillié, une vie pour Tombouctou* (Poitiers 1999).

60 M. Salinas, *Voyages et voyageurs en Algérie, 1830–1930* (Toulouse 1989).

61 J. Frémeaux, 'Souvenirs de Rome et présence française au Maghreb: essai d'interprétation', in J.-C. Vatin, (ed.), *Connaissances du Maghreb* (1984), pp.29–46; M. Greenhalgh, 'The new centurions: French reliance on the Roman past during the conquest of Algeria', *War and Society*, 16, 1 (1998), pp. 1–28; P.M. Lorcin, 'Rome and France in Africa: recovering colonial Algeria's Latin past', *FHS*, 25, 2 (2002), pp. 295–329.

62 F. Laurent, *Victor Hugo face à la conquête de l'Algérie* (2001), 18.

63 C.S. Andrew, *Théophile Delcassé and the Making of the Entente Cordiale* (1968).

64 R. Girardet, *Le nationalisme français: anthologie 1871–1914* (1966, repr. 1983), pp. 107–15.

65 Ruscio, *Que la France était belle*, pp. 103–13.

66 For an assessment of Ferry's role regarding the colonies, see T.F. Power, *Jules Ferry and the Renaissance of French Imperialism* (New York 1977); F. Manchuelle, 'Origines républicaines de la politique d'expansion coloniale de Jules Ferry 1838–1865', *Revue française d'histoire d'Outre-Mer (RFHOM)*, 75, 279 (1988), pp. 185–206.

67 Andrew and Kanya-Forstner, 'The French "Colonial Party"' and 'The Groupe Colonial, 1892–1932'; Lagana, *Le Parti colonial français*; August, *The Selling of the Empire*; L. Abrams and D.J. Miller, 'Who were the French colonialists? A reassessment of the Parti colonial, 1890–1914', *HJ*, 19, 3 (1976), pp. 685–725.

68 See for instance A.S. Kanya-Forstner, *The Conquest of the Western Sudan* (Cambridge 1969).

69 For a thorough appraisal of the role of the press in promoting the French conquest of Africa over the period, see W.H. Schneider, *An Empire for the Masses. The French Popular Image of Africa, 1870–1900* (Westport, CT 1982).

70 D. Lejeune, *Les sociétés de géographie en France et l'expansion coloniale au XIXe siècle* (1993), pp. 113–40. See also A. Murphy, *The Ideology of French Imperialism, 1871–1881* (Washington 1948).

71 M.J. Heffernan, 'The science of empire: the French geographical movement and the forms of French imperialism, 1870–1920', in Godlewska and Smith (eds), *Geography and Empire*, pp. 92–114.

72 A.L. Conklin, *A Mission to Civilize: The Republican Idea of Empire in France and West Africa, 1895–1930* (Stanford CA 1997).

73 M. Cornick, 'Representations of Britain and British colonialism in French adventure fiction, 1870–1914', *French Cultural Studies (FCS)*, 17, 2 (2006), pp. 137–54.

74 For a recent history of the White Fathers, see J.-C. Ceillier, *Histoire des missionnaires d'Afrique (Pères Blancs) (1868–1892)* (2008).

75 Lavigerie's key political role was noted from very early on: J. Tournier, *Le Cardinal Lavigerie et son action politique (1863–1892)* (1913).

76 R.E. Nwoye, *The Public Image of Pierre Savorgnan de Brazza and the Establishment of French Imperialism in the Congo* (Aberdeen 1981), pp. 103–12; H. Brunschwig, *Brazza explorateur: les traités Makoko 1880–1882* (1972), pp. 258–67.

77 P. Leroy-Beaulieu, *Le Sahara, le Soudan et les chemins de fer transsahariens* (1904). See also D. and P. Bejui, *Exploits et fantasmes transsahariens* (La Roche Blanche 1994). About the failure of the Flatters mission, see M. Cassou, *L'échec sanglant des missions Flatters* (2004).

78 M. Greenhalgh, *Epehemeral Vistas: The Expositions Universelles, Great Exhibitions and World's Fairs, 1851–1939* (Manchester 1988); P. Ory, *Les Expositions universelles* (1982).

79 C. Hodeir, 'Decentering the gaze at French colonial exhibitions', in P.S. Landau and D. Kaspin (eds), *Images and Empires: Visuality in Colonial and Postcolonial Africa* (Berkeley CA 2002), pp. 233–52. See also L.E. Palermo, 'Identity under construction: representing the colonies at the Paris Exposition universelle of 1889', in S. Peabody and T. Stovall (eds), *The Color of Liberty: Histories of Race in France* (Durham NC and London 2003), pp. 285–301.

80 V.a., 'Renoir et l'Algérie', in v.a., *De Delacroix à Renoir*, pp. 208–47.

81 J.-C. Humbert, *Jean Geiser: photographe, éditeur d'art, Alger 1848–1923* (2008).

82 R. Little, '"Tiens, Forestier!": Maupassant et la colonisation', *Plaisance*, III, 8 (2006), pp. 75–87.

83 J.-M. Seillan, *Aux sources du roman colonial (1863–1914): l'Afrique à la fin du XIXe siècle* (2006).

84 For more details on the influence of colonial ideology on Loti, see A.C. Hargreaves, *The Colonial Experience in French Fiction: A Study of Pierre Loti, Ernest Psichari and Pierre Mille* (1981).

85 For a general appraisal of the link between imperialism and literary production in the period, see M. Astier-Loutfi, *Littérature et colonialism: l'expansion coloniale vue dans la littérature romanesque française, 1871–1914* (1971).

86 One such instance being Raymonde Bonnetain's *Une Française au Soudan* (1894, repr. 2007).

87 R. Arié, 'L'opinion publique en France et l'affaire de Fachoda', *Revue d'histoire des colonies*, 41, 3–4 (1954), pp. 329–67, and G.N. Sanderson, *England, Europe and the Upper Nile* (Edinburgh 1965), p. 372. For an appraisal of French perceptions of England at the turn of the century, see M. Cornick, 'Les problèmes de la perception réciproque de la France et de l'Angleterre au seuil du XXe siècle', in M.-M. Benzoni et al., *Images des peuples et histoire des relations internationales du XVIe siècle à nos jours* (2008), pp. 239–52 and J. Guiffan, *Histoire de l'anglophobie en France* (Dinan 2004), pp. 137–48.

88 Girardet, *idée coloniale*, pp. 147–52.

89 On this question, see also J. Marseille, 'La gauche, la droite et le fait colonial en France des années 1880 aux années 1960', *Vingtième Siècle*, 24 (1989), pp. 17–28 and M. Michel, 'La colonisation', in J.-F. Sirinelli, *Histoire des droites en France* (1992), pp. 125–63.

90 M.J. Heffernan, 'The French right and the overseas empire', in N. Atkin and F. Tallett, *The Right in France* (2002), pp. 89–113.

91 L. Morando, *Les instituts coloniaux et l'Afrique, 1893–1940* (2007).

92 Among such examples were P. Gaffarel, *Les Colonies françaises* (1880) and A. Rambaud, *La France coloniale: histoire, géographie, commerce* (1886).

93 Such as M. Dubois and A. Terrier, *Les Colonies françaises: un siècle d'expansion coloniale* (1901); J. Darcy, *France et Angleterre, cent années de rivalité coloniale: l'Afrique* (1904); P. Gaffarel, *Histoire de l'expansion coloniale de la France depuis 1870 jusqu'en 1905* (1905).

94 M. Fallex and A. Mairey, *La France et ses colonies* (1902). For a general overview of the teaching about the colonies in France, see P. Singaravélou, Professer l'Empire: introduction à l'histoire de l'enseignement des sciences coloniales en France sous la IIIe République, doctoral thesis, University of Paris I 2007.

95 *Le Petit Parisien*, 11 January 1907.

96 On Marchand as a national hero, see Girardet, *idée coloniale*, pp. 148–9 and B. Sèbe, 'From Thoissey to the capital via Fashoda: Major Marchand, partisan icon of the right in Paris', in J. Wardhaugh (ed.), *Paris and the Right in the Twentieth Century* (Newcastle 2007), pp. 18–42.

97 P. Venier, 'A campaign of colonial propaganda: Gallieni, Lyautey and the defence of the military regime in Madagascar, May 1899 to July 1900', in Chafer and Sackur (eds), *Promoting the Colonial Idea*, pp. 29–39.

98 Sèbe, Celebrating, pp. 94–104 and 212–66.

99 With works by Jean Ricquebourg, Myriam Harry, Alfred Droin, Geneviève Lanzy and Pierre Loti.

100 With works by Raymond Marival, Henri Richardot and, most famously, the brothers Tharaud and André Gide.

101 Among the numerous biographies of Eberhardt, see E.C. Roux, *Isabelle du désert* (2003) and A. Kobak, *Isabelle: The life of Isabelle Eberhardt* (1987).

102 Anti-colonialism remained still present in the period (with works such as Paul Vigné d'Octon's *Les crimes coloniaux de la IIIe République*, published in 1911), although celebrations of the empire were in the majority: see Girardet, *idée coloniale*, pp. 156–67.

103 On the Tharaud brothers, see M. Leymarie, Jérôme et Jean Tharaud écrivains et journalistes: des années de formation à la notoriété, une marche au conformisme, doctoral thesis, IEP Paris 1994.

104 Especially in *Le Sang des races* (1899), *La Cina* (1901), *Pépète le Bien-Aimé* (1904) and *La Concession de Madame Petitgand* (1912).

105 M. Chevalier, 'Géographie et littérature', *Acta Geographica*, 1500 bis (2001), pp. 204–5.

106 M.-A. Leblond, *Le Roman colonial* (1926).

107 Ruscio, *Que la France était belle*, pp. 187–224.

108 J. Cowart et al., *Matisse in Morocco* (Washington 1990).

109 On Mangin's *La Force noire*, see A. Champeaux and E. Deroo, *La Force noire: gloires et infortunes d'une légende coloniale* (2006).

110 M. Michel, '1917: La "Force noire"', in Rioux, *Dictionnaire de la France coloniale*, 55–60. See also M. Michel, *Les Africains et la Grande Guerre* (2003).

111 Y. Holo, 'L'imaginaire colonial dans la bande dessinée', in Bancel et al., *Images et colonies*, pp. 73–6.

112 *A la baïonnette!*, 13 March 1915.

113 *Lectures pour tous*, 7 November 1914.

114 See the vivid contemporary account of Lucie Cousturier, *Des inconnus chez moi* (1920, repr. 2001). See also R. Little (ed.), *Lucie Cousturier, les tirailleurs sénégalais et la question coloniale* (2008); J. Riesz and J. Schultz, *Tirailleurs sénégalais: présentations littéraires et figuratives de soldats africains au service de la France* (Frankfurt 1989); C.J. Balesi, *From Adversaries to Comrades in Arms: West Africans and the French Military, 1885–1918* (Waltham MA 1979); and R.S. Fogarty, *Race and War in France*.

115 E.g. L. Gaillet, *Coulibaly: les Sénégalais sur la terre de France* (1917) and *Deux ans avec les Sénégalais* (1918); A. Séché, *Les Noirs, d'après des documents officiels* (1919).

116 Commery and J.P. Pinchon, *Bécassine pendant la Grande Guerre* (1915).

117 J. Garrigues, *Banania, histoire d'une passion française* (1991).

118 M. Le Van Ho, 'Le général Pennequin et le projet d'armée jaune (1911–1915)', *RFHOM*, 75, 279 (1988), pp. 145–67.

119 F. Neau-Dufour, *Ernest Psichari: l'ordre et l'errance* (2001).

120 See C.M. Andrew and A. S. Kanya-Forstner, *France Overseas: The Great War and the Climax of French Colonial Expansion* (1981).

121 Although the overall impact of 'popular imperialism' of French inter-war culture is still a matter of debate; see Thomas, *French Empire Between the Wars*, pp. 185–208.

122 Michel, 'La colonisation', 141.

123 August, *Selling of the Empire*, 69.

124 C.-R. Ageron, 'Les colonies devant l'opinion publique française (1919–1939)', *RFHOM*, 77, 286 (1990), pp. 31–73.

125 See S. Lemaire, 'Propager: l'Agence générale des Colonies (1920–1931)', in Blanchard, *Culture coloniale*, pp. 197–206 and L'Agence économique des colonies. Instrument de propagande ou creuset de l'idéologie coloniale en France (1870–1960)?, doctoral thesis, European University Institute, Florence 2000.

126 Morando, *instituts coloniaux*.

127 August, *Selling of the Empire*, 91.

128 August, *Selling of the Empire* and Ageron, 'Les colonies devant l'opinion'.

129 *Cahiers du centenaire de l'Algérie*, XII (1930), pp. 59–71.

130 G. Meynié, 'Volonté de propagande ou inconscient affiché? Images et imaginaire coloniaux français dans l'Entre-deux-guerres', in Blanchard, *Images et Colonies*, pp, 41–8.

131 August, *Selling of the Empire*, pp. 107–23.
132 Ageron, 'Les colonies devant l'opinion', p. 46.
133 *Cahiers du centenaire*, XII, pp. 59–71 and 'Cahier complémentaire', *L'Algérie du Centenaire vue par l'université de France* (1930).
134 L. Pyenson, *Civilizing Mission: Exact Sciences and French Overseas Expansion, 1830–1940* (Baltimore MD 1993).
135 C. Hodeir and M. Pierre, *L'Exposition coloniale* (Paris and Brussels 1991), p. 101. The 1931 colonial exhibition has recently attracted much scholarly attention as the embodiment of the triumph of an idealized 'Greater France': see Hodeir, 'Decentering the gaze', in Landau, *Images and Empires*, pp. 233–52; Thomas, *French Empire Between the Wars*, pp. 199–202. For the symbolic value of the event, see P. Morton, *Hybrid Modernities: Architecture and Representation at the 1931 Colonial Exposition, Paris* (Cambridge MA 2000); P. Norindr, 'Representing Indochina. The French colonial fantasmatic and the Exposition coloniale de Paris', *FCS*, 6, 1 (1995), pp. 35–60 and N. Cooper, *France in Indochina* (Oxford and New York 2001), pp. 65–90. For the value of the exhibition as a *lieu de mémoire*, see C.-R. Ageron, 'L'exposition coloniale de 1931: mythe républicain ou mythe impérial ?', in P. Nora (ed.), *Les Lieux de mémoire*, vol. I, (1984), pp. 561–91.
136 H. Lebovics, *True France: The Wars over Cultural Identity 1900–45* (Ithaca NY 1992), pp. 51–98. But Ageron had argued the opposite in the abovementioned *Lieux de mémoire*.
137 P. Blanchard et al., *Le Paris noir* (2001) and P. Blanchard et al., *Le Paris arabe* (2003).
138 P. Archer-Straw, *Negrophilia: Avant-Garde Paris and Black Culture in the 1920s* (2000); B. A. Berliner, *Ambivalent Desire: The Exotic Black other in Jazz-Age France* (Amherst and Boston 2002); and J. Blake, *Le Tumulte noir: Modernist Art and Popular Entertainment in Jazz-Age Paris 1900–1930* (University Park PA 1999).
139 On reactions to immigrants in metropolitan France, see P. Lawrence, '"Un flot d'agitateurs politiques, de fauteurs de désordre et de criminels." Adverse perceptions of immigrants in France between the wars', *French History*, 14, 2 (2000), pp. 201–21; Thomas, *French Empire Between the Wars*, pp. 279–80; R. Schor, *L'opinion française et les étrangers en France: 1919–1939* (1985) and N. MacMaster, *Colonial Migrants and Racism: Algerians in France 1900–1962* (1997).
140 Y. S. Fletcher, '"Capital of the colonies." Real and imagined boundaries between metropole and empire in 1920s Marseilles', in F. Driver and D. Gilbert (eds), *Imperial Cities. Landscape, Display and Identity* (Manchester 1999), pp. 136–54.
141 P. Blanchard et al. (eds), *Human Zoos. Science and Spectacle in the Age of Colonial Empires* (Liverpool 2008).
142 E. Furlough, '*Une leçon de choses*. Tourism, empire and the nation in interwar France', *FHS*, 25, 3 (2002), pp. 441–73.
143 G.-M. Haardt and L. Audouin-Dubreuil, *La première traversée du Sahara en automobile* (1923), *La Croisière noire: expédition Citroën Centre Afrique* (1927) and G. Le Fèvre, *Expédition Citroën Centre-Asie: la Croisière jaune* (1933).
144 See A. Audouin-Dubreuil, *La Croisière jaune* (Grenoble 2002), *La Croisière noire* (Grenoble 2004), *La Croisière des sables* (Grenoble 2005) and *Les Croisières Citroën* (Evreux 2004). On the cinematographic use of the *Croisière noire*, see M.-H. Piault, 'L'exotisme et le cinéma ethnographique: la rupture de La Croisière noire', *Journal of Film Preservation* (*JFP*), 63 (2001), pp. 6–16.
145 A. Murray, 'Le tourisme Citroën au Sahara (1924–1925)', *Vingtième Siècle*, 68 (2000), pp. 95–107.
146 A. Hugon, 'La propagande missionnaire', in Blanchard, *Images et colonies*, pp. 77–82.
147 Ruscio, *Que la France était belle*, pp. 235–51.
148 B. Boëhm, 'Arts et séductions', in Blanchard, *Images et colonies*, pp. 87–91.
149 See in particular Blanchard, *Images et Colonies* and E. Deroo, *L'Illusion coloniale* (2005).
150 E. Cazenave, *La Villa Abd-el-Tif* (1907–1962) (1998).
151 E. Cazenave, *Les artistes de l'Algérie* (2001), pp. 84–113. For sculptors, see also S. Richemond, *Les Salons des artistes coloniaux* (2003).

152 E. Bréon and M. Lefrançois (eds), *Coloniales 1920–1940* (Boulogne-Billancourt 1989).

153 E.g. J. and J. Tharaud, *Randonnée de Samba Diouf* (1922), B. Diallo, *Force-Bonté* (1926).

154 Especially André Gide, Albert Londres, Luc Durtain and Andrée Viollis and the Surrealists in general.

155 Catalogue of the French National Library, www.bnf.fr, entry 'Sur la route mandarine' (accessed 21 January 2009).

156 Chevalier, 'Géographie et littérature', p. 207.

157 See J. Déjeux, *La littérature algérienne contemporaine* (1975).

158 Sèbe, Celebrating, p. 107.

159 E. Cazenave, *Explorations artistiques au Sahara (1850–1975)* (2005).

160 See for instance P. Decraene and F. Zuccarelli, *Grands Sahariens à la découverte du "désert des déserts"* (1994); M. Roux, *Le désert de sable: le Sahara dans l'imaginaire des Français (1900–1994)* (1996); M. Tranchet, 'La représentation des Touaregs dans le roman saharien français. 1830–1998', in GEMDEV and Université du Mali, *Mali-France: regards sur une histoire partagée* (2005), pp. 183–99 and Pandolfi, 'mythe touareg'.

161 J. Germain and S. Faye, *Le Général Laperrine, grand Saharien* (1922). (Edition dated 1923 mentions 23rd edition).

162 R. Bazin, *Charles de Foucauld, explorateur du Maroc, ermite au Sahara* (1921). (Edition dated 1922 mentions 44th thousand).

163 Germain and Faye, *Général Laperrine*, p. 153.

164 Author of the best-seller *L'Atlantide* translated into twenty languages, which in the 1970s had sold 1,200,000 copies since its publication. See P. Boulanger, *Le cinéma colonial de 'l'Atlantide' à 'Lawrence d'Arabie'* (1975), p. 32.

165 A. de Meaux, *L'Ultime Désert: vie et mort de Michel Vieuchange* (2004).

166 Especially Théodore Monod, Henri Lhote, Emile-Félix Gautier and Robert Capot-Rey.

167 The role and place of colonial cinema has attracted much scholarly attention. Besides the pioneering M.-R. Bataille and C. Veillot, *Caméras sous le soleil* (Algiers 1956) and Boulanger, *Cinéma colonial*, more recent studies have approached the topic from a variety of points of views: A. Benali, *Le cinéma colonial au Maghreb: l'imaginaire en trompe-l'œil* (1998); D. H. Slavin, *Colonial Cinema and Imperial France 1919–1939* (Baltimore MD 2001); G. Gauthier and P. Esnault, 'Le cinéma colonial', *Revue du cinéma*, 394 (May 1984), pp. 83–94; P. Sorlin, 'The fanciful empire: French feature films and the colonies in the 1930s', *FCS*, 2 (1991), pp. 135–51; D. Sherzer, *Cinema, Colonialism, Postcolonialism* (Austin TX 1996); C. O'Brien, 'The "Cinéma colonial" of 1930s France: film narration as spatial practice', in M. Bernstein and G. Studlar (eds), *Visions of the East, Orientalism in Film* (1997). pp. 207–31; G. Wilder, 'Framing Greater France', *Journal of Historical Sociology*, 14, 2 (June 2001), pp. 198–225. On early colonial films, see M. Cadé, 'De la casquette du père Bugeaud aux moustaches du maréchal Lyautey', *Les Cahiers de la Cinémathèque*, 49 (1988), pp. 5–10.

168 P. Leprohon, *L'exotisme et le cinéma* (1945).

169 Based on Boulanger's chronology in *Cinéma colonial*, pp. 231–50.

170 Boulanger, *Cinéma colonial*, p. 123.

171 *Le Journal de Roubaix*, 17 February 1940.

172 Benali, *Cinéma colonial au Maghreb*, pp. 247–68.

173 See S. Ungar, 'Léon Poirier's L'Appel du silence and the cult of Imperial France', *JFP*, 63 (2001), pp. 41–6 and B. Sèbe, Celebrating, pp. 115–18.

174 Boulanger, *Cinéma colonial*, p. 123.

175 Especially *Les Sentinelles de l'Empire* (1938), *La France est un empire* (1939) and *Le Chemin de l'honneur* (1939).

176 C.-R. Ageron, 'La perception de la puissance française en 1938–1939: le mythe impérial', in R. Girault and R. Frank (eds), *La Puissance en Europe 1938–40* (1984), pp. 227–44.

177 M. Michel, 'La puissance par l'Empire: note sur la perception du facteur impérial dans l'élaboration de la défense nationale (1936-1938)', *RFHOM*, 64, 254 (1982), pp. 35–46.
178 K. K. Daouda and J. Thobie, 'Ouest-Éclair (Rennes) et l'empire colonial français de 1936 à 1939', *RFHOM*, 69, 255 (1982), pp. 115–27.
179 'Nous vaincrons parce que nous sommes les plus forts', *Pathé* newsreel, 1 January 1940, www.ina.fr (accessed 30 August 2009).
180 Michel, *Africains et la Grande Guerre*, p. 210.
181 P. M. de la Gorce, *L'Empire écartelé 1936–46* (1988). See also E. Jennings, *Vichy in the Tropics* (Palo Alto CA 2004) and J. Cantier and E. Jennings (eds), *L'Empire colonial sous Vichy* (2004).
182 See C. Levisse-Touzé, *Philippe Leclerc de Hauteclocque* (2002).
183 M. Thomas, *The French Empire at War 1940–5* (Manchester 1998), p. 224.
184 R. Ginio, *French Colonialism Unmasked* (Lincoln NE and London 2006), pp. 11–21.
185 Blanchard and Ginio, 'Révolution impériale', Blanchard, *Culture coloniale*, pp. 382–3 and Deroo, *Illusion coloniale*, pp. 152–3.
186 E.g. *Le Pavillon brûle*, *L'Homme sans nom*, *L'Appel du Bled*, *Le Chant de l'Exilé*, etc.
187 Bibliographical research undertaken on the online catalogue of the French National Library, www.bnf.fr (accessed 4 May 2009).
188 C.-R. Ageron, 'Vichy, les Français et l'empire', in J.-P. Azéma and F. Bédarida (eds), *Vichy et les Français* (1992), pp. 122–34.
189 Thomas, *French Empire at War*, pp. 253–4.
190 J. Marseille, 'Les images de l'Afrique en France (des années 1880 aux années 1930)', *Canadian Journal of African Studies*, 22, 1 (1988), pp. 121–30.
191 D.B. Marshall, *The French Colonial Myth and Constitution-making in the Fourth Republic* (New Haven CT 1973).
192 P. Tripier, *Autopsie de la guerre d'Algérie* (1972), p. 147.
193 On the consequences of the Algerian war on France, see T. Shepard, *The Invention of Decolonization* (Ithaca NY and London 2006).
194 F. Cooper, *Africa since 1940* (Cambridge 2002), pp. 66–132.
195 On Fourth Republic policies about sports, see M. Amar, *Nés pour courir: sport, pouvoir et rébellion 1944–1958* (Grenoble 1987).
196 See Cazenave, *Les Artistes de l'Algérie*.
197 Such as, for instance, *La Route inconnue* (1947), *L'Escadron blanc* (1949) and *Bob le flambeur* (1956).
198 J. Lenzini, *L'Algérie de Camus* (Aix-en-Provence 1987).
199 A. Haddour, *Colonial Myths: History and Narrative* (Manchester 2000) and J. Le.Sueur, *Uncivil War: Intellectuals and Identity Politics during the Decolonization of Algeria* (Philadelphia PA 2001), pp. 87–127.
200 See J. Frémeaux, 'The Sahara and the Algerian War', in M. Evans (ed.), *The Algerian War and the French Army 1954–1962* (Basingstoke 2002), pp. 76–87.
201 H. Lhote, *Vers d'autres tassilis* (1976).
202 Post-colonial literature has been the object of too many works to list them here. However, a useful overview to complement the present chapter can be found in M.A. Majumdar, *Postcoloniality, The French Dimension* (Oxford 2007).

CHAPTER 2

Passion or indifference?
Popular imperialism in Britain: continuities
and discontinuities over two centuries

John M. MacKenzie

Background

The concept of popular imperialism in Britain has stimulated considerable controversy.[1] There has long been, among British historians, an
apparent desire to separate domestic British history from that of its
empire. Such scholars, often occupying the political spectrum from both
left and right, have considered empire to be an inconvenient aspect of the
British past and one from which the British public could somehow be
absolved.[2] By this view, empire may have been a folly of the elite, for them
an expression of national power and economic importance, but it had
very little influence on the ordinary people, who were more concerned
with the basic problems of survival. While (this faction would argue) it
cannot be gainsaid that there were outbursts of apparently popular imperialism from time to time, these were very much restricted in their inci-
dence and swiftly evaporated after moments of threat on the
international stage passed. The elite, indeed, tended to lament the fact
that their interests did not seem to arouse much concern among ordinary
people. I have recently argued that these ideas (wrong-headed in my view)
were partly stimulated by the general rejection of the works of J.A.
Hobson, writing from the standpoint of the liberal left, by British historians in the twentieth century. Hobson's *Imperialism: A Study* was identified as a foundation of the unsustainable Marxist interpretation of
imperialism. His *The War in South Africa* represented a conspiracy
theory, linked to the investment practices of capitalists and their urge to
influence political processes that also did not fully fit the facts. His third
book of the period, spanning the turn of the nineteenth and twentieth
centuries, *The Psychology of Jingoism*, has been less noticed than the
other two, but has been rejected as yet another effusion of Hobsonian
obsessions.[3] In any case, his analysis of the public expressions of jingoism

was restricted to a narrow period and could indeed be confined to incidents of the 1890s and the years of the South African War. He was, however, a shrewd observer of a long-standing jingoist phenomenon.

In the quarter century that has elapsed since the publication of *Propaganda and Empire*, I have seen no reason to revise the interpretations unveiled in that book. Indeed, the conviction that popular imperialism was an abiding factor in British society has been confirmed by many subsequent studies and by the extension of the focus of the research. *Propaganda and Empire* was no more than a preliminary statement and it contained a number of gaps (including the very significant one of missionaries and the churches) which can now be filled.[4] Moreover, it is now possible to take more notice of the press and other aspects of print capitalism.[5] New research is appearing all the time and we shall shortly have a more convincing demonstration of the ways in which national imperial endeavour was expressed through educational processes.[6] There has also been a growing understanding of the character of national identity and the manner in which such identities are built up from a number of factors, including posturing on the international stage, as well as through processes of 'othering', both in respect of rival European nations and in relation to peoples of other races.[7] The fact is that imperial events slotted into an exciting adventure and militarist tradition which translated readily into other media, not just the stage and the press, but also popular literature, painting, prints, statuary, memorials and music.[8] As the nineteenth century wore on, this propensity to depict the world as essentially Britain's sphere of action was enhanced.

In considering whether there was popular support for and interest in empire, it is necessary to analyse the supply of material relating to empire as well as its potential consumption. In all my writings about popular imperialism, I have always been clear on a number of issues. The first is that the flow of information or references to empire was generalised, that it embraced both 'formal' and 'informal' empire, and that it inevitably failed to deal with the detailed principles and practices of imperial rule, which were the preserve of the elite. The second is that its span was both geographically and chronologically wide. Thus it embraced colonies of white settlement, the Empire of India, and, later, the so-called dependent territories. Its origins lay in the eighteenth century and it continued to be a significant aspect of British consciousness until the mid-twentieth. Third, it was closely bound up with the image and activities of the armed forces. Fourth, it was expressed in a wide variety of media, including entertainment, educational, and printed elements. Fifth, there was a significant literary dimension, both in the realm of canonical texts and in more popular literature, the latter being less recognised and understood than the former, but probably had greater circulation and penetration. Sixth, the various denominations of the Christian churches were highly influential in disseminating ideas and information about imperial territories and their peoples. And seventh, the scale of migration to the empire as well as the financial remittances that came back to families,[9] helped to keep the existence and significance of colonies continually in the forefront of the public imagination.

Earlier manifestations

It is important to recognise that in the British case, these imperial passions were not wholly new in the nineteenth century. Kathleen Wilson has charted the significance of aspects of popular imperialism in the eighteenth century and their close relationship with popular politics and the fortunes of administrations and their oppositions during that period.[10] She has identified a number of significant factors. In that century, empire was identified with manliness, with the avoidance of 'effeminacy' (though patriotic concepts were often represented in female form), with the liberties of the freeborn Englishman and their desire to spread them abroad in pursuit of a shadowy global salvation. It was also connected with a positive image of citizenship, with trading relations and sources of wealth and well-being. It constituted a source of identity in respect of rivals like the French and the Spanish and its possession and protection against assailants produced major public agitations during the War of Austrian Succession and the Seven Years' War. Empire was celebrated (and very occasionally attacked) in the streets and at fairs, in the theatre and in the press, in coffee houses and newsrooms, in ballads, tracts and novels.[11] Effigies of alleged villains were burned and heroes were exalted to the skies. Imperial enthusiasms also had the capacity to create Britons, to unite English with the Welsh and the Scots, at least lowland Scots. If empire was often depicted as a 'bulwark and emblem of English superiority and benevolence',[12] it also had the power to create a sense of British excellence and self-overvaluation in respect of the rest of the world. But empire was also fraught with ambiguities, sometimes representing freedom, sometimes autocracy, often promoting peaceful trade yet stimulating violence, in both conquest and in defence. Political identities associated with empire were also 'contested, fissured' and fraught with 'contending political identities'.[13] They were invariably seen as representing bourgeois ambitions and moralities against effete aristocratic opulence. The loss of empire might lead to the 'emasculation' of the nation. These ambiguities were particularly apparent during the American Revolutionary War when radicals supported the colonists to the rage of imperial loyalists. The entry of the French, the traditional enemy, into the war in 1778 helped to make the issues clearer, though not entirely so. Later, in the Napoleonic Wars, the initial support of the radicals for the revolutionary ideals in France was soon overwhelmed by the Bonapartist autocracy and the British fight for survival against the French dominance in Europe. The notion that 'imperial ascendancy and a populist virtuous polity'[14] should go hand in hand was to survive from the eighteenth into the nineteenth century.

It would be wrong to imagine that these various expressions of a popular imperialism within British culture were generally dormant, only to flare up during a colonial war, an indigenous revolt, or imperial competition with another European power. It is true that moments of jingoism tended to occur in response to just such climacterics, but they were only the periodic blazing of a continuing fire. There was, however, one great controversy and agitation which seemed to cut across enthusiasms for empire. This was the campaign against slavery which ran from the late eighteenth century until the abolition of the British slave trade in 1807 and the emancipation of slaves within the British Empire in 1833, after which the anti-slavery campaign moved against other empires, such as the Portuguese, the continuing Indian Ocean trade, and the existence of slavery in the southern United States, in Brazil and elsewhere. A large number of books were published in this area and, after 1833, the campaign contributed mightily to the British self-estimation as a just empire, one supposedly capable of showing the way to others. Thus, although the emancipation campaign seemed to contain anti-imperial elements from time to time, they were only traces, soon converted to a new sense of national justification. As Clare Midgley has demonstrated, women played an important role in the anti-slavery campaign, and after this women's campaigning organisations became a notable characteristic of British imperial discourses (perhaps culminating in the great controversies surrounding the South African War).[15] They were also involved in pro-imperial organisations like the Victoria League and (in Canada) the Imperial Order Daughters of the Empire.[16]

While there was a real dynamic in the nineteenth century, there were some essential ideological continuities. With the loss of the American colonies, the British concentrated on the Caribbean, on India, and increasingly on the territories of settlement in Canada, Australia, the Cape after 1815, and later New Zealand. In some respects, the aristocracy restored their association with empire through the military, through colonial governorships, and through gentlemanly migration. Whereas the Scots in the eighteenth century had been divided into the virtuous urban traders and the 'barbaric' and popish Highlanders of the 1745 rebellion, they became united both in a single culture (itself influenced by the cultural tropes of Jacobitism) and in an adherence to the opportunities afforded by empire. Modes of administration and law were transformed; after the Durham Report settlers were given a modicum of internal self-government; and the images of the military and of the navy were progressively enhanced (though the latter had traditionally been seen as the protector of British freedoms). There was a major shift from mercantilism to free trade and the old monopolistic companies progressively disappeared (though replaced later in the nineteenth century by the new chartered companies). The franchise was progressively extended after 1832 and the reputation of the monarchy increased under Victoria even as its power declined. Traditional rulers among indigenous people were taken into partnership and where they did not exist they were often invented. Through missionary endeavour, the Christian churches became much more associated with, if not entirely seduced by, the empire. Racial ideas and associated racism were transformed as they were influenced by pseudo-scientific social derivations of dominant scientific ideas. Yet, although imperial forms were very different, the cultural expression of empire remained remarkably similar. The fantasies of freedom, of the spreading of peace and civilisation, of promoting rights and legal protections, and the dissemination of Christianity, education and moral values, continued to feature strongly in the propaganda. An extensive range of media continued to be bent to imperial ends. Hero-worship remained a rallying point, often with appeals to historic precedents, and public excitements could be readily whipped up when imperial reverses seemed to threaten national integrity and security. We can also identify continuities in the presentation of fiction on imperial themes.[17]

Migration and the 'British World'

What were the dimensions of this imperial imaginary? It is clear that we should be thinking in terms of awareness rather than knowledge, of a generalised support rather than (except at specific historical moments) a detailed passion, of a sense of national superiority instead of overweening pride. It may well be true that those at the bottom of the social heap in Britain, those lost in the predicament of poverty, were far too concerned with the business of survival to take much interest in this. But for them, as for many others, there might be the possibility of emigration in search of better circumstances. The 'empire of settlement' presented what looked to be a life's oyster of opportunity, a place to which it was possible to migrate – if the passage money could be found – without any need of passports, visas, or adherence to quotas.

That was indeed the impression that some emigration recruiters wished to convey. Such propaganda had its origins as far back as the early decades of the seventeenth century and was conveyed at that time through handbills, ballads, sermons and cheap advertising.[18] It continued, off and on, until the post-Second World War period of the twentieth century. The whole business of emigration and the information and recruitment mechanisms associated with it have been largely ignored in the discussion of popular imperialism. Yet they were highly significant in keeping the existence of the empire, and its possibly beneficent effects, before the British public. In the nineteenth century, recruiting agencies and their agents were widespread phenomena. Lectures were given throughout the country and were well attended. Leaflets were issued. Newspaper articles were common and advertisements appeared not only in the public prints, but also in shops (photographic evidence demonstrates this)[19] and, in the twentieth century, on large public street hoardings.[20] Thus, few can have been unaware that these opportunities were available, even if only a minority, albeit a large one, took them up.

Among the majority who stayed at home, almost everybody must have had relatives who migrated overseas. Countless letters were exchanged. Chains of migration were established as remittances helped those at home to follow. While there are very real instances of virtually enforced migration, from Scotland during the Highland Clearances and from Ireland during the Hungry Forties, most migration was voluntary. Although it has seemed almost invisible to some historians, it was highly visible to contemporaries. Emigration statistics are notoriously slippery, but it has been estimated that in the classic age of migration from 1815–1930, the British Isles (that is, including Ireland) sent some 18,700,000 people overseas, over one-third of all migrants from Europe. The English figure for that period might be over ten million with the Scots contributing at least two million. The result is that hundreds of millions of people in the world claim descent from English, Scots, Irish and Welsh migrants, while well over 350 million people speak English as a first language.[21] It would seem unlikely that such major movements of people had no effects upon the home populations.

Moreover, it reveals the extent to which the British were able to see the wider world in general, and increasingly the empire in particular, as vast free regions over which to roam. This was one of the great migrations of human history, curiously less prominent than the historic migrations of peoples in Africa, Asia, the Americas, North Africa and the Middle East, partly because it was seaborne. Moreover, until the period after the Second World War, colonies of settlement did their best to concentrate on the immigration of people of British stock, a policy only abandoned when it was obvious that the British could no longer supply the numbers required. In addition to this great movement of ordinary people, the

British Empire (and also non-imperial countries) became a vast zone of opportunity for professionals and other members of an elite.[22]

The world of formal and informal empire also became a great scientific laboratory available to scientists from Britain (and elsewhere in Europe). The process of engrossing an imperial world into scientific (and medical) endeavour was a significant part of its 'domestication'.[23] But there was of course much ordinary careering too, both by 'sojourners' who went to the empire temporarily and migrants who stayed in order to create fresh opportunities for themselves and their descendants. The key to an understanding of this major migration is that it involved us and us, us here and us there. Migrants made the 'othering' of indigenous peoples come much closer to home. Moreover, the migrants set out to create a familiar world, a world in which the built environment (particularly the urban) soon came to reflect the architectural forms of home, a world of societies and cultural events, sports and horse racing, civic organisation, of institutions like schools, universities, museums, art galleries, libraries and zoos, of gardens and familiar plants and animals (through 'acclimatisation'). All of these mushroomed not just in the colonies of settlement, but also in India and the so-called 'dependent territories'. Migrants and sojourners were truly in the business of creating a wider zone of familiar domesticity even in very different environments, climates and ethnic contexts. However, it is true that local modifications (often connected with the existence of indigenous people) soon made their appearance.[24] In all of these ways, popular imperialism became a global phenomenon, one which ensures that the dichotomy between the 'domestic' and the 'overseas' should not be emphasised too much.[25] In so many cultural forms, here was indeed a British World, one which inevitably had its effects upon a home population.

Yet emigration presents a number of problems in a discussion of popular imperialism. Like the empire itself, emigration for the British was always there, initially to Ireland or parts of Europe, then to the American colonies, and later to the 'territories of settlement' in the nineteenth and twentieth centuries. But if it was a continuing possibility, it was also in some respects a hidden phenomenon. Conventional approaches to British domestic history have often ignored it. The second difficulty is that the post-independence United States figured so strongly in this migration, at least until the early years of the twentieth century. For some commentators, migration was an essentially non-imperial process because of this significance of the USA. There are two answers to this. The United States, given its history and Anglophone status, could almost be seen by contemporaries as part of a British imperial world.[26] Anthony Trollope virtually treated it as such.[27] Cecil Rhodes and others believed passionately that it could be brought back within the imperial orbit.

Moreover, emigration to British colonies was nonetheless a major phenomenon in the nineteenth century and would ultimately outrank that to the USA in the twentieth. The third difficulty is that emigration could often be double edged. Many emigrants found new and satisfying lives. Others were gravely discontented and considerable numbers returned to Britain, particularly when travel became less problematic in the late nineteenth and twentieth centuries. At times, return migration could be as high as 40 per cent.[28] There is no evidence, however, that such return movements generated any form of anti-imperialism. The fact is that knowledge of the empire, even through somewhat mixed emotions, was enhanced. Moreover, emigrants, particularly those heading for the colonies, saw themselves as simply moving to a different part of Britain. As we have seen, theirs was invariably a move across a British World, not an alien globe. Language and cultures, religion and social relations were familiar, even if in seemingly alien geographical regions. Emigration had a tendency to heighten the notion that Britishness had become a global category. To some extent, these sensations even survived into the era when the former dominions had transparently become independent nation states, in the years after the Second World War. The continuing status of Queen Elizabeth II as Queen of Canada, New Zealand and Australia helped to preserve this atavistic view. Only in Australia was there a concerted effort to remove her, but even here it failed.

The theatre and literature

If emigration throws up problems of imperial focus, still its contribution to an understanding of Britain's imperial status and its supposed advantages was ever-present. The visibility of empire in other cultural forms can also be presented as having ambiguities which can be stressed by those seeking to deny the existence of a popular imperialism. But we would be wrong to interpret ambiguity as representing the negative. If we take the case of the theatre, it is abundantly apparent that from the eighteenth century, it demonstrated a fascination with an outer world newly unveiled in the exploratory, military and conquest events of the age. Kathleen Wilson has written of the 'centrality of theater in English culture'.[29] Indeed, theatrical interpretations of imperial events became almost legion, not only in England, but throughout Britain and in some parts of the empire. But the formal theatre was not the sole medium for such performances: we must add the theatricality of public performance, of shows and ceremonies which developed increasingly as a key medium of both local and national character in the course of the nineteenth century. These public performances of patriotic identity in global context took the form of the immensely popular panoramas (many of which featured spectacular imperial events),[30] of elaborate civic ceremonials, of celebratory regimental departures and arrivals (particularly after regiments were localised after the reforms of 1871), of exhibitions in London and many provincial cities, of the unveiling of memorials and monuments,[31] and of pageants of nation and empire. It is the universality of all these forms, plus the interest of the local press, that ensures that aspects of popular imperialism were distributed throughout the country and not just in the coastal ports which had clear and direct economic and shipping connections with imperial possessions. Inland counties, for example, had local regiments, all of which participated in colonial campaigns at one time or another. Their exploits, acts of heroism, sacrifices and losses, and it must be said aspects of their disillusion with the campaigns thrust upon them, appeared in newspapers exhibiting local chauvinisms in an imperial context. Such materials were produced, sold and read throughout the country.

Thus both formal and informal stages became a setting for repeated representations of empire and imperial events, all of them contributing to a fascination with adventure and militarist traditions which became increasingly prominent in all media of the time. Indeed, a number of characteristics of the theatre of the eighteenth and nineteenth centuries led to these repeated celebrations of empire. The prime focus was topicality: in the absence of modern aural and visual media, it was in the theatre that the great events of the day were re-created. This is certainly the case from the 1740s onwards when the climactic events of the War of Austrian Succession, the Seven Years' War and the American Revolutionary War were staged in melodramatic and spectacular form.[32] Admiral Vernon's success against the Spaniards at Porto Bello in 1740 was celebrated in a play entitled *The Play of the British Hero; or, Admiral VERNON'S Conquest over the Spaniards* and a number of others followed in succeeding decades.[33] This phenomenon became even more prominent during the Napoleonic Wars and events in India were followed with considerable interest. As one example of many, in the year of the Battle of Seringapatam (1799) and the fall of Tipu Sultan, the ruler of Mysore, no fewer than six plays based on these events appeared on the London stage. A similar staging appeared in Dublin and there are indications that such displays went round the empire.[34] In 1800, *The British in Egypt* portrayed the events associated with Napoleon's assault on Egypt and his efforts to secure a route to threaten the British position in India. These were frustrated by Nelson's victory at the Battle of the Nile and Nelson certainly became a major theatrical hero of the age. Thus imperial and naval events set within the vastness of the outer world were contained within the proscenium arch or the tanks of the aquatic theatres.

There was indeed a major fascination with spectacle which was expressed in the extraordinary aquatic performances that took place in London and elsewhere, invariably depicting great naval encounters in the European battle for the control of the outer world. One example of many is thrown up in the career of the Italian explorer and primitive archaeologist of Egypt, Giovanni Belzoni, who helped to create the dramatic hydraulic effects for a theatrical representation of the Spanish siege of Gibraltar during the American Revolutionary War.[35] This was matched by military and equestrian performances which often sought to recreate battle scenes. This fascination with spectacle grew in the nineteenth century. Stage effects and props, developing lighting and staging technology, all offered visual splendours designed to overawe and thrill an audience.[36] These mirrored the characteristics of industrialism, so well represented in factory production and what were seen as the transport marvels of the age. Worship of heroes and also of the heroic possibilities of ordinary people fitted with this. The grandeur of perceived moral character could be set against thrilling backdrops that were exotic and colourful.

A related feature of the period was the centrality of melodrama as the characteristic theatrical form of the age.[37] Melodrama featured major struggles between good and evil, which readily fitted the notion of a moral imperialism battling with the supposedly violent and atavistic 'others' of empire. Even pantomime, and certainly music hall, increasingly portrayed aspects of empire and imperialism by the end of the nineteenth century.[38] All of these fitted the nationalist patriotic mood of the time. They also ensured that, in an era of theatrical censorship, common ground could be found among writers, performers, rulers and consumers. In other words, such theatrical performances were both popular and acceptable. It is possible, for example, to identify a decline in plays representing class tensions (perhaps more common in the early nineteenth century) and their transformations into transnational racial conflict instead.[39] Plays based on imperial events often brought together these spectacular and melodramatic traditions. It would be tedious to list the many plays which illustrate this phenomenon, but all the great imperial moments of the nineteenth century appeared on the stage, including the Burma War of 1824, the so-called 'Kaffir Wars' on the eastern Cape frontier, the Indian 'Mutiny', campaigns on the North-West frontier of India, the Maori and Zulu Wars, the fate of General Gordon at Khartoum, events in Central Africa associated with Cecil Rhodes's conquest of what would become Southern Rhodesia (Zimbabwe) and with the South African War of 1899–1902.[40] The titles of many of these are seldom a good guide to the content. Neither *Youth* nor *Cheer, Boys, Cheer* immediately suggest that they are entirely set in imperial contexts, but they are. Often major playwrights turned their attention to such material. One example would be Dion Bouccicoult's *Jessie Brown; or the Relief of Lucknow;*[41] another would be Hall Caine's *The Mahdi* of 1894.

Most of these plays went on national tours and were performed even in quite small towns. To give just one example, a museum in Arbroath, a fishing town on the East Coast of Scotland, contains a playbill relating to plays performed at the beginning of the twentieth century. One week featured an 'important engagement of the eminent author-actor, Fred Cooke, with the original London Company, comprising real Blacks (Kaffirs) from Darkest Africa' in *Briton and Boer in Peace and War*. The performance would feature 'special new scenery, elaborate mechanical effects, correct military uniforms and accoutrements'. The act titles indicate that the play covered both the first (culminating in the battle of Majuba Hill) and second 'Boer Wars', together with the British advance into central Africa, and clearly involved considerable scene changes. The second play featured was called *The Diver's Luck*, which claimed to have had 5,000 performances. This play featured diamonds, an ocean voyage, and dives to the bottom of the sea. Among the characters are a Malay, a 'Coloured Coon', 'a Jew', a 'native of the island of Borneo'. Thus the empire features as the origin of priceless stones, of oceanic adventure, and in the shape of exotic and racialised figures.[42] This portrayal of blacks and other exoticised figures on the stage is part of a long tradition and cannot be separated from the experience of empire.[43]

The appearance of such plays in Arbroath represents the quite extraordinary penetration of such performances throughout the country. There is no evidence that such plays were received in a hostile spirit. It has been truly said that the box office does not lie and the lengthy runs of such plays, together with their extensive tours, reflect the very considerable popularity they enjoyed. Even more popular was the universal music hall which underwent a number of changes in the later nineteenth century.[44] Grander theatres were built and more elaborate performances staged. The halls began, in effect, to indulge in self-censorship and came to feature patriotic song scenes and tableaux which frequently adopted imperial subjects. It was indeed in the music hall that Hobson most closely identified his psychology of jingoism, a phenomenon which spanned the period from at least the 1880s to the First World War. Music hall performances penetrated other locations, such as the working men's clubs, indicating the manner in which these institutions lost their radical thrust in the high noon of empire.[45]

While it is true that the popular culture of empire does become more prominent in the later nineteenth century, it unquestionably had a longer life-span between the eighteenth and twentieth centuries. But in the second half of the nineteenth, a particular conjunction became apparent.

Queen Victoria increasingly became one of the embodiments of empire, particularly after she was elevated to the status of Empress of India. In the nationalist conditions of late nineteenth-century Europe, a greater patriotic fervour infused the culture of the period. This embraced the militarism associated with an increased visibility and reputation for both the army and the navy.[46] At the same time social Darwinian theories served to heighten racial ideas in the period. This was also a high point of Christian missionary endeavour, featured strongly in churches and local newspapers throughout the land. Hence the culture of empire was strongly influenced by a potent compound of monarchism, militarism, expansive missions and the associated major theory of social Darwinism. Intriguingly, the play *The Diver's Luck*, discussed above, had the slogan 'The Survival of the Fittest' prominently displayed beneath its title. The combined notion of British fitness to rule and the possibility of the decline and disappearance of 'unfit' peoples features prominently in much of the literature of the period.

An excellent example of the presence of empire in a popular play occurs in Arthur Wing Pinero's *The Magistrate*. First produced in 1885, it brought Pinero fame and wealth, enjoying no fewer than 363 performances on its first run. A key point in the plot is that Agatha Posket has spent time in India, had a son and was widowed there. The distance of India from English society enabled her to lop five years off the ages of both herself and her son, thereby making her more attractive in the marriage market at home. This device helps her to trap the magistrate, Aeneas Posket, into marriage. All the farcical aspects of the plot are based on this deception.[47] If a sojourn in India offers opportunities for such playful reinvention of the past, the empire later forms another function. Posket is outraged by the antics of his stepson and ultimately gives in to his desire to marry his piano teacher on one condition, that he emigrate to Canada with a £1,000 subvention to get him out of the way. Thus empire becomes a convenient emigration bin for ne'er do wells. This play was no doubt seen by thousands of members of the British middle classes, whose pretensions and manipulations of empire were being punctured and satirised, while many representatives of the working classes would have occupied cheap balcony seats. Such conventions and others like them are commonplace in nineteenth-century literature. Emigration, for example, is often used to tie up the loose ends of plots.

Plays constitute a popular literature of performance. The nineteenth century, however, also inaugurated a great age of reading, of cheaper publications, of public and circulation libraries, of increased literacy, and of the appearance of large quantities of material projected at the young. As the technology of printing and binding facilitated mass production, unit costs came down and literary works for both adults and juveniles became much cheaper. This ensured that they became a ready source of prizes and presents in schools, Sunday schools and among family members. In the realm of the high literary canon, empire becomes a sort of background noise, a presence which received regular allusions because of the exploits of characters, but which, it can be argued, is not necessarily central to plots. Nevertheless, fortunes are made in the empire; characters go there and return; fabulous jewels emanate from imperial places, and surprising (but usually distant) events can occur. The implication that the empire is an everyday phenomenon which can influence, for good or ill, the lives of the central characters of plots is seldom far away throughout nineteenth-century literature.[48] Thus empire is a place where amazing things can happen. Such conceits appear in the novels of Jane Austen, Dickens, Thackeray (who was born in India, the son of an East India Company Collector),[49] Wilkie Collins and many others.

Dickens never set a novel in the empire, perhaps because he had not visited colonial territories. With the exception of Thackeray, Trollope and the obvious case of Kipling, this was true of most authors in the high canonical tradition (though imperial travels and residence were much more common among popular writers). Nevertheless, Dickens had a considerable interest in empire and its existence is woven in and out of his novels. He particularly believed in emigration as a regenerative, morally improving experience. He supported and virtually managed a Home for Homeless Women for twelve years from 1847 and promoted its central programme of assisted emigration for 'fallen women'.[50] He collected emigration circulars and invited Samuel Sidey, an emigration propagandist, to publish articles on the subject in *Household Words* (which Dickens founded and edited). He also collaborated with Caroline Chisholm on articles on emigration and the processes of migration overseas form an important regenerative aspect of *David Copperfield* (several characters leave for Australia). Mr Brownlow in *Oliver Twist* sends his son to the West Indies. Characters also have a habit of emerging from the colonies. Magwitch in *Great Expectations* is the obvious example: an escaped convict from Botany Bay he returns with a fortune and sets about educating Pip with it, raising him up the social scale in the process. Empire, and even transportation, thus facilitate the fantasy of upward social mobility while throwing up dilemmas of class. This device is crucial to the plot. Characters in *Little Dorrit* and *Our Mutual Friend* return from the West Indies or the East. Dickens's family practised what he preached. Two sons emigrated to Australia; one went to India in the army, was involved in the Indian 'Mutiny' and died there in 1863; another joined the Bengal police and later emigrated to Canada. Dickens very nearly decided to go to Australia for a public reading tour, but drew back from such an adventure.[51] The obverse of Dickens's support for emigration was his view of black people. Whites had a right and duty to move across the world precisely because black people were either unfit or were doomed to extinction (Trollope had similar, though perhaps more complex, views). This helps to explain Dickens's fierce support for Governor Eyre in the controversy following Eyre's brutal suppression of the Morant Bay rebellion in Jamaica in 1865.[52]

Anthony Trollope travelled much more extensively than Dickens, his job in the Post Office taking him around the world conducting surveys of the arrangements for the imperial mails. Having lived in Ireland for a number of years, he journeyed to Egypt in 1857 to examine the postal route to India. In 1858 he was in the West Indies and Central America. He sailed to Australia and New Zealand in 1871 and was back in Australia in 1875 (his son had emigrated there).[53] In 1877 he travelled extensively in South Africa. He also spent time in the United States and briefly visited Ceylon (Sri Lanka).[54] He published books on all of these journeys, including *The West Indies and the Spanish Main* (1860),[55] *Australia and New Zealand* (1873), and *South Africa* (1878).[56] He also published 'letters' on his colonial tours in the *Daily Telegraph* and other papers. While it could be said that his Barchester and Palliser series of novels were little influenced by these imperial journeys, there is no doubt that many of his short stories were derived from them, as were aspects of his characterisations. His novel *John Caldigate* was partly set in the Australian gold fields. Moreover, judging by the scale of the publishers' advances he received, his travel books sold in large numbers and have indeed remained in print until modern times. Few readers of Trollope would have been unaware of the fact that he was a proponent of the British Empire, even if an acute and at times critical one.

Rudyard Kipling is of course the great laureate of empire, extolling imperial ideas in his prose, his poetry, and his novels while also satirising many of the inhabitants of empire. With his close connections with India, the place of his birth and early writings (apart from his schooling in England he was there from 1865–71 and 1882–89), with South Africa (from 1900) and also North America, he became the embodiment of British patriotic visions of empire, while constantly worrying and warning about decline. His collections of Indian short stories were widely read, as were his stories for children, his characterisations of the common soldiery ('Tommy Atkins') and his masterpiece, the novel *Kim*.[57] He was particularly enthralled by all things technical, by the machinery (both at sea and on land) that both proved the superiority of the British and rendered the empire amenable to control. He admired engineers and bridge builders for the controls they exerted upon the environment through transport systems and hydrographic works.

But Kipling was not the only immensely popular imperial writer of the late nineteenth and early twentieth centuries. We must add many of the works of Robert Louis Stevenson, Sir Henry Rider Haggard and John Buchan.[58] All of these were interested in powerful invocations of people in exotic places, in alien landscapes tamed by colonial authority. As popular writers they wrote within the dominant ideology of their age. They were instrumental in promoting the political concerns of an elite among a wider readership, even if their works offered the occasional subtle (and not so subtle) critiques of imperial policy. These authors have stimulated most attention from scholars, but we should not forget the considerable influence of popular writers upon a wider reading public. The Scot of Irish extraction, Sir Arthur Conan Doyle was a protagonist of empire who volunteered for medical service in the South African War (for which he won his knighthood). During this war he published a propagandist pamphlet defending British tactics and the behaviour of the military, seeking to counteract the attacks of the 'pro-Boers', Emily Hobhouse and anti-British propaganda from continental Europe. 'The War in South Africa: its Causes and Conduct' immediately sold nearly 400,000 copies, almost 100,000 of which were sent to the United States, Canada, Germany and France.

Doyle also visited West Africa, Egypt, Canada and Australia, and later travelled extensively in Africa.[59] His book *The Tragedy of Korosko* is redolent of his imperial philosophy. Moreover, the Sherlock Holmes stories are full of imperial references.[60] Both Holmes and Dr Watson are patriotic, royalist and imperialist. Watson was apparently injured at the Battle of Maiwand in 1880 and bought a portrait of General Gordon, the martyred hero of Khartoum to install in Holmes's Baker Street rooms. Yet again, the empire seems always to be there, a tangible presence. People enter plots from the empire and leave them to go there. The British Empire is depicted as a source of great wealth, which inevitably arouses the interest of scoundrels. It is also a locus of violence, of big game hunting, and a place where dangerous tropical diseases are rife. Tropical medicine had emerged as a new discipline and studies of micro-biology raised hopes for solutions but also fears of contamination. If these themes are woven into the immensely popular Holmes stories, Doyle's imitators took up imperial settings even more explicitly. The Sax Rohmer Fu Manchu novels dealt with the 'yellow peril' (a fear emanating from both formal and informal imperialism in the East) while the detective Sexton Blake, the creation of Harry Blyth under the pseudonym Hal Meredith, ranged widely across the empire.

While there are many ambiguities present in all this imperial literature, certain values are prominent. They include worship of the work ethic, 'manliness' and masculinity, patriotism, loyalty to Queen, King, country and empire, duty, self-discipline and the potential for sacrifice. It seems hard to believe that the readership failed to recognise that these were the ideals of the authors, presented as imperial values that the citizens of the British Empire should revere and follow. The social penetration of these works must have been profound, given their extensive circulation figures. But there was also another tradition which emphasised women's responses to and roles in empire.

This is a highly influential and little noticed area of popular literature, embracing a vast corpus of novels, largely set in India, by women writers and published by Mills and Boon, as well as mainstream publishers like Heinemann and Chatto. This tradition runs from Flora Annie Steel in the late nineteenth century through to M.M. Kaye in more modern times, and both of these were perhaps the most notable members of this 'school'. Steel was widely read and admired: she emerges as a woman so unwilling to accept the secondary role expected of the colonial female that she played a significant part in the inspection of schools and educational policy in British India. Kaye was also extensively read and represents perhaps the nostalgic dying fall of British India in the mid-twentieth century.

But there are many more writers in this group: it embraces such figures as Maud Diver (whose prolific output was widely read), Bithia Mary Croker, Alice Perrin, Christine Weston and F.E. Penny. To these writers of prose we can add the celebrated poet Laurence Hope (the nom de plume of Adela Florence Cory). Hope's poetry was popular in its own right, but it had a new infusion of fame when four of the poems from her collection *The Garden of Karma* (1901) were set to music by Amy Woodforde-Finden. They were so popular – particularly the Kashmiri Song – that Finden subsequently set four more poems from Hope's collection *Stars of the Desert* (1903). This was not only a British phenomenon: the tradition also included Sara Jeanette Duncan, who was a Canadian, Ida Ross Wiley, born in Melbourne, and Catherine Mayo, an American. Dominic Omissi has estimated that there were at least 120 novels in this canon, all set in India.[61] They were immensely popular (one edition of a Savi novel proclaims a print run of 45,000) and would have been staple fare in circulating and public libraries. They were presumably mainly read by women (although there is no evidence to confirm this). While they fully exploited the potential of India as a romantic and exotic location, they can also be analysed in terms of their handling of the notion of imperial rule, of particular landscapes, of tropical medicine, and above all attitudes towards indigenous people.[62] They deserve a great deal more attention than they have received, not least because it is possible to discern attitudes which are in some respects 'anti-canonical', different from those of male authors like Kipling and others. In this consideration of female authors, we should include one who was read by men, Olive Schreiner, an

2.1 Cover of the *Wonder Book of Empire*, popular children's publication. This edition was published in the 1920s. (Courtesy John M. MacKenzie)

influential woman in South Africa in the late nineteenth and early twentieth centuries who wrote vividly about Africa, but was also highly critical of Rhodes's methods (though not necessarily of the imperial thrust in general) in his grasp for Central Africa.

If there was a considerable literature by women, often catering to female readers, throughout the last eighty years of imperial rule, there was also a vast corpus of works directed at children. These caught a veritable publishing flood in the last few decades of the nineteenth century when books began to appear in almost every home, when schools and Sunday schools offered large numbers of improving prizes for their charges. Writers such as W.H.G. Kingston, G.A. Henty, R.M. Ballantyne and Gordon Stables (among many others) produced a considerable body of work.[63] Any suggestion that these 'ripping yarns' failed to convey an imperial ideology to their readers surely demeans the capacity of that audience to understand the contemporary contexts, generally imperial, in which the plots are worked. Even when the stories of Henty and others were set in the ancient world or the Middle Ages, the patterns of dominance and subordination, of supposed moral authority, of good and evil, and of chivalric heroism clearly parallel the themes of the more explicit imperial tales.

Advertising, exhibitions, streetscapes and music

The writing, marketing and selling of these books is closely implicated with the burgeoning of the mass market.[64] And the lubricant of the mass market is advertising. The whole business of advertising was revolutionised in this period, with strikingly new images, the beginnings of the use of colour, with slogans and fonts that caught the eye. Robert Opie, the major collector of packaging and advertising of the period, has said that the three most prominent themes in the late nineteenth century were the Queen, sentiment and the empire.[65] There can, indeed, be little doubt that imperial images and patriotic slogans, often relating to contemporary events, became a key fare of advertising in newspapers and magazines, on streets and railway stations, on shop fronts and elsewhere. Consumers cannot have been unaware of the origins of these products because advertisers in so many media were at pains to tell them.

In some instances, imperial images were specifically used to sell products whose ingredients were sourced in the empire. Several companies turned such associations into their house style. These included soap,[66] cocoa and chocolate, tea and tobacco advertising.[67] Other producers created the connection through the suggestion that their products were beneficially used in the empire. This would include such items as Camp

Coffee, Bovril meat extract, and various biscuits. Many of these images had racist connotations reflecting the tight connection between aspects of racial imaging and the economics and marketing strategies of empire.[68] Advertising and the associated consumption constituted forms of self-flattery, promoting an awareness of the useful commodities of empire and of their connection with exotic and supposedly glamorous locations. As it happens, such commodities also produced significant changes in social practices and class relations.[69] In the inter-war years, these characteristics received semi-official endorsement through the advertising campaigns of the Empire Marketing Board which stressed the importance of imperial produce for British trade and consumption, including aspects of diet.[70] To some extent this was also true of the Post Office propaganda campaigns in the same period.[71] It is the widespread prevalence of such advertising which suggests that the imperial ethos was attractive to a general public. No company is going to link its name to an ideology which its customers will find inimical. Such advertising campaigns were based on the notion that images of empire and of imperial 'others' were sufficiently appealing that they helped to sell products. A similar argument can be used of the box office success of plays and, later, films that adopted imperial themes.[72] All were based on the expectation that the sweeping up of the adventurous, spectacular and melodramatic potential of empire helped to draw in sizeable audiences. This has remained true in the post-colonial resurgence of nostalgic films of empire, on television and in the cinema, which have proved strikingly popular in modern times.[73]

This persistence of imperial imagery and propagandist/entertainment themes can also be identified in the continuing significance of empire exhibitions into the twentieth century.[74] From the Colonial and Indian of 1886, exhibitions were strongly focused upon the imperial relationship. These reached a high point with the Wembley Empire Exhibition in London in 1924–25 and continued until the Glasgow Empire Exhibition of 1938. Official events were supplemented by the remarkable sequence of commercial exhibitions at Olympia and the White City. All these immensely popular shows offered a visual encyclopaedia of industry, commerce, technology, transport, ethnography, crafts, women's work and art, marshalling the global panoply of the imperial relationship. Colonial products were highlighted while beverages and foodstuffs were sold in dedicated 'kiosks', often with sales people from the country concerned. The exhibitions also embraced theatrical events in the shape of grand pageants of empire, often involving hundreds of performers acting out events in the history of Britain and her empire in spectacular displays sometimes involving animals, and always music, processions and dance. The key point that may be made about the exhibitions is that, as well as representing the patterns of dominance and subordination of the imperial

Courtyard of Indian Pavilion

2.2 Exotic architecture comes to London: the Indian Pavilion at the Wembley Empire Exhibition of 1924–25. (Postcard, courtesy John M. MacKenzie)

connection, they marked an interleaving of the modern and the pre-modern which so often runs through the whole of experience of empire. On the one hand, they celebrated modernism in all its forms. Yet they presented indigenous peoples as performers and as craftspeople.[75] It is obvious that this can be interpreted as acting out the operation of Social Darwinian laws, the superiority of the modern pulling 'native' peoples of empire into the contemporary world or alternatively subjecting them to extinction through a deterministic interpretation of the 'survival of the fittest'. But a more subtle analysis is possible. Modernism had produced anxieties since the middle of the nineteenth century and there were frequent attempts (for example in the Arts and Crafts movement) to hark back to a purer pre-industrial age marked by handwork and crafts, which Sir George Birdwood saw as best represented in India.[76] John Ruskin was the prophet of such a movement and William Morris and his followers were its prime exemplars. The beauty of oriental crafts from both India and the Middle East were much admired (and celebrated in Orientalist paintings of the period). Thus, while the exhibitions certainly presented empire in miniature (even to the extent of trying to recreate aspects of the landscape of colonies), they were also displaying some of the anxieties of the age, including the appeal to a healthy ruralism in contrast to the unhealthy environment of the city.

[76]

The exhibitions set out to recreate in fantastical form the built environment of empire, whether in the Orientalist extravaganzas of the entrepreneur Imre Kiralfy at the White City or in the colonial pavilions and other structures of the Coronation exhibition of George V, or those of Wembley and Glasgow. So-called 'native villages' presented the supposedly primitive built environment of indigenous peoples. This was even applied to backward whites: the 'clachan' at the Glasgow Exhibition contained 'black houses' and other structures emblematic of a more 'barbarous' Scottish past. But the structures of empire were also represented in British cities. The 'imperial city' could not fail to display aspects of the imperial relationship in its factories, products, shipping headquarters, architecture, statuary, street furniture, societies, institutions, regiments and ceremonials.[77] Street naming often represented heroes and events of empire, as almost any British town and city demonstrates. Statues and memorials frequently commemorate notable imperial figures. Glasgow is full of them, notably 'Lord Roberts of Kandahar and Pretoria', high above Kelvingrove Park, David Livingstone, and Lord Clyde of Indian 'Mutiny' fame, while London presents a positive Valhalla of such heroic personalities commemorated in stone. These imperial associations of British cities are also represented in paintings. One notable one by Sir John Lavery depicts the opening of the Glasgow Exhibition of 1888 by Queen Victoria. The scene, with its grand throne, city dignitaries, military and heraldic figures, represents a municipal durbar, in which the echoes of India are abundantly apparent.

Exhibition pageants and theatrical events as well as civic and military ceremonies inevitably made use of the beguiling characteristics of music to offer entertainment and spread patriotic and imperial sentiment.[78] Victorian times were indeed the great era of public music, when composers who were, in effect, musical laureates wrote music to order. Music was specifically written for official occasions, such as royal events and jubilees, for celebratory days like Queen Victoria's birthday, later Empire Day, for exhibitions and festivals throughout the country, and for military events such as the Aldershot Tattoo. Music with connotations of empire was also written for operettas, musical plays and other theatrical events, and for military marches. Some hymns incorporated an essentially imperial vision and all of these musical forms were propagated throughout the population by the explosion in sales of sheet music in the period. Piano pieces were written to celebrate significant imperial events and many examples can still be found in the ephemera collections of book and antique shops. Moreover, major composers such as Sir Edward Elgar (whose wife came from a family with close connections with India) were sucked into this imperial ideology, writing marches and other works for patriotic use. All of these forms were also a means of bringing together the British World, for such music went around the British Empire, through the medium of the military band as well as through travelling theatrical and musical troupes. In turn, colonial territories gave musical forms and performers back to the metropolitan state.

Christian missions and youth organisations

Music was of course a vital part of Christian worship and among the hymn writing of the day was the genre of missionary hymns, extolling the church's evangelical thrust. All of the Protestant denominations, and later the Roman Catholic Church too, set out to establish missions throughout the world, notably in Africa, the Caribbean, China, South Asia, Pacific Islands, and also in respect of indigenous peoples in Canada, Australia and New Zealand. These ambitious objectives, which had faltering precedents within Britain and North America in the eighteenth century, were clearly apparent in the early decades of the nineteenth century and built up to a virtual torrent of missionary foundations by the twentieth.[79] A large number of missionary societies were founded, many of them publishing magazines and other publications. The concept of the missionary hero fed into the generalised hero-worship of the imperial era and contributed to the tremendous range of books about or by missionaries (including many memoirs) published in the late nineteenth and early twentieth centuries. Charlotte M. Yonge, whose novels set on mission stations were published in the 1850s and were immensely popular, set a significant precedent. All such books were used in the prize and present market, offering stories of improvement, often of rise in the social scale, and above all of grappling with the climatic, medical and ethnic dangers of the missionary lifestyle, invariably in remote places. Missionaries were also involved in heroic acts of exploration (Livingstone is but the most visible example of many) which fed into the adventure tradition of the age. They became notable exemplars of moral virtues and authority which were propagated to the public, notably the young.

Specific denominations and individual churches often specialised in particular areas of the globe, though some extended over several regions. Metropole and mission field were closely intertwined while missionaries (not always justifiably) developed reputations as 'friends of the natives' even when they propagated a culturally racialised view of those whom they sought to convert.[80] Catherine Hall has mapped in considerable detail the connections among the Baptist Missionary Society, some of its leading and controversial clergy, Jamaica, and the Midlands.[81] Hall has argued that aspects of metropole and colony can only be understood in relation to each other and has used the Baptist missionary focus to illustrate a point which can also be demonstrated in so many other ways. Susan Thorne's *Congregational Missions and the Making of an Imperial Culture* neatly offers her thesis in the title.[82] She has set the bourgeois, philanthropic, social imperial and gender aspects of missionary endeavour into a strongly imperial frame. Moreover, the fact is that missionaries on furlough, pursuing the necessity of raising money, spoke everywhere in churches and halls on the necessity of their work in 'saving' and ameliorating the lives of the otherwise benighted peoples of empire. They wrote articles in missionary magazines and their work was often highlighted in the local press. There is a very strong tradition of this in Scotland, where it continued until the 1950s.[83] There is a considerable debate about the contribution made by missionaries to imperial ideology, but we can be sure that many missionaries came to realise that their cause had the best hope of success within imperial territories.[84] They were frequently critical of colonial policies and of dominant imperial personalities (such as Cecil Rhodes), but they still often adhered (as they revealed in their memoirs) to the redemptive potential of imperial power. While they were seldom popular among settlers, still they performed functions, mainly respecting education, technical training, and medical services that were valuable to colonial administrations and societies.[85] It is also apparent that their lectures, their 'newsworthiness', the support of their churches, their many publications, and the sermons of their clerical supporters served to spread information and certain types of knowledge about a wider world which embraced the imperial connection. At certain climactic moments, missionary agitation could be important in political events, as with aspects of the scramble for Nyasaland (Malawi) in Central Africa in 1890 and the controversy over Uganda in 1893. It is also apparent that missionary activity, both in the field and in the support systems of home, tended to break down the gendered separation of spheres. Women were highly active both in overseas missions and in campaigning and raising funds.[86] But as European imperialism tottered to its fall in the twentieth century, missionaries often helped it on its way by supporting nationalist movements, having in many cases educated their leaders.[87]

Missionaries were also active in propagating youth movements and sports among the indigenous young whom they sought to influence.[88] These were yet further respects in which metropole and colony were tied together in a common culture. In both Britain and the colonies, certain youth movements and days associated with imperial celebration were held in common. The Boys' Brigade and other similar brigades dated from the 1880s. These were followed by the highly influential Boy Scouts, founded in 1908 by a notable imperial figure, Sir Robert Baden Powell. The idea of Scouts was based upon his experience in southern Africa, particularly during the South African War. This rapidly became a world-wide movement, both within and outside the British Empire, and carried within its ethos key aspects of notions of colonial environments, the military and social and ethnic attitudes.[89] The Scouts took a frontier ethos (not least in their uniform and in responses to the natural world) to the metropole and it was then in turn transmitted back to colonial frontiers. There can be little doubt that such youth movements and their public processions and displays were reminiscent of the rehabilitation of the military during this period. Once again, metropole and colony were tied together in these respects. Concepts of martial races were applied to both settings.[90] The image of the military became a highly positive one, partly through colonial wars, the widespread publications associated with them, and through the paintings of the period.[91] The organisation of the Royal Navy, the uniforms and presentation of officers and sailors and their involvement in public ceremony also came to be regularised in this period, a development connected with the navy's imperial role.[92]

Heroes, rhetoric and the empire at home

These phenomena were closely connected with the cult of the hero, which in British culture invariably meant imperial heroes. There was nothing new in this. Heroes had been notably celebrated in the eighteenth century and during the Napoleonic period, but in the later nineteenth century there was a prominent move to revive the reputations of the heroes of the past and create new ones for a contemporary generation. Heroes are, of course, viewed as the embodiment of the virtues, the indomitable spirit and the self-sacrifice of the patriot, emblematic representatives of the national character. They therefore offer models to be emulated and constitute supreme exemplars of national identity. This cult of the hero saw the resurrection of historic figures like Admiral Vernon, General James Wolfe, Captain James Cook and Admiral Horatio Nelson. The latter three were given special status because they met their deaths in the course of their national service to the military, exploration and the navy.[93] Geographical discovery continued to be (as in the days of Cook) a prime location for heroic endeavour, now given wider prominence through the sensationalism of the popular press.[94] David Livingstone is a prime example, combining indomitable travels with the resonance of slave trade suppression.[95] These were joined by major figures of colonial campaigns, particularly those who were supposedly martyred during their efforts to extend or 'protect' the British Empire. These included, most notably, Generals Havelock and Gordon.[96] 'Books of heroes' were repeatedly produced by British publishers and were distributed among the young as part of the wave of juvenile literature of the period.

The empire penetrated Britain in many other ways. For example, colony and metropole were mutually constituted through ideas of social reform and progress.[97] The rhetoric of 'backwardness' and deprivation, of improvement and amelioration were used in similar ways at both the centre and the so-called periphery. Indeed, empire was repeatedly reconstituted in adjacent space, both in the built environment[98] and also through the presence of the peoples of empire in metropolitan communities. There had been black people in Britain since the eighteenth century. Their numbers escalated in the nineteenth and twentieth centuries, particularly in the port cities where sailors were sometimes discharged or 'deserted'. They were joined by increasing numbers of Asians, notably Indians who arrived in Britain for a wide variety of reasons.[99] While there has been a good deal of work on these 'internal others', more remains to be done on the effects of their presence upon racial ideas, anxieties about inter-racial sexual encounters, employment and competing social relations.

The others of empire were also encountered in the museums of the metropole where, increasingly, ethnographic and other displays sought to reveal alien and exotic cultures, usually in separate compartments from the mainstream of European traditions. A severe separation was created between 'us' and 'them' either within the museum or indeed in separate buildings. It is only in modern times that such separations have been broken down.[100] Such constructions of race and ethnicity within museums were also designed to indicate not only the character of imperial rule, but also the economic and shipping relationships that brought the British into contact with exotic peoples.[101] Moreover, they offered a sense of possession. Just as the artefacts were 'possessed' in the public collection, so were the peoples who had produced them rendered 'possessions' in the colonial setting.[102] Racial hierarchies were clearly established through the taxonomies of artefacts, even if, at times, there was some sneaking admiration for the craftsmanship displayed in their production. In the captions in museums and in countless other texts, including the press and many of the books for adults and juveniles already mentioned, ideas and ideologies of empire were conveyed through specific forms of language and expression. Empire was so pervasive that the English language not only picked up words from the empire, but linguistic forms came to reflect the patterns of dominance and subordination within the ethnic, social, gender, and environmental mix of the colonies in their interaction with the metropole.[103]

Conclusion

But of course all of this was still heavily contested. The political stage was often agitated by colonial excitements, but run-of-the-mill imperial matters seemed to cause boredom and a failure of interest. Majority identities invariably coalesced around the imperial state, but minorities always fiercely opposed the violence, brutality and authoritarianism of empire, although such opposition was sometimes expressed in terms of a search for a more ethical empire. But until the mid-twentieth century, one political factor seems to be clear. No party expressing outright opposition to empire ever secured much support in the British political process. By the twentieth century, there was a high degree of convergence among the political parties in this area. Conservatives, Liberals (and even 'pro-Boer' Liberals were not necessarily opposed to empire in itself), and Labour all united on a patriotic programme of continuing imperial duties, even if individual policies were inevitably the cause of dissension.

Moreover, issues of Irish independence and partition were not only deeply woven into British politics, but also played a part in the cultural, religious and political lives of British cities such as Glasgow and Liverpool. Ireland was invariably constructed as a major problem of empire at a time when imperial issues constituted a significant aspect of British constructions and rhetoric of citizenship.[104] Popular imperialism was not a brief, jingoistic and aberrant phenomenon. It was a continuing factor in British society and politics from the mid-eighteenth to the mid-twentieth centuries. If it has seemed invisible or non-functioning to many historians, it is simply because it was always there, a continuing tradition which inevitably underwent changes over time, but which contained more continuities of expression than have been recognised.

Notes

1 The extensive literature defies a full listing. My *Propaganda and Empire* (Manchester 1984) and the edited volume *Imperialism and Popular Culture* (Manchester 1986) were among the earliest statements of the influence of empire upon metropolitan culture and national identities. Many detailed studies have appeared in the Manchester University Press 'Studies in Imperialism' series, numbering eighty volumes. Catherine Hall and Sonya O. Rose (eds), *At Home with the Empire: Metropolitan Culture and the Imperial World* (Cambridge 2006) is a valuable recent study, while Kathleen Wilson (ed.), *A New Imperial History: Culture, Identity and Modernity in Britain and the Empire 1660–1940* offers new perspectives. Bernard Porter, *The Absent-Minded Imperialists: Empire, Society and Culture in Britain* (Oxford 2004), constitutes the alternative statement, at least prompting us to re-evaluate and perhaps re-affirm the interlinking of British imperial and domestic history. See also Porter's 'Further thoughts on imperial absent-mindedness', *Journal of Imperial and Commonwealth History* (*JICH*), 36, 1 (March 2008), pp. 101–17 and my reply: 'Comfort and conviction: a response to Bernard Porter', *JICH*, 36, 4 (December 2008), pp. 659–68. Traditional historians who had sought to separate British domestic history from its imperial context immediately seized upon Porter's book as supporting their position.

Some have seen Andrew Thompson's book *The Empire Strikes Back? The Impact of Imperialism on Britain from the Mid-Nineteenth Century* (Harlow 2005) as offering a 'third way'. See also Andrew S. Thompson, *Imperial Britain: the Empire in British Politics, c. 1801–1932* (Harlow 2000) and Anthony Webster, *The Debate on the Rise of the British Empire* (Manchester 2006).

2 Sheryllynne Haggerty, Anthony Webster and Nicholas J. White (eds), *The Empire in One City? Liverpool's Inconvenient Imperial Past* (Manchester 2008).

3 MacKenzie, 'Comfort and conviction', p. 661.

4 See, among others, Catherine Hall, *Civilising Subjects: Metropole and Colony in the English Imagination 1830–1867* (Cambridge 2002), Susan Thorne, *Congregational Missions and the Making of an Imperial Culture in 19th-Century England* (Stanford 1999), and John M. MacKenzie with Nigel R. Dalziel, *The Scots in South Africa: Ethnicity, Identity, Gender and Race* (Manchester 2007), Chapter 4.

5 Simon J. Potter (ed.), *Newspapers and Empire in Ireland and Britain: Reporting the British Empire c. 1857–1921* (Dublin 2004); Chandrika Kaul (ed.), *Media and the British Empire* (Houndmills 2006); and Chandrika Kaul, *Reporting the Raj: The British press and India, c. 1880–1922* (Manchester 2003). See also John M. MacKenzie, 'Empires of travel: British guide books and cultural imperialism in the 19th and 20th centuries', in John K. Walton (ed.), *Histories of Tourism: Representation, Identity and Conflict* (Cliveden 2005), pp. 19–38.

6 Peter Yeandle, *Citizenship, Nation and Empire: The Teaching of History 1850–2002* (Manchester, 2011, forthcoming).

7 Linda Colley, *Britons* (New Haven CT 1992) was an influential statement of such a concept in relation to Europe. Edward Said's much discussed *Orientalism* (London 1978) dealt with similar issues in respect of the Middle East. Martin Daunton and Rick Halpern (eds), *Empire and Others: British Encounters with Indigenous Peoples 1600–1850* (London 1991) contains valuable contributions, as does (with different perspectives) Elizabeth Hallam and Brian V. Street (eds), *Cultural Encounters: Representing Otherness* (London 2000). See also Tony Ballantyne, *Orientalism and Race: Aryanism and the British Empire* (Houndmills 2002). Issues of the racial othering have been explored in an extensive literature.

8 Martin Green, *Dreams of Adventure, Deeds of Empire* (London 1980).

9 For remittances, see Gary B. Magee and Andrew S. Thompson, '"Lines of credit, debts of obligation": migrant remittances to Britain, c. 1875–1913', *Economic History Review*, LIX, 7 (August 2006), pp. 539–77. Such remittances were a widespread phenomenon.

10 Kathleen Wilson, *The Sense of the People: Politics, Culture and Imperialism in England, 1715–1785* (Cambridge 1995). There were three times as many provincial presses in operation in 1800 than in 1750, while in the later nineteenth century press technology progressed so rapidly that unit costs came down, illustrations could be included more readily, and topical reading matter became available to all.

11 Wilson, *Sense of the People*, p. 282.

12 Ibid., p. 139.

13 Ibid., p. 157.

14 Clare Midgley, *Women Against Slavery: The British Campaigns, 1780–1870* (London 1992); Midgley (ed.), *Gender and Imperialism* (Manchester 1998), particularly her own chapter 'Anti-slavery and the roots of imperial feminism', pp. 161–79; and Midgley. 'Bringing the Empire home: women activists in imperial Britain 1790s to 1930s', in Hall and Rose (eds), *At Home with the Empire*, pp. 230–51; also Paula Krebs, *Gender, Race and the Writing of Empire: Public Discourse and the Boer War* (Cambridge 1999).

15 Eliza Riedi, 'Women, gender and the promotion of empire; the Victoria League, 1901–1914', *Historical Journal*, 45, 3 (2002), pp. 569–99; also Katie Pickles, *Female Imperialism and National Identity: Imperial Order Daughters of the Empire* (Manchester 2002).

16 Cora Kaplan, 'Imagining empire: history, fantasy and literature', in Hall and Rose (eds), *At Home with the Empire*, pp. 191–211. Kaplan helpfully concentrates her discussion on the early nineteenth and later twentieth centuries.

18 Eric Richards, *Britannia's Children: Emigration from England, Scotland, Wales and Ireland since 1600* (London 2002), p. 44.
19 There were shipping and emigration agencies in most towns. A postcard of one in Inverness displays prominent shipping and emigration posters as well as a rack for leaflets for 'The Empire's Greatest Railway' (the Canadian Pacific) and is published in Nigel Dalziel and John MacKenzie, *Inverness and District in Old Photographs* (Thrupp 1998), p. 16. The nineteenth-century Smail's printing works in Innerleithen, the Borders, Scotland, a property of the National Trust for Scotland, was an emigration agency and there are ledgers of emigration customers still extant there.
20 Marjory Harper 'Enticing the emigrant: Canadian agents in Ireland and Scotland, c. 1870–c. 1920', *Scottish Historical Review*, LXXXIII, 1, 215 (April 2004), pp 41–58 offers many examples of the operations of agents. For advertising, see Eric Richards, *Destination Australia* (Manchester 2008), pp. 48, 82, 94, 104, 112 and passim; also *Britannia's Children*, pp. 80–1, 166, 185.
21 Richards, *Britannia's Children*, pp. 6–11.
22 For examples, see David Lambert and Alan Lester (eds), *Colonial Lives Across the British Empire* (Cambridge 2006).
23 Robert A. Stafford, *Scientist of Empire: Sir Roderick Murchison, Scientific Exploration and Victorian Imperialism* (Cambridge 1989); Richard Drayton, *Nature's Government; Science, Imperial Britain, and the 'Improvement' of the World* (New Haven CT 2000); John M. MacKenzie (ed.), *Imperialism and the Natural World* (Manchester 1990); and Saul Dubow (ed.), *Science and Society in Southern Africa* (Manchester 2000). For missionary involvement, see John M. MacKenzie, 'Missionaries, science and the environment in nineteenth-century Africa', in Andrew Porter (ed.), *The Imperial Horizons of British Protestant Missions, 1880–1914* (Cambridge 2003), pp. 106–30. There is also a growing literature on science and the Indian Empire. It is noticeable how far the protagonists of a 'new imperial history' often miss these significant phenomena.
24 For examples of social and cultural context, see John M. MacKenzie, *Museums and Empire: Natural History, Human Cultures, and Colonial Identities* (Manchester 2009). Museums constituted a means whereby science and anthropology were popularised.
25 There is, for example, a tendency to do this in the introduction to Hall and Rose (eds), *At Home with the Empire*, pp. 23–5.
26 After all, in Colonial Office surveys conducted in Britain in 1948 and 1951, some of those interviewed thought that the USA was still in the empire. David Goldsworthy, *Colonial Issues in British Politics, 1945–61* (Oxford, 1971), p. 399.
27 According to Graham Handley, Trollope 'regarded America as a triumph for England'. Graham Handley (ed.), *Trollope the Traveller* (London 1993), p. xxiv.
28 Marjory Harper (ed.), *Emigrant Homecomings: The Return Movement of Migrants, 1600–2000* (Manchester 2005).
29 Kathleen Wilson, *The Island Race: Englishness, Empire and Gender in the Eighteenth Century* (London 2003), p. xii.
30 Panoramas were used to encourage emigration. They also displayed military events and journeys, such as Egypt and the route to India. Alan Thomas, *The Expanding Eye* (London 1978); Bernard Comment, *The Panorama* (London 1999).
31 Many graveyards contain stones commemorating people who had died in the empire, had pursued their careers there, or were killed in colonial campaigns. Nigel Dalziel and I are compiling a database of such inscriptions, particularly in Scotland.
32 Handel's 'Music for the Royal Fireworks' was composed to celebrate the end of the Austrian Succession War while 'Rule Britannia' was composed and first sung in this era. 'God Save the King' came to be used increasingly as the national anthem.
33 Kathleen Wilson, *Sense of the People*, p. 147. Wilson has identified this play being performed in Norwich and Newcastle in 1741. There were also pamphlets, ballads, press notices and commemorative ceramic material and medals celebrating Vernon's victory, which was celebrated in public rejoicings and in pantomimes in open-air theatres until 1788. This deeper history of popular imperialism in Britain exposes problems for historians hermetically sealed in the nineteenth-twentieth century period.

34 Maya Jasanoff, *Edge of Empire: Conquest and Collecting in the East 1750–1850* (London 2005), pp. 174–5.
35 Ibid., p. 148. See also Kathleen Wilson's forthcoming *The Colonial Stage: Theater, Culture and Modernity in the English Provinces, 1720–1800*, in which the author proposes to look at theatrical performances in Cork, St Helena, Jamaica, Calcutta and Sumatra. For the Napoleonic period on the stage, see Gillian Russell, *The Theatres of War; Performance, Politics and Society, 1793–1815* (Oxford 1995). See also David Bradby et al. (eds), *Performance and Politics in Popular Drama* (Cambridge 1980), notably J.S. Bratton's chapter on 'The theatre of war'.
36 Michael Booth's pioneering *Victorian Spectacular Theatre* (London 1981) first unveiled these phenomena.
37 Michael Booth, *English Melodrama* (London 1965). It is noticeable that Porter makes his assertions about the alleged absence of empire in the theatre without making reference to any sources in theatrical history. This is symptomatic of the manner in which historical fields such as those relating to the theatre, to emigration, and to science are not taken up by conventional historians.
38 For imperial and racial aspects of late nineteenth-century pantomime, see Jim Davis, 'Imperial transgressions: the ideology of Drury Lane pantomime in the late nineteenth century', *New Theatre Quarterly*, 12 (February 1996), pp. 147–55. See also the appendix to Jill A. Sullivan, 'The Business of the Pantomime: Regional Productions 1865–1892', PhD thesis, University of Nottingham, 2005), which contains a number of references to pantomime's treatment of empire. I am indebted to Jeffrey Richards and Peter Yeandle for these references, and to Jill Sullivan for permission to refer to her thesis.
39 MacKenzie, *Propaganda and Empire*, Chapter 2.
40 Many of these plays are analysed in MacKenzie, *Propaganda and Empire*, Chapter 2. Large numbers of them were researched in the Lord Chamberlain's Collection at the British Library; Marty Gould, *Nineteenth-Century Theatre and the Imperial Encounter* (New York forthcoming).
41 This and many other plays and pageants relating to empire are analysed in J.S. Bratton, Richard Allen Cave, Breandan Gregory, Heidi J. Holder and Michael Pickering, *Acts of Supremacy: The British Empire and the Stage, 1790–1930* (Manchester 1991).
42 Playbills for these plays are in the Signal Tower Museum, Arbroath, Angus and are the only such items on display there.
43 This receives a sophisticated analysis in Felicity A. Nussbaum, 'The theatre of empire: racial counterfeit, racial realism', in Wilson, *New Imperial History*, pp. 71–90.
44 Penny Summerfield, 'Patriotism and empire: music-hall entertainment, 1870–1914', in MacKenzie (ed.), *Imperialism and Popular Culture*, pp. 17–48.
45 This case is argued in MacKenzie, *Propaganda and Empire*, pp. 61–3.
46 Mary A. Conley, *From Jack Tar to Union Jack: Representing Naval Manhood in the British Empire, 1870–1914* (Manchester 2009).
47 This play was performed at the Pitlochry Festival Theatre in 2008.
48 For the extensive range of literary imperial content, see Patrick Brantlinger, *Victorian Literature and Postcolonial Studies* (Edinburgh 2009), particularly parts 1 and 3.
49 In his novel *Vanity Fair*, one of Thackeray's principal characters has been a collector in India, while another becomes a minor colonial governor.
50 Jenny Hartley, *Charles Dickens and the House of Fallen Women* (London 2008).
51 Details of Dickens's connection with the empire can be found in Paul Schlicke (ed.), *The Oxford Reader's Companion to Dickens* (Oxford 1999), particularly pp. 217–18. See also D.H. Simpson, 'Dickens and the British Empire', Royal Commonwealth Society *Library Notes*, new series 162–3 (1970). Various other works have charted Dickens's interest in the empire.
52 Dickens joined John Ruskin and Thomas Carlyle in supporting Eyre. John Stuart Mill and David Livingstone, among others, were in the opposite camp.
53 P.D. Edwards, *Anthony Trollope's Son in Australia: the Life and Letters of F.J.A. Trollope, 1847–1910* (Queensland 1982); Marcie Muir, *Trollope in Australia* (Adelaide 1949).

[85]

54 These travels are well covered in Victoria Glendenning, *Trollope* (London 1992). See also Handley, *Trollope the Traveller* and Betty Dreyer (ed.), *Anthony Trollope: Tourists and Colonials*, volume 3 of the Complete Short Stories (London 1991).

55 Republished in New York in 1999 with an introduction by Fred D'Aguiar.

56 Republished in Stroud in 2005. South Africa contains so many interesting insights that it has been much quoted by modern historians. There have been other modern re-issues, as for all Trollope's travel works.

57 Among a vast bibliography, see Lewis D. Wurgaft, *The Imperial Imagination: Magic and Myth in Kipling's India* (Middleton CT 1983); Andrew Rutherford (ed.), *Kipling's Mind and Art* (Stanford 1964); B.J. Moore-Gilbert, *Kipling and 'Orientalism'* (London 1986) and Bart Moore-Gilbert, *Writing India 1757–1990* (Manchester 1996). Among many biographies, Martin Seymour-Smith, *Rudyard Kipling* (London 1989) has useful observations on the ideology of Kipling's writings. See also Rudyard Kipling, *Something of Myself and other Autobiographical Writings*, edited by Thomas Pinney (Cambridge 1990).

58 See, for example, the compendium of Stevenson stories *In the South Seas* (London 1986, first published in 1900). For Rider Haggard, see Peter Beresford Ellis, *H. Rider Haggard: A Voice from the Infinite* (London 1978) and Tom Pocock, *Rider Haggard and the Lost Empire* (London 1993). For Buchan, Juanita Kruse, *John Buchan (1875–1940) and the Idea of Empire: Popular Literature and Political Ideology* (Lampeter 1989); Andrew Lownie, *John Buchan: The Presbyterian Cavalier* (London 1995). Among the many scholarly works on imperial literature, Alan Sandison, *The Wheel of Empire: A Study of the Imperial Idea in Some Later Nineteenth and Early Twentieth-Century Fiction* (London 1967) remains useful. One of Sandison's themes is the influence of Darwinian ideas upon many of these writers.

59 Arthur Conan Doyle, *Our African Winter* (London 1929, republished 2001). Doyle visited South, Central and East Africa, mainly pursuing his interests in spiritualism.

60 Jeffrey Richards, 'Sherlock Holmes, Conan Doyle and the British Empire: An investigation into Conan Doyle's links with the British Empire as expressed through his Sherlockian and other literature' (Musgrave Monograph number eight, Huddersfield 1997). I am indebted to Jeffrey Richards for supplying this item.

61 Dominic Omissi, 'The Mills and Boon Memsahibs: Women's Romantic Indian Fiction, 1877–1947', PhD thesis, University of Lancaster, 1995.

62 Omissi's reading of these novels is significantly different from that of Benita Parry, *Delusions and Discoveries: India in the British Imagination 1880–1930* (London 1972). See also Patrick Brantlinger, *Rule of Darkness: British Literature and Imperialism 1830–1914* (Ithaca 1988) and Allan J. Greenberger, *The British Image of India: Studies of India in the British Imagination 1880–1930* (Oxford 1969).

63 MacKenzie, *Propaganda and Empire*, Chapter 8; Joseph Bristow, *Empire Boys: Adventures in a Man's World* (London 1991); Bob Dixon, *Catching Them Young: Sex, Race and Class in Children's Fiction*, particularly the Race chapter (London 1977) and Jeffrey Richards (ed.), *Imperialism and Juvenile Literature* (Manchester 1989)

64 W. Hamish Fraser, *The Coming of the Mass Market, 1850–1914* (London 1981).

65 The Robert Opie Collection is now housed in the Museum of Brands, Packaging and Advertising in London. There are many related publications and reproduction collectibles associated with this museum. See Opie, *Rule Britannia: Trading on the British Image* (Harmondsworth 1985) for imperial imagery. Opie argued for this three-fold specialisms of advertising in a television programme on Victorian art and design fronted by Jeremy Paxman, March 2009. Jeremy Paxman, *The Victorians: Britain Through the Paintings of the Age* (London 2009), particularly Chapter 4, 'The world of wealth and power'.

66 Brian Lewis, *'So Clean': Lord Leverhulme, Soap and Civilisation* (Manchester 2008), particularly Chapter 4.

67 Anandi Ramamurthy, *Imperial Persuaders: Images of Africa and Asia in British Advertising* (Manchester 2003).

68 Anandi Ramamurthy, *Black Markets: Images of Black People in Advertising and*

Packaging in Britain 1880–1990 (Manchester 1990); Jan Nederveen Pieterse, *White on Black: Images of Africa and Blacks in Western Popular Culture* (New Haven CT 1992).

69 Joanna de Groot, 'Metropolitan desires and colonial connections: Reflections on consumption and empire', in Hall and Rose (eds), *At Home with the Empire*, pp. 166–90.

70 Many of these images are published and analysed in Stephen Constantine, *Buy and Build: The Advertising Posters of the Empire Marketing Board* (London 1986) and Ramamurthy, *Imperial Persuaders*, Chapter 5.

71 The GPO issued a magnificent series of posters illustrating the heroic delivery of the posts around the empire in the 1930s. Films were also produced in these years.

72 MacKenzie, *Propaganda and Empire*, Chapter 3; Jeffrey Richards, *Visions of Yesterday* (London 1973).

73 Jeffrey Richards, 'Imperial heroes for a post-imperial age: films and the end of empire'; John M. MacKenzie, 'The persistence of empire in metropolitan culture'; Tsu Ming Tao, 'Wandering in the wake of empire: British travel and tourism in the post-imperial world', all in Stuart Ward (ed.), *British Culture and the End of Empire* (Manchester 2001), respectively pp. 128–44, 21–36, and 163–79 (particularly p. 170). Several other chapters in this collection are also relevant.

74 MacKenzie, *Propaganda and Empire*, Chapter 4; Paul Greenhalgh, *Ephemeral Vistas: the Expositions Universelles, Great Exhibitions and World Fairs, 1851–1939* (Manchester 1988); John E. Findling (ed.), *Historical Dictionary of World's Fairs and Expositions 1851–1988* (Westport CT 1990, second edition 2008).

75 Pascal Blanchard, Nicolas Bancel et al. (eds), *Human Zoos: Science and Spectacle in the Age of Colonial Empires* (Liverpool 2008, originally published in French and Italian, 2002 and 2004) deals with this phenomenon across Europe as well as Britain.

76 John M. MacKenzie, *Orientalism: History, Theory and the Arts* (Manchester 1995), Chapter 5. See also the Asian chapter of John M. MacKenzie, *Museums and Empire: Natural History, Human Cultures and Colonial Identities* (Manchester 2009). I delivered a keynote on modernism and anti-modernism in a conference at the University of Tours in October, 2008, to be published in a volume edited by Trevor Harris.

77 John M. MacKenzie, '"The Second City of the Empire" – Glasgow, imperial municipality', in Felix Driver and David Gilbert (eds), *Imperial cities* (Manchesterr 1999), pp. 215–37. See also the chapters on London by Iain Black, Deborah S. Ryan, Andrew Hassam and Jonathan Schneer in the same volume. See also Haggerty et al. (eds), *The Empire in One City?* and Miles Taylor (ed.), *Southampton: Gateway to the British Empire* (London 2007) which similarly has chapters on shipping, pageants, connections with imperial heroes, the military, and aerial transport.

78 Jeffrey Richards, *Imperialism and Music: Britain 1876–1953* (Manchester 2001)

79 Some idea of the prolific nature of these foundations, as well as the earlier precedents, can be derived from Stephen Neill, *A History of Christian Missions* (Harmondsworth 1964).

80 Hilary M. Carey (ed.), *Empires of Religion* (London 2008).

81 Hall, *Civilising Subjects*.

82 See footnote 4 above. See also Susan Thorne, 'Religion and empire at home', in Hall and Rose (eds), *At Home with the Empire*, pp. 143–65.

83 Personal memory of the Church of Scotland in Glasgow in the 1950s. For an invocation of the earlier and extensive propagandist travels of a missionary, see A.A. Millar, *Alexander Duff of India* (Edinburgh 1992).

84 Contrast, for example, Andrew Porter, *Religion versus Empire? British Protestant Missionaries and Overseas Expansion 1700–1914* (Manchester 2004) with Brian Stanley, *The Bible and the Flag: Protestant Missions and British Imperialism in the Nineteenth and Twentieth Centuries* (Leicester 1990).

85 For a recent work on the medical activities of missionaries, see David Hardiman, *Missionaries and their Medicine: A Christian Modernity for Tribal India* (Manchester 2008).

86 Lesley A. Orr Macdonald, *A Unique and Glorious Mission: Women and Presbyterianism in Scotland 1830–1930* (Edinburgh 2000), particularly Chapter 3.

[87]

87 Brian Stanley (ed.), *Missions, Nationalism and the End of Empire* (Grand Rapids 2003).

88 J.A. Mangan, *The Games Ethic and Imperialism: Aspects of the Diffusion of an Ideal* (London 1986), particularly Chapters 4 and 7. Also contributions to J.A.Mangan (ed.), *Benefits Bestowed? Education and British Imperialism* (Manchester 1988) and Mangan (ed.), *Making Imperial Mentalities: Socialisation and British Imperialism* (Manchester 1990).

89 Among many sources, see Robert H. Macdonald, *Sons of the Empire: The Frontier and the Boy Scout Movement* (Toronto 1993) and Allen Warren, 'Citizens of the Empire: Baden-Powell, Scouts and Guides, and an imperial ideal', in MacKenzie (ed.), *Imperialism and Popular Culture*, pp. 232–56.

90 Heather Streets, *Martial Races: The Military, Race and Masculinity in British Imperial Culture, 1857–1914* (Manchester 2004).

91 Again the literature is considerable, but see Edward M. Spiers, *The Victorian Soldier in Africa* (Manchester 2004), Spiers, *The Scottish Solder and Empire, 1854–1902* (Edinburgh 2006), Stuart Allan and Allan Carswell, *The Thin Red Line: War Empire and Visions of Scotland* (Edinburgh 2004), Graham Dawson, *Soldier Heroes: British Adventure, Empire and the Imagining of Masculinities* (London 1994) and J.W.M. Hichberger, *Images of the Army: The Military in British Art, 1815–1914* (Manchester 1988).

92 Conley, *From Jack Tar to Union Jack*.

93 For naval heroic myths in general, see C.I. Hamilton, 'Naval hagiography and the Victorian hero', *Historical Journal*, 23, 2 (1980), pp. 381–98. For Nelson, David Cannadine (ed.), *Admiral Lord Nelson: Context and Legacy* (London 2005) and Holger Hoock (ed.), *Trafalgar 1805–2005: History, Commemoration and National Preoccupation* (Oxford 2007). See also Huw Lewis-Jones, '"Displaying Nelson": Navalism and "The Exhibition" of 1891', *Trafalgar Chronicle*, 14 (2004), pp. 53–86. For Captain Cook, Nigel Rigby and Pieter van der Merwe, *Captain Cook in the Pacific* (London 2002) and Nicholas Thomas, *Discoveries: the Voyages of Captain Cook* (London 2003). For Wolfe, Nicholas Rogers, 'Brave Wolfe: the making of a hero', in Wilson (ed.), *A New Imperial History*, pp. 239–59.

94 Beau Riffenburgh, *The Myth of the Explorer: the Press, Sensationalism, and Geographical Discovery* (London 1993).

95 John M. MacKenzie, 'David Livingstone and the construction of the myth', in Graham Walker and Tom Gallagher, *Sermons and Battle Hymns* (Edinburgh 1990), pp. 24–42; MacKenzie, 'The iconography of the exemplary life: the case of David Livingstone', in Geoffrey Cubitt and Allen Warren (eds), *Heroic Reputations and Exemplary Lives* (Manchester 2000), pp. 84–104.

96 John M. MacKenzie, 'Heroic myths of empire', in MacKenzie (ed.), *Popular Imperialism and the Military* (Manchester 1992), pp. 109–38. I have always argued that T.E. Lawrence failed to get into the supreme canon of heroes because he missed out on martyrdom – and he knew it. John M. MacKenzie, 'T.E. Lawrence: the myth and the message', in Robert Giddings (ed.), *Literature and Imperialism* (London 1991), pp. 150–81.

97 John Marriott, *The Other Empire: Metropolis, India and Progress in the Colonial Imagination* (Manchester 2003).

98 Jane M. Jacobs, *Edge of Empire: Postcolonialism and the City* (London 1996) which also compares London with Australian cities, Perth and Brisbane.

99 Shompa Lahiri, *Indians in Britain: Anglo-Indian Encounters, Race and Identity, 1880–1930* (London 2000) and Rosina Visram, *Asians in Britain: 400 Years of History* (London 2002); also Laura Tabili, 'A homogeneous society? Britain's internal "others", 1800 – present', in Hall and Rose, *At Home with the Empire*, pp. 53–76 and Diane Frost, 'The maligned, the despised and the ostracised: working-class white women, interracial relationships, and colonial ideologies in nineteenth and twentieth century Liverpool', in Haggerty et al. (eds), *The Empire in One City?*, pp. 143–64. For a specific case of an African in Britain, Ben Shephard, 'Showbiz imperialism: the case of Peter Lobengula', in MacKenzie (ed.), *Imperialism and Popular Culture*, pp. 94–112.

100 The contents of the Museum of Mankind in London have only recently been reintegrated into the main body of the British Museum.

101 Zachary Kingdon and Dmitri van den Bersselaar, 'Collecting empire? African objects, West African trade and a Liverpool museum', in Haggerty et al. (eds), *The Empire in One City?*, pp. 100–22.

102 A. Coombes, *Reinventing Africa: Museums, Culture and the Popular Imagination in Late Victorian and Edwardian England* (New Haven CT 1994).

103 David Spurr, *The Rhetoric of Empire: Colonial Discourses in Journalism, Travel Writing, and Imperial Administration* (Durham NC, 1993); Robert H. Macdonald, *The Language of Empire: Myths and Metaphors of Popular Imperialism, 1880–1918* (Manchester 1994).

104 Christine Kinealy, 'At home with the empire: the example of Ireland', James Epstein, 'Taking class notes on empire' and Keith McClelland and Sonya Rose, 'Citizenship and empire, 1867–1928', all in Hall and Rose (eds), *At Home with the Empire*, pp. 77–100, 251–74, 275–97.

CHAPTER 3

Songs of an imperial underdog: imperialism and popular culture in the Netherlands, 1870–1960

Vincent Kuitenbrouwer

Introduction

Around 1900 the Dutch expressed their feelings about world affairs in song. At that time the public was captivated by two major conflicts, both of which must be seen in the context of modern imperialism; the campaigns of the colonial army against the Sultanate of Aceh in Northern Sumatra (1873–1904) and the South African War (1899–1902) between the Boer republics and the British Empire. Popular songs showed a strong sense of moral judgement, a deep belief in the righteousness of the Dutch cause and a denunciation of the perceived enemy. One tune that was openly sung in the streets called for the hanging of a local ruler in Aceh, Toekoe Oemar, who was considered to be an untrustworthy traitor.[1] At the same time the Boers in South Africa were celebrated as heroes and the Dutch public knew their songs by heart. Edward VII was introduced in an unpleasant manner to this folklore when he disembarked from the royal yacht at the port of Vlissingen in 1901, where a large crowd received him singing the Transvaal anthem. One British diplomat who was present recalled it as 'the most disgraceful scene I have ever witnessed in my life'.[2]

The popularity of such patriotic songs throws up the question in what ways overseas issues affected society in the Netherlands at the time. From the seventeenth century onwards, the Dutch had been involved in colonialism, but there was a growing drive for expansion during the last decades of the nineteenth. Historians consider this to be the Dutch incarnation of modern imperialism, and there has emerged a substantial body of secondary literature about this topic. Not surprisingly, the main focus of historiography is on the Dutch East Indies, which became the jewel of the formal colonial empire during an unprecedented period of expansion between 1870 and 1910. There is general consensus that South Africa also played an important role in the Dutch imperial mentality at the period. Although there was no concrete desire to establish a territorial presence, there were structural attempts to expand cultural influence in order to strengthen the ties with the Boer republics. This, contemporaries hoped, would serve as a bulwark against British expansion in the region so that an independent Dutch presence would be guaranteed which would open up possibilities for emigration and trade. This chapter will analyse how Dutch historians have written about the centripetal effects of these two overseas adventures during the late nineteenth and first half of the twentieth century.

The Dutch Empire also included possessions in the Caribbean: Surinam and the Netherlands Antilles. These colonies had been established during the early modern period and the Dutch policy at the end of the nineteenth century was mainly aimed at consolidation. There were diplomatic conflicts with Venezuela and France about the demarcation of borders and worries about the growth of American influence in the region, which shows that the Netherlands did not want to give up its possessions in the West.[3] It seems, however, that events in the Dutch Indies and South Africa did attract more attention amongst policy-makers and the public. In addition, there are few studies on the impact of the Caribbean on the Netherlands, which means that it falls largely out of the scope of this chapter, which is based on historiography.

The secondary literature reveals two themes that will serve as *leitmotivs* in the following paragraphs. The first one is chronology. Martin Bossenbroek, who has written the most extensive overview of Dutch imperial culture, has provided a rather peculiar metaphor for a timeline, namely the 'hop-skip-jump'; according to him the first steps were taken in the 1870s, the jump took place in the 1880s and 1890s and the 'landing' in the early 1900s.[4] In general most authors confirm that the Dutch interest in overseas matters emerged in the 1870s, when modern imperialism took shape. At that time both the Dutch Indies and South Africa underwent great socio-economic and political transformations, which were connected with the development of the colonial state. In many ways this process reached its climax around 1900 when it led to large-scale violence in both regions, which attracted much attention. It is an open question, however, when such issues lost their relevance. Some agree with Bossenbroek that the interest of the Dutch public ended in the 1900s. By 1910 the territorial expansion in Dutch Indies was completed, which meant a drop in media attention, so some argue.[5] Likewise, many historians are of the opinion that the public lost interest in the Boer cause after the republics in South Africa had been annexed by the British in 1902.[6] Others hold that the interest in overseas matters that emerged during the late nineteenth century had a longer lifespan. Such authors emphasise that contemporaries in the Netherlands considered themselves directly related with events in the Indonesian archipelago and South Africa, which suggests that imperial culture had a lasting impact on national identity.[7]

This brings forward a second issue that is discussed in the historiography, the way in which overseas experiences were connected to feelings of nationalism. At the end of the nineteenth century the Netherlands underwent a process of centralisation and modernisation.[8] These socioeconomic changes were accompanied by a sense of chauvinistic optimism and many Dutch people experienced the *fin-de-siècle* as a 'new start' rather than the end of the old century. In their eyes the grandeur of the 'Golden Age' of the mid-seventeenth century, when the Dutch ruled the waves, re-emerged. In this context the expansion of overseas spheres of influence was seen as a clear indicator of revival, which stimulated the unity of the nation. Niek van Sas has argued that in this period, which coincided with the emergence of modern political parties, imperial aspirations transcended partisanship and so acted as a truly national symbol.[9] As it will be seen below, there was a lot of discussion about the ways in which the Dutch overseas ambitions should be given shape, but except from certain groups within the nascent Socialist movement, there was no fundamental criticism of colonialism as such. In addition it was associated with other national symbols, such as the monarchy. Queen Wilhelmina, who ascended the throne in 1898, embodied the close ties between the Royal House. Throughout her reign – which ended in 1948, on the eve of decolonisation in Indonesia – she expressed great personal interest in overseas matters.[10]

The Dutch Indies and South Africa also served as a mirror for the Dutch nation in other ways. As has been pointed out, these regions underwent great transformations at the end of the nineteenth century. As a result, the public was confronted with questions about modernity in a global context. Such issues were not unique for the Dutch experience because all colonial powers at that period were faced with similar questions. The Dutch came up with ideas, mainly derived from evolutionary theory, that fitted a broad Western world-view on the differences between 'self' and 'other'.[11] Nevertheless, such issues also gave rise to contemporary ideas about the peculiar nature of the Dutch colonial experience and its superiority over other models of expansion, which was seen as a question of national prestige. This was clearly reflected in the colonial vocabulary. With the exception of some Socialist critics, the word 'imperialism' at that time was used to refer to other empires, particularly the British and French.[12] Instead, the Dutch Indies was known under poetic names as '*Ons Indië*' ('Our Indies') or '*De gordel van smaragd*' ('The emerald belt'). The euphemism '*ethische politiek*' ('ethical policy'), introduced in the 1900s, referred to colonial rule. The ambitions in South Africa were phrased in terms of racial kinship, '*Stamverwantschap*'. In this imagery, the Dutch-speaking population in the Boer republics and the Cape Colony were seen as part of the same linguistic and cultural community as the inhabitants of the Low Countries, which was known as '*Groot-Nederland*' ('Greater Netherlands'). Such semantics show that overseas issues generated questions about Dutch identity in the international context.

These issues were not unproblematic for contemporaries and the ideas that surrounded the Dutch imperial experience were highly ambivalent. Despite a general belief in progress and technological advance, there were also doubts about some aspects of modernity. Both the indigenous cultures of the Indonesian archipelago and the archaic lifestyle of the Boers were thought to contain antidotes to the social illnesses of Western society.[13] Again, such considerations were not unique at that time, but there were more specific problems that were associated with the international status of the Netherlands. While amongst the European powers it took a second-rank position, it had the greatest colonial empire after Britain and France: a contradiction that affected the form and content of imperial propaganda. In order to preserve the status as neutral power in Europe, the government acted reluctantly towards the organisations that supported expansion. Although high-ranking politicians, and the Queen herself, were involved in such initiatives on their own accord, they were constantly walking a diplomatic tightrope to defend the position of the Netherlands as a colonial nation and at the same time not to offend other countries in order to avoid conflict. The historian Maarten Kuitenbrouwer has asserted that this constant balancing act was typical for the Dutch situation, which he has called the 'imperialism of a small power'.[14]

While there is a substantial number of books that mention the cultural aspects of the Dutch form of imperialism, it remains an issue to what extent it actually affected 'the People'. In the historiography there is a noticeable lack of quantitative data, which could provide insights into the importance of imperial culture. Although important work remains to be done in this respect this chapter aims to give an overview of the secondary literature on this topic and therefore it would go too far to try to compile a representative cross-section to examine in what ways public opinion was influenced by overseas issues. It has emerged in recent British historiography that such an enterprise entails more than many historians realise and that quantitative measurements have to be put firmly into historical context in order to assess them properly.[15] In this sense there are additional difficulties for historians in the Netherlands because not much is known about how the public debate was structured during the colonial period. Certain topics, such as imperial imagery in cinema and advertisement, have received particularly little attention and research is needed to get an overview of the available sources. But there might also be a deeper issue at hand, which says something about the meaning of Dutch imperialism. Compared with the British Empire its so-called 'cultural economy' was rather small.[16] Contemporaries were certainly aware that Dutch was no world-language and that as a result the market for its cultural institutions was limited. Although there were exceptions, such as the rapid growth of steamboat companies, it was hard to generate capital or political will to invest in global lines of communication. One of the most apparent deficiencies in this sense was the lack of an independent network of intercontinental telegraph lines, which made the Netherlands dependent on foreign news agencies, such as Reuters.[17]

Despite the absence of such imperial hardware there are indications that the Dutch Indies and South Africa had an effect on the Dutch mindset. Susan Legêne has argued that there was a 'silent consensus' about colonial rule that was omnipresent.[18] Choosing a different line of argument Bossenbroek has shown that images of the Dutch Empire reverberated in a great variety of cultural genres and amongst many social groups. This suggests that there was no clear separation between so-called 'high' and popular cultures, which means that ideas about 'Dutchness' in colonial context were disseminated throughout all walks of society.[19] Therefore the small involvement of the government and the limited strength of the cultural institutions did not prevent the emergence of a clear imperial imagery. It will be argued that this was part of the Dutch way of empire building. The boisterous tone of the songs mentioned above to an extent covered up the great uncertainties that bothered many contemporaries, who were confronted with the question how the Netherlands as a small nation was to retain its presence amongst the great colonial powers. In this sense these were the songs of an imperial underdog.

The Dutch Indies, 1870–1910

The emergence of public interest in the Dutch Indies must be considered as part of the transformation of the old mercantile empire of the seventeenth century into a modern colonial state. Legêne argues that this process already started in 1815, when the Dutch established formal rule on the island of Java, the economic heartland of the Indonesian archipelago. Some aspects of colonial rule caused embarrassment, so she continues, and although representations of the East were meant to provide legitimacy, criticism was shunned, which revealed this 'uncertainty'.[20] The unease with expansion can be clearly detected in the so-called 'abstention policy', to which the government adhered. This meant that the establishment of formal rule was confined to Java only and presence on islands in the so-called 'outer regions' remained limited to trade posts. The Dutch presence on Java was characterised by the 'cultivation system', which obliged farmers to produce commercial crops on their land for the Dutch authorities. These two principles of colonial policy during the early nineteenth century did receive quite a lot of attention in other countries. In Britain, France and Belgium there developed a considerable appreciation of how the colony on Java was 'managed'.[21]

Nonetheless this so-called 'conservative' view of the Dutch Empire in South-East Asia came under increasing pressure during the second half of the nineteenth century. For a large part this can be explained from the shifting international situation that accompanied the emergence of modern imperialism.[22] There are also clear indications, however, that from the 1850s an increasing number of people in the Netherlands started to think differently about such matters, and more importantly, started writing about it too. In a biography about the internationally renowned ethnologist P.J. Veth, Paul van der Velde has argued that this scholar played an important role in the popularisation of the Indies.[23] It certainly seems that Veth took a central position in the network of the so-called 'progressive' liberals that advocated the reform of the colonial possessions and put increasing pressure on the government to do so. He did, for example, a lot to promote the work of his old friend E. Douwes Dekker, who, under the pseudonym Multatuli, wrote the most famous book about the excesses of the cultivation system, the semi-autobiographical novel *Max Havelaar* (1860). From 1870 onwards the cultivation system was gradually abolished when legislation was passed that introduced free trade in the Dutch Indies. Although it is hard to assert if the book actually influenced this shift, it is clear that it inspired many people who read it, and even today *Max Havelaar* is considered as one of the most important works of Dutch literature.[24]

Another change took place when war erupted between the Dutch colonial authorities and the independent Sultanate of Aceh in Northern Sumatra in 1873. This conflict descended into a bloody guerrilla war that lasted for more than three decades. Already during the 1870s the prolonged military intervention raised questions about the merits of the abstention policy. Veth jumped on this issue right from the start and wrote a famous essay to advocate the conquest of Aceh. The war, so he argued, was totally legitimised as the region was known as a notorious 'pirate's nest' and it was up to the Dutch to bring order there.[25] In 1873 he also was one of the founding members of the Royal Dutch

Geographical Society (KNAG), which initially presented itself as an active lobby group for territorial expansion. During the founding meeting it was decided that 'even the appearance of a learned society was to be avoided', so clearly was it intended as a propagandist organisation. The most spectacular attempt of Veth to break the abstention policy was his plan for an expedition into the interior of Sumatra (1877–79), led by his son Daniël. The party set out on a gunboat, but was held back by a large group of armed men. Just around that time there was a change of government and the new minister of colonial affairs withdrew the funding, which forced the expedition to return. This failed example of gunboat diplomacy signalled the end of the propagandistic era of the KNAG, and when Veth died in 1895, its members had retreated completely in the ivory towers of academia, so Van der Velde argues.[26] By that time, however, the abstention policy had become untenable for other reasons.

Historians agree that it was the public enthusiasm about the so-called Lombok expedition that caused a breakthrough.[27] In August 1894 Dutch troops on the island were attacked in a night raid by the local princes. The news of this defeat was passed on to the Netherlands via newspapers on Java. Journalists there had already been arguing for the conquest of Lombok for months and took the opportunity to advocate it once more. In their words the attack had been nothing less than 'treason' that had to be 'revenged' in order to 'restore national prestige'. Such vocabulary was completely taken over by public opinion in the Netherlands. Everywhere around the country Lombok committees were founded that collected money for widows and veterans, which gathered a grand total of around fl.300,000 (at the time the equivalent of approximately £25,000). In the Indies a similar fund raised fl.220,000 (£18,000). At the same time hundreds of young men volunteered for the colonial army to punish the 'savages'. Barely a month after the attack the Dutch invaded Lombok and rooted out all local opposition. The most famous event was the destruction of the palace at Tjakranegara, which was looted. The royal treasure was taken back as a trophy and put in display in the National Gallery of the *Rijksmuseum*. This time the news from Lombok was met in a haze of triumph and all around the Netherlands spontaneous celebrations started. The climax took place in July 1895 when the victorious soldiers were welcomed back with a grand parade in The Hague where they received medals from the royal family, cheered by thousands of spectators.

The excitement over Lombok gave the advocates of a more active policy of expansion in the outer regions more leverage. The most famous protagonist of such an approach became General J.B. van Heutsz, who was a seasoned officer in Aceh. He developed a strategy of total warfare, in which the civilian population was not spared in order to stamp out the

De verovering van Tjakranegara op Lombok

3.1   Classroom poster depicting Dutch colonial troops taking the palace
at Tjakranegara on Lombok, published in 1911.
(Courtesy Tropenmuseum, Amsterdam)

guerrillas. In 1896 he was appointed as the commander-in-chief of the
forces on Sumatra, which marked the beginning of the so-called 'pacification policy'. His feats of arms aroused much enthusiasm amongst the
Dutch public and they were celebrated in books, songs and, to a lesser
extent, cartoons in which the colonial army was glorified and the
Indonesian adversaries insulted.[28] In 1904 Van Heutsz declared victory in
Aceh and the Sultanate was officially annexed. The general received a
hero's welcome in the Netherlands where he made a tour around several
towns where he was cheered by large crowds.[29] After this enthusiastic
reception he returned to the Indies as governor-general, oversaw the
'pacification' of other islands and by 1910 the conquest was completed.
Some people obviously were proud at this achievement, the most graphic
illustration of which was a map of Europe over which the archipelago was
projected. This showed that the Dutch possessed a colony that would
stretch from Scandinavia to Istanbul. There was, however, considerable
unease about the gross violence that accompanied the process of expansion. In 1905 it emerged that the new governor in Aceh, G.C.E. van

[97]

Daalen, in the previous year had led an expedition to the hinterland during which several villages were destroyed and the inhabitants killed. He was forced to resign after this 'murderous history' was exposed in pamphlets, which led to a tumultuous debate in parliament.[30]

The violent conquest of the Indonesian archipelago did have a more peaceful counterpart, the so-called 'ethical policy'. In 1901 the Queen mentioned this term for the first time in her annual address to the nation. The policy can be seen as a direct extension of the ideas that 'progressives' such as Veth started to develop from 1870 onwards. The traditional conservative colonial policy mainly drew in ideas of 'association', whereby the Dutch and indigenous cultures existed separately from each other. Although 'progressive' scholars did recognise the differences between the white and the indigenous population, they also to an extent advocated the principle of 'assimilation', which aimed to westernise the Indies.[31] One of the most famous protagonists of the latter principle was the Arabist Christiaan Snouck Hurgronje, who acted as an advisor of Van Heutsz in Aceh. Under his influence Dutch colonial rule was reformed into the 'ethical policy', which was aimed at the education and elevation of the indigenous population.

A century after he wrote his works about these issues there is still controversy amongst scholars about how to interpret Snouck's close involvement in the formation of the colonial state, which has led to a short but fierce round of the Orientalism debate in the Netherlands. In 1995 the sociologist Pieter van der Veer wrote an essay, mainly drawing on the theory of Edward Said, in which he presented Snouck as a henchman of the colonialists and so responsible for an oppressive and exploitative régime.[32] This provoked a reaction by historians from Leiden, the university where Snouck spent most of his academic career, who defended his reputation as a talented academic.[33] Others have pointed out that this polarisation obscures the complexity of the work of Snouck, which reflected upon deep notions of the colonial state and modernity in a global context.[34]

The issues Snouck and other contemporary intellectuals grappled with did generate fundamental questions about the relations between the cultures of the Western 'self' and the Eastern 'other'. One of the main issues was the possibility for indigenous people to reach a higher level of 'civilisation'. As in other countries these ideas fitted the evolutionary model of Social Darwinism, which presented a hierarchy between the different 'races' of the world. Departing from such ideas, practically all scholars that studied the Indies during the colonial era considered the Dutch superior to the indigenous people of the archipelago, who needed guidance of the colonial state one way or another.[35] Despite this apparent Euro-centrism there were a lot of ambiguities, which ensured that the discourse was not monolithic and was characterised by a strong dynamism. There was, for example, genuine respect for some aspects of Indonesian cultures, which were considered as an antidote to certain 'illnessess' of modern life in Europe. Frances Gouda has argued that such complex ideas were formulated in metaphors that portrayed the indigenous people both as children that needed education and as exotic mystics with great ancient wisdom. According to her this reveals 'a discourse of control and dominance, on the one hand, and a "rethoric of desire" on the other'.[36]

Obviously such ideas were mainly discussed by academics. In this respect, the *Koninklijke Instituut voor Taal- Land en Volkenkunde* (KITLV, Royal Netherlands Institute of South East Asian and Caribbean Studies) in Leiden, founded in 1851, was one of the first platforms where such debates took place. During its long existence it has established itself as the most important centre for the study of overseas anthropology in the Netherlands. In his history of the KITLV Maarten Kuitenbrouwer has argued that this institute shows how anthropologists in the nineteenth and first half of the twentieth century moved 'in between orientalism and science', as they did do serious research, but their views were also shaped by and applied in the colonial context.[37] As has been mentioned prominent academics such as Snouck, and also C. van Vollenhoven, were important advisors to the government and their views were largely reflected in the reforms that took place under the 'ethical policy'. At other levels their influence also became apparent. In 1864 two competing courses for colonial administrators were started in the towns of Delft and Leiden. By 1900 both these institutes were moribund and in 1902 a new course was started at the University of Leiden. Although in the first two decades of its existence it did not lead to an academic degree and the numbers of students was rather small, it clearly indicated that at the beginning of the twentieth century Leiden became the most important centre for the study of the Dutch Indies and the training of colonial officials.[38]

At the end of the nineteenth century there were other groups that clearly were connected to the expansion of the colonial state in the Indonesian archipelago, such as missionaries. In the Dutch Indies, a great variety of denominations was active, which reflected the fragmented religious landscape in the motherland. But despite the differences all such organisations reported about their edifying work in the archipelago in magazines and during public meetings. In this way their efforts can be seen as a strong support for the emergence of the 'ethical policy', which emphasised the civilising duty of the Netherlands as a Christian nation.[39]

The representation of the Dutch Indies also spread to the arts. In Dutch literature Indonesian themes took a distinctive place, and still do.

Many authors who wrote about the colonies had themselves spent time there. In a pioneering study of this genre Rob Nieuwenhuys has argued that their work can only be fitted partially into an Euro-centric model of literary analysis as they had been influenced by a different social structure.[40] More recently Pamela Pattynama has put forward another view and characterised this body of literature as a 'travel archive', which transferred images of the Indies to the Netherlands that have nestled into the collective memory.[41] One of the most famous examples is Louis Couperus, who spent much of his youth in the Dutch Indies. His best-known novel is *De Stille Kracht* (translated in English as *The Hidden Force*) in which he described the downfall of a Dutch administrator on Java, who gets entangled in an intricate love web between his half-blood children, an indigenous concubine and a local aristocrat. Pattynama considers it as a prime example how the Dutch audience was presented with notions about gender and race in a colonial context.[42]

The colony in the East was also a source of inspiration for other artists. The Netherlands is not a country that is well known for its monuments and in comparison with other colonial powers few statues were erected to commemorate colonial heroes, with the noticeable exception of Van Heutsz.[43] In other forms of Dutch architecture, however, Indonesian motifs were increasingly incorporated, particularly in the ornaments of buildings that housed trading and shipping companies.[44] The influential designer C.A. Lion Cachet was heavily influenced by Oriental themes in his Art Nouveau creations, which ranged from wallpapers to stamps.[45] Also a significant number of Western painters went to the Dutch Indies, which generated cultural exchange. Societies and museums were created in Java, which stimulated the spread of Western arts. At the same time many artists were influenced by indigenous crafts and designs, especially from the island of Bali.[46] And last but not least there were the gamelan orchestras that performed in Europe from the 1880s. Although it took the Western audience a while to get used to the peculiar sounds, this traditional Indonesian music has greatly influenced modern composers.[47]

Despite the great variety of the genres mentioned above, many contemporaries considered them as part of the same *gesamtkunstwerk*. The most obvious form in which such a synthesis took shape were colonial exhibitions. Marieke Bloembergen has written the most extensive study of the Dutch 'colonial spectacles' at world exhibitions between 1880 and 1931, which contains lively descriptions of the exotic splendour of the pavilions in which the Indies were represented. The exhibits were rather differentiated as they were meant to draw people from all walks of life. They accommodated intellectuals who discussed highbrow matters during academic conferences and at the same time tried to lure people from lower classes with so-called 'native villages' where Indonesians showed their music and dance. The objects on display gave facts and figures about the advance of Western technology and trade in the archipelago as well as a taste for indigenous crafts. The bottom line of this bewildering mix of information and entertainment was rather straightforward though; the Netherlands presented itself as a colonial power and tried to brush up its national prestige.[48] As most of the world exhibitions took place in foreign countries, this message was not for domestic use only. In this respect the diplomatic balancing act of neutrality was clearly apparent. In the pavilions at foreign exhibitions almost nothing could be found about the military conquest of the archipelago, which could provoke criticism from other colonial powers. It was the civilising mission that took centre stage, which served as a legitimation of Dutch rule in the Indies because it promoted 'effective government'.[49]

Such messages were conveyed to the Dutch public too although the tone was slightly less cautious. The only colonial exhibition ever to be held in the Netherlands (Amsterdam 1883) attracted one-and-a-half million visitors. Aside from a large ethnological exhibition and an eclectic 'native village' with houses and people from throughout the archipelago, they were presented with a large statue that was erected to symbolise 'victory in Aceh' – rather premature considering it would take another two decades before the Sultanate was annexed.[50] Although such an event was never repeated in the Netherlands it did lead to attempts to present the colonial enterprise in Asia to a wider public. Already in the 1860s and 1870s several museums had been founded which aimed to do so. An extremely important ethnographic collection was situated in Leiden, and in Haarlem there was a permanent display that represented aspects of colonial trade. Initially these institutions were rather poorly organised and, inspired by the 1883 exhibition, their directors became members of the newly founded *Nederlandsche Koloniale Vereeniging* (Dutch Colonial Association) that wanted to inform the public about the Dutch Indies. During the following two decades, however, this lobby was largely torn by the question of which city should host the most important museum. In the 1900s it became clear that for the time being nothing would change and that the Haarlem and Leiden museums would stay put. It was only then that the professionalisation of these institutions began.[51]

Bossenbroek has argued that the press offered an effective way to propagate Dutch expansion at the end of the nineteenth century. As in other countries the media in the Netherlands underwent great changes at the time caused by technological advance and lower taxes, which led to a far wider distribution. At the same time the great events that took place in the archipelago received a lot of attention in various periodicals. Although many newspapers and magazines were allied to a political party, there was general support for the expansion of Dutch rule in the Indies, with the exception of a few Socialist journalists. Although the tone could be quite boisterous, such as in the patriotic editorials of the famous journalist Charles Boissevain, elitist newspapers in general supported the government in its cautious policy of neutrality. There was, however, also an emergent popular press that was less circumspect in its patriotic outbursts. Such media increasingly used visual material to attract readers and illustrated magazines became a popular medium to disseminate pictures of colonial life. In this way photography, so Bossenbroek argues, became an important genre in Dutch imperial culture.[52]

Despite the apparent influence of the press, it can well be argued that the main target of the groups that wanted to promote overseas expansion was the nation's youth. After the introduction of compulsory education in 1901, schools became the most important place to do so. During history lessons pupils were presented with a patriotic vision of the Dutch past. These featured several heroic episodes from the early colonial days of the East India Company in the seventeenth century. Less popular topics were the cultivation system and early nineteenth century rule on Java. Classes about more recent events, such as the wars on Aceh and Lombok, provided biased views on the situation in Indonesia in which the indigenous population was blamed for the violence and the colonial army praised for its gallant conduct. In geography lessons the colonies in the East, and West, also featured heavily and children were taught about the rich produce these regions yielded. Aside from these facts and figures many classrooms were decorated with patriotic pictures on the walls. Colonial themes were popular here too. One of the most famous of such plates depicts the taking of Tjakranegara on Lombok with furious looking Indonesians throwing themselves on cool Dutch bayonets.[53] Also outside the schools the youth was exposed to heroic stories from the Dutch Indies in children's books. Until the 1870s, one title appeared annually in which the Indies featured. After that there was a steady growth up to six titles a year. Historical adventure books were the most popular genre, followed by travelogues and stories of daily life of the European population.[54]

The great variety of media that presented the expansion of the Dutch Indies to the public suggests that the message that the colony was there to stay was widely disseminated from the late nineteenth century. As Bossenbroek has pointed out one should not go too far in making a distinction between elitist expressions of these issues and more popular genres. The presence of colonial issues in the classroom is probably the most tangible expression of this. Apparently, the Dutch Indies was considered an intricate part of the education of the young, which says something about the significance of the colony for the formation of national identity. The questions that were generated by looking at the colonial 'other' contained relevant issues for the mother country because at the time the Netherlands itself underwent great social change. In this way the transformation of the old mercantile empire into a modern colonial state served both as a mirror and as a source for national pride. In such ideas the image of the 'self' was no less important than that of the 'other', which points out that they were not monolithic or strictly binary. Such complexities are even more apparent while looking at the representation of the Boers in South Africa.

South Africa, 1880–1902

Another part of the pre-modern mercantile empire that was rediscovered by the Dutch public at the end of the nineteenth century was South Africa. The turnaround, however, was more sudden than the emerging interest in the Dutch Indies. Unlike the possessions in the East and West Indies, the Cape Colony had not been given back by the British, who occupied the Dutch overseas territories during the Napoleonic Wars. In the six decades or so that followed the official handover in 1814, the public in the Netherlands hardly paid attention to the Dutch-speaking descendants of the East India Company colonists who by then lived in a colony where English was the official language. Some individuals, the most famous of whom was U.G. Lauts, showed interest in the political developments when the Boers moved inland during the Great Trek to establish two independent republics, the Transvaal (ZAR) and the Orange Free State (OVS). He applauded this effort to escape British dominance and tried to persuade people from the Netherlands to go there and help the Boers. Most of the few individuals who did so, however, came back with negative stories about the republics where they thought life was expensive, work was hard and the inhabitants were undeveloped and rude to outsiders. So when Britain annexed the Transvaal in 1877 there was hardly any protest against it.[55]

This changed all of a sudden when the Boers in the Transvaal took up arms to end the annexation in December 1880 and a wave of enthusiasm hit the public in the Netherlands.[56] Everywhere around the country committees came into being that expressed their support for the Boer cause. The most successful initiative was by Professor P. Harting in Utrecht. He wrote an address to the British people to ask for the restoration of independence in the Transvaal which was signed by 6,082 people, amongst whom were many influential politicians, army officers and academics. The nation-wide success of the address was such that Transvaal committees from several cities decided to co-operate and start

3.2   Dutch youngsters dressed like Boers around 1896.
(Photograph courtesy of Zuid Afrika Huis, Amsterdam)

the Dutch South Africa Association (*Nederlandsch Zuid-Afrikaansche Vereeniging*, NZAV).

The ideals that were behind this support were summarised in terms of racial kinship; '*Stamverwantschap*', a word that cannot be translated. The Boers were seen as 'cousins in South Africa' as they descended from the colonists of the old Dutch East India Company and, despite their heavy dialect, still used high Dutch as their official written language. In addition their archaic lifestyle was seen as a leftover from the glorious Golden Age, which earned them the honorary title of 'the Gueux of the nineteenth century', a reference to the pre-modern freedom fighters that defeated the Spaniards. This last issue also had to do with the position of the Netherlands as a second-rank nation, which cheered the brave Boers who fought the great British Empire. The victory at Majuba Hill therefore was seen as a glorious feat of arms that would give the Dutch race new 'élan'.

The vulnerable international position of the Netherlands, however, was seen as a problem in this respect. Around the time of the Transvaal War Britain and the Netherlands were in the process of demarcating the borders between their empires in South East Asia. The government was extremely cautious not to offend the British as it was feared that they would annex parts of the Indonesian archipelago and it adhered to a strict policy of neutrality towards the South African question.[57] This did not prevent politicians becoming members of the NZAV on a personal basis. Although there were political groups who were somewhat reluctant to support the Boers, such as the Socialists who considered them 'Feudalistic' and the Catholics who objected to their fundamental Calvinism, sympathy for the republics was widespread even within these parties. Henk te Velde and Chris Koppen have shown that leading figures in the Liberal fractions and the Protestant party were greatly influenced by their pro-Boer sympathies. In this way the South African question played a significant role in the development of Dutch political culture and nationalism.[58]

Aside from this domestic aspect, it can be argued that the pro-Boer movement in the Netherlands was a form of informal and cultural imperialism.[59] Members of the NZAV expressed hoped for the existence of an independent state in South Africa where Dutch was spoken, where the influence of the Netherlands in that region would grow and economic opportunities develop. Such sentiments were clearly reflected in a public letter by a number of intellectuals who in 1886 asserted that the ties between the people in the Netherlands and the Boers were mutually beneficial.[60] In its statutes the NZAV wrote that one of the main goals was to mobilise support for initiatives to boost emigration and enterprise. The actual effects of this propaganda, however, were disappointing. The most important company that was active in South Africa, the Dutch South African Railway Company that built a line between Pretoria and Delagoa Bay, was unable to raise enough capital in the Netherlands and mainly drew its investments from Germany. Also the emigration numbers remained low. An estimated 6,500 people left for South Africa between 1881 and 1899, most of whom went to Transvaal.

In that republic the situation was not as most pro-Boers in the Netherlands hoped. Many Boers were suspicious of outsiders and amongst certain groups there was a deep resentment of the so-called *Hollanders*, who they considered to be arrogant meddlers. Nevertheless President Paul Kruger, who was in power between 1881 and 1900, thought that it was necessary to attract people from the Netherlands to help out with the modernisation of the republic, especially after gold was found at the Rand in 1886, which speeded up developments enormously. As a result of this 'hate and love relationship', Gerrit Schutte shows, *Hollanders* played a considerable role in the development of administration, infrastructure and education in the Transvaal.[61] The majority of these emigrants were well educated and started to write about their experiences in South Africa, either as correspondents for newspapers, or in travelogues. In this way a line of communication was set up between the republics and the Netherlands, which led to the formation of a body of Dutch literature about the South African question. The contents of this literature were highly coloured by concepts of race. Although the dichotomy between black Africans and white colonists was an important theme, there was more to it than that. The English-speaking and Dutch-speaking communities in South Africa were at that time known as 'the two white races', which shows that race in this context did not only refer to physical features, but also to culture and heritage.

The great question that emerged was how to 'civilise' South Africa, to use a term of the time. In this sense Dutch authors that wrote about the Boers had an ambivalent attitude towards their 'kinsmen'. In general the inhabitants of the republics were described as a simple and illiterate people with an archaic lifestyle, which prevented their development. Many travellers complained about the lack of interest in education and culture, which made life in South Africa a bore. On the other hand there was much admiration for the skills the Boers had developed during their outdoor life, such as shooting and horse riding. In this sense many authors in the Netherlands certainly saw them as an example to invigorate their own nation that had been weakened by modern society.[62]

Such ambivalent ideas, however, did fall away to some extent while looking at the overall picture of South Africa. To many contemporaries the main question was which 'white race' would be able to become the dominant colonial power in the region, the British or the Boers. In this sense the propaganda had another function, namely to counter the descriptions – 'slander' in the eyes of the Dutch public – that British authors produced of the Boers in which they portrayed them as half-savages, who were not capable of 'responsible government' or as cruel oppressors of the black population. In Dutch sources the Boers, who had been in Africa for centuries, were presented as far better colonisers than the British 'newcomers'. Such authors tried to show how the British had oppressed the Dutch-speaking population in South Africa since taking over the Cape Colony. The Great Trek was described as a justified flight into the interior to escape from tyranny. Moreover, it was argued, the pioneers were the first to bring the light of 'civilisation' to these 'savage' lands for which they had to pay with 'martyrs-blood' in the wars they fought with black Africans. As a result of these experiences, it was argued, the Boers had learned to consider black people as their inferiors in order to guard the social order in the republics. Siegfried Huigen has shown that this heroic account of the colonial past in which racial antagonism was the leading theme, served to provide an alternative to the Anglo-centric literature about South Africa and legitimise the existence of an independent Dutch-speaking entity in the region.[63]

It seems that such ideas spread widely throughout public opinion in the Netherlands in the 1880s and 1890s.[64] The most apparent sign of this was the outcry about the mounting tensions between the British Empire and the Boer republics. The first outburst took place in 1896, after the Jameson Raid, when Kruger and his men were praised in the newspapers for their victory over the 'Buccaneers' of the British South Africa Company. But this was just a foretaste of what was to come during the South African War (1899–1902). In the run-up to that conflict another address to the British people was published in an effort to stop the conflict from breaking out and this time more than 140,000 people signed it. When hostilities started in October there were other signs of massive support for the embattled Boers. Churches all across the country organised meetings to pray for their survival. In a few months the membership of the NZAV leaped from 1,600 to more than 6,000 and many other pro-Boer organisations sprang up. The combined efforts to collect money for the republics yielded approximately fl.2,000,000 (at the time approximately £165,000). As a result of this great commotion the Dutch government was caught between a rock and hard place as it would not abandon its policy of neutrality, but at the same time was pressured by the public to do something on behalf of the Boers. In 1900 a cunning solution was found when President Kruger, who had been forced to leave his republic, was offered asylum and was brought to Europe on the Dutch cruiser *Gelderland*. Kruger's popularity became clear when he visited The Hague where he was granted an audience by one of his greatest admirers, Queen Wilhelmina, and gigantic crowds cheered him continuously.

Some historians see this enormous outburst of pro-Boer enthusiasm in the Netherlands as a temporary phenomenon during which the public was caught by a collective form of hysteria.[65] Although it can be argued that support for the Boers and dislike of Great Britain during the South African War was an European-wide phenomenon, this overlooks the continuity between the propaganda of 1899 and 1902 and the period that preceded it. Ulrich Kröll has argued that the situation in the Netherlands differed from that in Germany and France where the agitation about the South African War was respectively less widespread and the result of Anglophobia rather than the result of support for the republics. In this way, he has asserted that organisations in the Netherlands – who worked closely together with the minister plenipotentiary of the Transvaal, W.J. Leyds – took a central position in the continental pro-Boer propaganda campaign.[66] Indeed, the Netherlands was flooded by a tidal wave of publications that was fed by information coming from South Africa. Although it became increasingly hard to do so because the British cut off the telegraph lines and censored the regular mail, reports from Boer generals and letters from eyewitnesses continued to be published in newspapers and in pamphlets throughout the conflict.

My own research suggests that the contents of such publications must be seen in the light of the view of South African history that emerged in Dutch publications during the 1880s and 1890s.[67] One famous pamphlet that was published, written by the young statesman Jan Smuts, was titled *A Century of Wrong* and portrayed the war as a result of the British oppression of the Boers that had started when they took over the Cape Colony. Such views clearly captured the hearts and minds of the Dutch public in the first months of the conflict, when battles took place, during which the Boer commandos managed to withstand the mighty British army. In Dutch descriptions of such events the slanted view on the South African question clearly emerged. Although some commentators worried about the discipline of the Boer forces, they were seen as skilful and gallant fighters. One theme that emerged in many accounts was their humanitarian approach to wounded adversaries, which showed that they were only fighting for self-preservation. In contrast the British army was described as thoroughly corrupt, the soldiers blinded by indoctrination and jingo-propaganda. This 'racial hatred' resulted in 'atrocities' on and off the battlefield, it was thought.

After the British had occupied the territory of the Boer republics by June 1900, the war descended into a guerrilla conflict. To quell opposition the army command implemented harsh measures such as farm burning and concentration camps. In Dutch publications such methods were also seen as a result of the struggle between the 'white races', which marked the nineteenth-century history of South Africa. The tone of many authors became more radical and terms such as 'extermination' and 'mass murder' were increasingly used in relation to the way the British tried to subdue the commandos. Moreover, the image of the Boers shifted in this period. Those who surrendered, so-called *'Handsoppers'*, were seen as cowards who embodied all the bad traits of the Boer character, such as narrow-mindedness and egocentrism. In contrast, commandos who continued fighting, so-called *'Bittereinders'*, were seen as true patriots who never would give up their freedom. The women in the concentration camps shared in the same heroism. Heartbreaking accounts that came in from the camps exposed their suffering, but also mentioned that they remained confident that the Boers would persevere in the end.

Bossenbroek has argued that in the years between 1899 and 1902 the war in South Africa truly set public opinion 'alight'.[68] Indeed the conflict was represented in a wide range of media and there are numerous examples that show that pro-Boer propaganda affected daily life in different ways. Paul Kruger became a brand name for items such as tobacco, wallets, beer, and 'refreshing' lemonade. In addition the exiled president received an enormous volume of cards, honorary diplomas and other gifts at his villa in the Dutch town of Hilversum.[69] In addition the Boer commandos seemed to have inspired a substantial group of enthusiasts to do their bit for their own country. In 1900 the *Vereeniging voor Volks-weerbaarheid* was founded, an organisation that aimed to train Dutch men in order to improve their military skills. One of the main reasons to do so was that the war in South Africa showed how important this had become in modern warfare. Leaders from the three biggest political parties joined its executive committee, and it soon boasted that it had no less than 14,000 members. There was a distinctive South African touch as participants in training camps liked to wear broad-brimmed slouch hats and bandoliers when they went out into the 'veldt' of the Low Countries.[70]

Despite these signs of feverish patriotism, many historians argue that after the Peace of Vereeniging had been signed (31 May 1902) the pro-Boer movement ended as suddenly as it had started. In this treaty the republics surrendered their independence and officially became part of the British Empire. The initial reactions in Dutch newspapers certainly did contain great disappointment about this outcome, which practically shut off the possibilities for the Dutch to try to enlarge their influence in South Africa.[71] But this was not the only sentiment that resounded in contemporary critiques. One of the most famous journalists at the time, C. Boissevain, thought that the heroic fight and the great suffering of the republics also had a positive effect on the unity of the Dutch-speaking people, in both the former republics and the Cape Colony, who had been 'hammered into the race that eventually will civilise and rule South Africa'.[72] Such references stimulate the question whether 1902 really was the end of pro-Boer sentiments in the Netherlands. The same question can be asked about the public interest in the Dutch Indies. The following paragraphs will explore Dutch imperial culture after the turbulent period between 1870 and 1910.

The Dutch Indies, 1910–40

The most extensive study of Dutch imperial culture, by Bossenbroek, signals the demise of the interest in the Dutch Indies in the first decade of the twentieth century.[73] Bob de Graaff agrees with this view and argues that after the territorial conquest of the archipelago the coverage of current affairs in the East lessened and so the public interest dwindled. According to him one could even speak of 'indifference' towards colonial issues.[74] Other authors have different views. Te Velde has argued that the Dutch public did take pride in their colonial possessions in South East

Asia, but that this enthusiasm was not enough to lead to such strong nationalist feelings as there had been at the close of the nineteenth century.[75] In her study of colonial exhibitions, Bloembergen signals more continuity and argues that the display of the Dutch Indies remained firmly embedded in the debate about the principles on which Dutch colonial rule should be established.[76] Seen from such a perspective, there seems to have been less of a discontinuity during the 1900s than others suggest.

The political developments in the Indies continued to give rise to controversy. Although it remains to be seen to what extent the two processes were actually related, the 'ethical policy' – which aimed to provide more education to the indigenous population – was accompanied by the rise of a modern nationalist movement, based on Islamist principles. A development that ran parallel was increasing agitation against colonial rule from the upcoming Communist movement in the colony. During the first decade of the twentieth century most Social-Democrats became supporters of the 'ethical policy' and ended their demands for more political rights for the indigenous population. The Communists, however, did not cease their campaign and agitated more radically. Official fears about this movement climaxed in 1926 when a Communist revolt was quelled.[77] But it already became apparent during the First World War that the pressure on the colonial government in the Dutch Indies had grown considerably, mainly because the ties with the motherland were largely cut off. In 1918 the governor-general therefore saw himself forced to create a parliament for Indonesian representatives, the so-called *Volksraad*.

In the Netherlands there was an outcry amongst certain groups over this development. Such reactionary ideas mainly existed amongst businessmen who were active in the archipelago. At the end of the nineteenth century a relatively small group of capitalists dominated the economic ties with the colonies and made great profits.[78] These men considered the ´ethical policy´ to be dangerous for their interests. Their main principle was the *Rijkseenheidgedachte*, the idea that the Netherlands and her possessions in the East should be tied together in closer union. In his study of this 'colonial lobby', Arjen Taselaar has argued that it was quite influential and yielded significant political weight, particularly before the economic crisis of 1929. One of the main results was that free trade was restricted considerably, which seems to echo the international trend towards autarky at the time. Moreover, the tolerance towards the nationalist movement faded during the inter-war years and the colonial government became increasingly repressive.[79]

The colonial lobby also sought other ways to propagate the necessity to strengthen the ties with the Dutch Indies. A main thorn in the side of the unionists was the 'progressive' bulwark at the University of Leiden, which dominated the academic study of the Dutch Indies. That is why the lobby collected money amongst big companies to start a new faculty of Indology at the University of Utrecht, which opened in 1925. The professors at this new institute made propaganda about issues concerning colonial policy and engaged in polemics with their colleagues from Leiden. They also started a magazine to put forward their views, which clearly had the unionist signature of the *Rijkseenheidgedachte*. In addition, a course for colonial administrators was started in Utrecht to break the Leiden monopoly in this field. Soon, it counted a similar number of students as its competitor.[80]

Another big project of the business lobby was the foundation of the Colonial Institute in Amsterdam, which was meant to reach out to the wider public. In 1910, one of the most influential entrepreneurs in the Netherlands, J.T. Cremer, collected the necessary funds amongst his colleagues. The organisation was divided into three parts. The department of tropical medicine soon acquired international fame because of its education and research. Another section was an ethnological museum, which combined the collections of the colonial museum in Haarlem and the zoo in Amsterdam. And lastly there was a department for the promotion of trade, with its own museum and a propaganda bureau for tropical produce. The realisation of the two latter sections, that were interlinked, would take considerable time because the building that housed them was only finished in 1926. The impressive looking structure, in neo-renaissance style, was opened by Queen Wilhelmina and the speeches that were given at the ceremony emphasised the unity between the Netherlands and her colony in the East.[81]

By the time the Colonial Institute was fully operational such ideas had firmly taken shape. As a result the divide between the 'progressives' who supported the 'ethical policy' and 'conservatives' who propagated the unionist vision became less stringent. Many historians argue that at the end of the 1920s both camps had reached a general consensus as a reaction against the increasing uncertainties in the relations between the Netherlands and its colony in the East. This consensus was based on racialist and paternalistic views of the Indonesians and it was argued that for the time being they needed colonial guidance as they were not able to rule themselves.[82] Another shared idea was that the wealth of the mother country largely depended on the income derived from the colony.[83] These feelings were summarised in the famous catchphrase '*Indië verloren rampspoed geboren*' ('Indies thorn, calamity born').[84] However, Bob de Graaff argues that such sentiments only affected a limited circle of government officials and that there were no attempts to spread them to a larger audience.[85] Similarly, Taselaar seems to consider the Colonial

Institute mainly as a toy of a wealthy business lobby that was not really serious about making propaganda. According to him, the Institute was already in decline in the 1930s when the economic depression made people reluctant to spend money on such projects.[86] This view is supported by statistics about the number of people who visited the Colonial Institute, which declined from 81,000 in 1927 to 45,000 in 1932. Although there was a small rise again in the late part of the 1930s there were complaints that the exhibits were too elitist and academic to attract a large audience.[87]

Looking at other projects, however, it appears that propaganda from the Institute in fact did reach a wider audience than the people who actually visited the museums. One of the most important activities of the organisation was to supply schools with information about the colonies. Between 1918 and 1922 several thousands of geography teachers received a course on how to teach their pupils about the colonial possessions in the classroom. In addition, samples of colonial produce were circulated among the schools, which seems to have been successful; in 1917 there were 2,200 of such parcels, in 1940 4,300.[88] Taselaar considers these initiatives to be 'elitist' as they were top-bottom aimed at building patriotic citizens.[89] Notwithstanding the intentions of this propaganda, however, one can argue that the unionist view that the colonies were of vital importance for the economy of the motherland reached a wider audience.

In literature the Dutch Indies remained a prominent topic too. Some writers who had been born and raised there, such as E. du Perron, became dissatisfied with the increasing repression of the colonial state and started to criticise the *Rijkseenheidgedachte*.[90] It seems, however, that the majority of publications did not contain such dissent. Jur van Goor has argued that because of the improvements of the infrastructure in the archipelago it became easier for Dutch opinion makers to go and travel there, which led to a growing number of publications during the inter-war years. Despite the great variety of sources there was a central message in the majority of publications of the time, which was that the Dutch Indies were important for the motherland and vice versa and that the colonial state should stay in existence.[91] After the First World War there was also a marked rise in the number of children's books in which the archipelago featured; from six annually in 1914, to thirteen in 1930 and twenty-four in 1940.[92] As mentioned before, such books gave a highly patriotic vision of the Dutch colonial presence in the East.

The new media contributed to this image too. Because the Netherlands did not possess an independent network of submarine cables, there were many experiments with the wireless, which made the Dutch leaders in this field. In March 1927 a milestone was reached when a radio broadcast from the Philips factory in Eindhoven was received on Java. Two months later Queen Wilhelmina and Princess Juliana addressed the people in the overseas territories and emphasised that the radio waves strengthened the ties between the colonies and the motherland. In addition the fact that even the BBC had to ask Philips to transmit their signal to parts of the British Empire filled many people in the Netherlands with pride about this achievement.[93] In the same period handheld film cameras were introduced in the Indies and it seems that a substantial number of people owned one. Films with scenes from the daily life of the colonial elites were sent home where the family could enjoy these exotic pictures. Many reels have survived in the archives, but no thorough study of this material exists. There are several compilations though, which show that these films provided the public in the Netherlands with a romantic picture of day-to-day life in which depicted the differences between the white elites and indigenous people.[94]

It can well be argued that the Dutch increasingly lost sense of what was actually going on in the Dutch Indies during the inter-war years. While the motherland revelled in the imagery of the mystic and profitable possessions in the East, it ignored the rise of Indonesian nationalism and the increasing pressure coming from Japan and the United States of America. There is controversy over the question as to how far such views actually disseminated through society. Both Bob de Graaff and Taselaar argue that the unionist view was only shared by a small elite of conservative politicians, government officials and colonial businessmen, who were reluctant to make propaganda. On the other hand, however, this lobby did found the Colonial Institute, which was aimed at spreading knowledge about the Dutch Indies, particularly amongst the nation's youth. Looking at other media, the idea that the colonial possessions were inextricably bound with the Netherlands seems to have been more widespread than Bob de Graaff and Taselaar argue. When the process of decolonisation took off after the Second World War, the public slowly came to realise that colonial rule in Indonesia was not self-evident anymore. But by then it proved to be too late for them to wake from the collective colonial dream.

South Africa, 1902–40

Some argue that the interest of the Dutch public in South Africa had a marked conclusion when the South African War ended in 1902. The most extensive study about the ties between the Netherlands and the Afrikaners in the first three decades of the twentieth century is by Bart de Graaff. He argues that after the conflict was over, feelings of racial kinship were marginalised. The annexation of the Boer republics by the British Empire meant that the hopes for a Dutch sphere of influence in the region vanished. Looking at trade and migration this certainly seems to have been the case. Exports to South Africa during that period did not exceed 1 per cent of the total Dutch volume and the number of settlers remained extremely low until the 1930s. In addition several leading figures in the Afrikaner nationalist movement were increasingly averse to any external meddling in their affairs.[95]

One of the most apparent changes that took place was the development of Afrikaans as an official language, by the so-called second *Taal*-movement. Gradually the written form of the Dutch dialect that was spoken in South Africa replaced high Dutch, which was the language spoken and written in the Netherlands. Ingrid Glorie in this respect even writes of a 'double process of decolonisation of the Afrikaans language and culture with regard to English as well as Dutch cultural dominance'.[96] It certainly is true that such developments caused tensions between the Dutch and the Afrikaners. Some literary critics in the Netherlands did not conceal their contempt for Afrikaans, which they considered an ugly and retarded dialect. On the other hand Afrikaner nationalists underwent a process of radicalisation, which led to expressions of their dislike of high Dutch. The climax of this antagonism took place around the law that made Afrikaans an official language in 1925. A year before a teacher at Rustenburg ordered his pupils to burn all books they could find that had been published in the Netherlands.[97]

Despite these examples of overt hostility from both sides the ties between the second *Taal*-movement and the literary establishment in the Netherlands were not all bad. During the first decade of the twentieth century many Dutchmen reacted to Milner's policy of Anglicisation by providing external help to the Afrikaners to rebuild their own institutions. In the course of that decade the former minister plenipotentiary of the Transvaal in Europe, W.J. Leyds, sent millions of guilders from the leftovers of the state assets of the republic to help Dutch-speaking schools and newspapers.[98] Looking at the new circumstances in South Africa, he and others accepted the development of Afrikaans. In 1906, the former superintendent for education in the Transvaal, Nicolaas Mansvelt, compiled a songbook with rhymes in vernacular set to music in order to stimulate the patriotic feelings of the Afrikaners. This initiative was welcomed in the Netherlands and there was genuine appreciation for the poetic potential of Afrikaans. At that time Afrikaner song evenings were well attended and some of the rhymes became part of the curriculum at primary schools where they were sung up to the 1950s.

There was also appreciation for Mansvelt's volume in South Africa. Gustav Preller, one of the main protagonists of the *Taal*-movement used it as a source of inspiration for his efforts to popularise Afrikaans. Moreover, his famous historical work was greatly influenced by Dutch literature about the history of South Africa. Several authors have pointed out that in this way authors from the Netherlands significantly influenced Afrikaner nationalism, which incorporated a highly coloured vision on the past.[99] One of the most famous to do so was Leyds, who dedicated his life to history writing after his political career ended in 1902. Up to 1919 he published two voluminous works about the relations between the British and the Boers from the Great Trek up to the eve of the South African War. In it he provided a legitimation of the policy of the two republics, especially under the Kruger government, of which he was an important member himself. This biased view of that history has had a lot of influence on the way Afrikaner historians wrote about it.[100]

The heroic view of South African history also remained popular in the Netherlands, which is illustrated by the work of L. Penning. This Dutch writer started publishing about the struggle between the Boers and British after the Jameson Raid, an event which infuriated him. During the South African War he rose to fame with a chronology of the conflict and a series of semi-historical adventure books about a fictive Transvaal officer, who participated in real battles. The series, which counted five books, became hugely popular and was reprinted in large numbers until the 1950s. In all, Penning wrote twenty books about South Africa and his beloved Afrikaners. Although his brothers had emigrated to the Transvaal in the 1880s, he himself never went to South Africa until just before his seventieth birthday in 1923. Several literary scholars have argued that this means that his work provides a simplistic view that is detached from reality and is full of gross stereotypes of heroic Boers, wicked British and inferior black Africans.[101] Despite these biases, or maybe thanks to them, the work of Penning remained hugely popular, which is illustrated by a highly successful lecture tour he made after his trip to South Africa, which continued until his death in 1927. Penning himself explained the enthusiasm of the sold-out audiences as follows: 'Their [the Afrikaners'] history is one of continuous struggle for freedom and justice, a mighty fight of blood and tears. That struggle has found resonance in the hearts of our people [in the Netherlands].'[102]

The ongoing popularity of Penning's work shows that there remained a strong undercurrent of sympathy for the Boers in the Netherlands after 1902, which was based on a biased view on South Africa and its recent history.[103] The perpetuation of this heroic image created possibilities for closer ties between the Netherlands and South Africa. It can therefore be argued that the language law of 1925 was the low point in the relationship, but got better again afterwards. People in the Netherlands accepted that Afrikaans had become an official language in South Africa, which helped to ease many tensions. Moreover, Afrikaner leaders signalled that the literature in their new language had not yet enough critical mass to stand on its own.[104] During the 1930s the ties grew more intense and there were serious plans for an official cultural treaty.[105] It was the outbreak of the Second World War which prevented that from happening.

Post World War Two:
the traumas of decolonisation and apartheid

In many ways the Second World War was a great disruption in Dutch history. Even today the experiences of the Nazi occupation of the motherland and the Japanese conquest of the Indonesian archipelago stand out as the most important traumas in public memory of the Netherlands. Although critical reflection on such topics was taboo for decades, they implicitly led to a reappraisal of notions of 'self' and 'otherness' that have had an impact on ideas about national identity in the Netherlands and its place in the wider world. This, combined with specific events in Indonesia and South Africa, undermined the ideas about these countries that had developed in the late nineteenth and early twentieth centuries.[106]

When the Indonesian leader Sukarno declared independence, two days after Japan had surrendered in August 1945, it initially caused an outcry in the Netherlands, in which the phrase 'Indië verloren, rampspoed geboren', clearly resonated. In the months after their own liberation from the Nazis most Dutch people hoped that things would return to 'normal', meaning the situation before the war. The nostalgic image of the Indies under colonial rule fitted this attitude well and the riches of Indonesia were considered necessary for the reconstruction of the mother-country after the war. Also many people still thought that Indonesians could not cope without the guidance of the colonial administration. In such responses the nationalists were seen as henchmen of the Japanese who had poisoned them with subversive ideas about independence. Such notions have undoubtedly influenced the government when it decided to send troops to restore order.

It would soon become clear that these visions did not chime with reality at all. The conflict rapidly became a bloody guerrilla war for which the weakened Dutch army was badly prepared. Moreover international pressure mounted on the government to hand over Indonesia's sovereignty. After this had happened on 27 December 1949, there was an initial silence for almost two decades. In 1969, the past war in Indonesia re-emerged in the public debate when an army veteran appeared on television describing the 'excesses' committed by the Dutch army, which was followed by a parliamentary enquiry. This clearly signalled a shift in public opinion about the history of the Dutch Indies. Whereas before the war people talked of 'development' and 'harmony' between coloniser and colonised, terms such as 'exploitation' and 'oppression' became the norm.

The relations with South Africa also did not change immediately after the Second World War. There was some discomfort about the election victory of the *Nasionale Party* in 1948 as its leaders had not protested against the Nazi occupation of the Netherlands. Also its first steps on the road of apartheid were not uncontroversial. Nevertheless, the ties between the Netherlands and South Africa were strengthened in the 1950s when the plans for a cultural treaty that had emerged before the war were realised. It was significant that one of the main initiators of this plan, Prime Minister W. Drees, had enthusiastically cheered a deputation of Boer generals as a young boy when they visited the Netherlands in 1902 and remembered it as his first introduction with politics.

The real turnaround came in 1960 with the Sharpeville massacre, when dozens of black demonstrators were shot dead while protesting against the segregation laws. Suddenly, the Dutch changed from the most loyal friends of the Afrikaners into their fiercest critics. Although the anti-apartheid movement was an international phenomenon, it was particularly active in the Netherlands. As had been the case around 1900, public opinion put much pressure on the government, which even abandoned its policy of non-involvement. After the Soweto uprising in 1976 it withdrew the cultural treaty and in the 1980s implemented boycotts on certain South African goods. But even amongst the most radical activists there seems to have been a lingering sense that there was a special relationship between the Netherlands and South Africa. Looking back in 1992, one of the leaders of the anti-apartheid movement explained his zeal as follows: 'If someone from your family commits a murder you obviously care more about that than when a complete stranger does it.'[107]

Such quotes suggest there was a greater measure of continuity between the ideas about the Netherlands and the wider world before and after the decolonisation of Indonesia and the emergence of apartheid in South Africa than seems the case at first sight. The complete reversal of the post-colonial narrative tends to obscure the significance of the imperial mindset of the Dutch public between roughly 1870 and 1960. It has been argued in this chapter that imperial ideology played an important role in the development of national identity in the Netherlands during that period. The far horizons of the Dutch Indies and South Africa served as a source of inspiration and pride for Dutch nationalism, which revelled in the heroism of colonial warfare – whether it was on the winning or losing side. The development of the colonial state in these regions also brought home ideas about modernity in global context and as such served as a mirror for the nation. Such ideas were not straightforward, however, and also touched upon many uncertainties, especially about the position of the Netherlands as a small nation with a big colonial empire. A difficult question is in what ways such ideas actually reached a wider audience and influenced public opinion. In historiography not much has been written on the nature of Dutch cultural institutions overseas and international avenues of information. Compared with nations whose language was spoken more widely, the development of such infrastructure seems to have been rather limited. Still there is historical evidence that a substantial amount of material from overseas territories reached the Netherlands and that these sources were spread throughout a great variety of genres.

Obviously, groups that had direct links with the Dutch Indies, such as the military, anthropologists and missionaries, openly showed their interest in the colonial possessions in the region. Images of the East also disseminated through the arts, exhibitions, museums and the press. Maybe the clearest indicator that colonialism actually contributed to nation-building in the Netherlands was the fact that the nation's youth was fed with a heroic vision of the 'civilising duty' that their mother country was performing, both inside and outside the classrooms. The bonds between the Netherlands and the Boer republics in South Africa were less formalised, but during the last two decades of the nineteenth century a great amount of information was transferred by a small but highly literate group of emigrants. In this way, it became generally accepted that the Boers, although they were considered backwards in some respects, were better suited than the British to take the lead in the development of South Africa and control the black majority. Such views reached all walks of society, particularly during the South African War, when the public was flooded with propagandistic material.

Many historians have argued that the popularity of such ideas largely ended after the first decade of the twentieth century, when the colonial conquest of the Indonesian archipelago was completed and the Boer republics were annexed by the British Empire. There are, however, indications that imperial culture in the inter-war period was more significant than is often suggested. Many contemporary Dutch publications about the Indies tended to overlook the nationalist movement that increasingly challenged colonial rule there. Instead the public in the Netherlands was presented with the idea that the possessions in the East were essential, both for the indigenous populations that needed Western guidance and for the wealth of the motherland. In the inter-war period a main target of propagandists seem to have been the youth, who were presented with an exotic image of the East at schools and in children's books. Also the heroic version of the Boers remained in vogue. Although there were tensions with radical Afrikaner nationalists, who rejected High Dutch, publications in Afrikaans were available in the Netherlands and appreciated for their poetic qualities. In addition the glorified past of the former republics remained hugely popular, especially amongst young people, who devoured Penning's adventure stories until the 1950s.

Both the wide variety of genres in which imperial culture was represented, and its long lifespan show that it had impact on society in the Netherlands. Such ideas are supported in a body of secondary literature that is growing. Still, it seems that historians have only seen the tip of the iceberg of primary material that is available. Many sources have been left untouched and much research remains to be done in order to get a clearer picture of Dutch identity in global context. At the start of the twenty-first century old certainties seem to crumble rapidly, which is all the more reason to dig into the historical question how people in the Netherlands tried to deal with their complicated status of an imperial underdog.

I would like to thank Marieke Bloembergen and Niek van Sas for their comments on previous versions of this chapter.

Notes

1 B. Paasman, 'Wij gaan naar Achin toe. De Atjeh-oorlog in liedjes verbeeld', in L. Dolk (ed.), *Atjeh. De verbeelding van een koloniale oorlog* (Amsterdam 2001), pp. 46–63, p. 51.

2 M. Kuitenbrouwer, *Nederland en de opkomst van het moderne imperialisme. Koloniën en buitenlandse politiek 1870–1902* (Amsterdam 1985), p. 187.

3 Ibid., pp. 57–9, 94–7, 150–2.

4 M. Bossenbroek, *Holland op zijn breedst. Indië en Zuid-Afrika in de Nederlandse cultuur omstreeks 1900* (Amsterdam 1996), pp. 344–52.

5 Bob de Graaff, *'Kalm temidden van de woeste golven'. Het ministerie van koloniën en zijn taakomgeving, 1912–1940* (Den Haag 1997), pp. 241.

6 Bart de Graaff, *De mythe van de stamverwantschap. Nederland en de Afrikaners, 1902–1930* (Amsterdam, 1993), pp. 10.

7 For the Dutch Indies: L. Blussé and E. Locher-Scholten, 'Inleiding', *Tijdschrift voor Geschiedenis*, 105 (1992), pp. 341–45; for South Africa: W. Jonckheere, *Van Mafeking tot Robbeneiland. Zuid-Afrika in de Nederlandse literatuur 1896–1996* (Nijmegen 1999), p. 15.

8 H. Kippenberg and B. de Pater, *De eenwording van Nederland. Schaalvergroting en integratie sinds 1860* (Nijmegen 1988).

9 N.C.F. van Sas, 'Fin-de-siècle als nieuw begin. Nationalisme in Nederland rond 1900', *Bijdragen en Mededelingen betreffende de Geschiedenis der Nederlanden*, 106 (1991), pp. 595–609.

10 For the most extensive publication about the ties between the colonies and the royal house: G. Oostindië, *De parels en de kroon: Het koningshuis en de koloniën* (Amsterdam 2006).

11 F. Gouda, *Dutch Culture Overseas: Colonial Practice in the Netherlands Indies* (Amsterdam 1995); M. Bloembergen, *Colonial Spectacles: The Netherlands and the Dutch East Indies at the World Exhibitions, 1880–1931* (Singapore 2006).

12 M. Kuitenbrouwer, *Nederland*, pp. 201–02.
13 For the Dutch Indies: Gouda, *Dutch Culture*, p. 119; Bloembergen, *Colonial Spectacles*, p. 14; for South Africa: H. te Velde, *Gemeenschapszin en plichtsbesef: liberalisme en nationalisme in Nederland, 1870–1918* (Den Haag 1992), pp. 79–82.
14 M. Kuitenbrouwer, 'Het imperialisme van een kleine mogendheid: de overzeese expansie van Nederland 1870–1914', in N.C.F. van Sas (ed.), *De kracht van Nederland: internationale positie en buitenlands beleid in historisch perspectief* (Haarlem 1991), pp. 42–72.
15 A. Thompson, *The Empire Strikes Back? The Impact of Imperialism on Britain from the Mid-Nineteenth Century* (Harlow 2005), p. 239.
16 A. Thompson, 'A "Cultural Economy" of the British World, c.1850–1914', keynote delivered at the conference: 'Defining the British World', University of Bristol/University of West England, 11–14 July 2007.
17 Bossenbroek, *Holland*, pp. 199–202. For the development of steamboat lines: J.N.F.K. à Campo, *Koninklijke Pakketvaart Maatschappij. Stoomvaart en staatsvorming in de Indonesische archipel 1884–1914* (Hilversum 1992).
18 'zwijgende consensus'. S. Legêne, *De bagage van Blomhoff en Van Breughel. Japan, Java, Tripoli en Suriname in de negentiende-eeuwse cultuur van het imperialisme* (Amsterdam 1998), p. 15.
19 Bossenbroek, *Holland*, pp. 19–20.
20 'onzekerheid'. Legêne, *De baggage*, pp. 395–6.
21 H.L. Wesseling, 'Nederland als koloniaal model', in H.L. Wesseling (ed.), *Indië verloren rampspoed geboren* (Amsterdam 1988), pp. 140–76; C. Fasseur, 'Gemengd onthaal: de weerklank op Money's "Java" in Nederland', *Bijdragen en Mededelingen betreffende de Geschiedenis der Nederlanden*, 105 (1990), pp. 368–77.
22 M. Kuitenbrouwer, *Nederland*, passim.
23 P.G.E.I.J. van der Velde, *Een Indische Liefde. P.J. de Veth (1814–1895) en de inburgering van Nederlands-Indië* (Amsterdam 2000), p. 326.
24 Bloembergen, *Colonial Spectacles*, pp. 28–9. For the popularisation of the Max Havelaar after decolonisation: P. Pattynama, '"Max Havelaar" of de invloed van de populaire media op de herinnering aan Indië', *Indische letteren*, 21 (2006), pp. 169–85.
25 Velde, *Een Indische*, p. 226.
26 Ibid., pp. 229–56; P.G.E.I.J. van der Velde, 'The Royal Dutch Geographical Society and the Dutch East Indies, 1873–1914: from colonial lobby to colonial hobby', in M. Bell, et al. (eds), *Geography and Imperialism, 1820–1940* (Manchester 1995), pp. 80–92.
27 This paragraph is based on: J. van Goor, 'De Lombokexpeditie en het Nederlandse nationalisme', in J. van Goor (ed.), *Imperialisme in de marge* (Utrecht 1985), pp. 19–70; M. Kuitenbrouwer, *Nederland*, pp. 160–4.
28 For an overview of the representation of the Aceh War: Dolk (ed.), *Atjeh*. Critics of Van Heutsz's strategy produced many cartoons in which they depicted the Dutch colonial army as butchers.
29 Bossenbroek, *Holland*, p. 322.
30 Ibid., pp. 43–5.
31 Bloembergen, *Colonial Spectacles*, pp. 41–8.
32 P. van der Veer, *Modern oriëntalisme: essays over westerse beschavingsdrang* (Amsterdam 1995), pp. 167–202.
33 H.W. van den Doel, 'Christiaan Snoeck Hurgronje: De stralende zon van het Leidse heelal', in H. Beliën et al. (eds), *In de vaart der volkeren: Nederlanders rond 1900* (Amsterdam 1998), pp. 215–29.
34 M. Kuitenbrouwer, *Tussen oriëntalisme*, pp. 11–12.
35 Ibid., p. 304; Bloembergen, *Colonial Spectacles*, pp. 38–9.
36 Gouda, *Dutch Culture*, pp. 119–20.
37 M. Kuitenbrouwer, *Tussen oriëntalisme*, pp. 4–5. An English translation of this work is forthcoming.
38 For an overview of the education of colonial administrators: C. Fasseur, *De Indologen. Ambtenaren voor de Oost, 1825–1950* (Amsterdam 1993).

39 T. van den End, 'Transformatie door informatie? De bijdrage van de Nederlandse zending aan de opinievorming over het koloniale bestel', *Tijdschrift voor Geschiedenis*, 105 (1992), pp. 429–55; Bossenbroek, *Holland*, pp. 117-37.

40 R. Nieuwenhuys, *Oost-Indische Spiegel. Wat Nederlandse schrijvers en dichters over Indonesië hebben geschreven vanaf de eerste jaren der compagnie* (Amsterdam 1978), pp. 16–17.

41 'reisarchief'. P. Pattynama, '..de baai...de binnenbaai...'. *Indië herinnerd* (Amsterdam 2005), p. 7.

42 P. Pattynama, 'Secrets and danger: interracial sexuality in Louis Couperus's "The Hidden Force" and Dutch colonial culture around 1900', in J. Clancy-Smith and F. Gouda (eds), *Domesticating the Empire: Race Gender and Family Life in French and Dutch Colonialism* (Charlottesville/London 1998), pp. 84–107.

43 M. Bloembergen, 'Amsterdam: het Van Heutszmonument: het Nederlandse koloniale geheugen', in *Nederland in de twintigste eeuw* (2005), pp. 72–87.

44 Y. Koopmans, 'Koloniale expansie en Nederlandse monumentale sculptuur', *Tijdschrift voor Geschiedenis*, 105 (1992), pp. 383–406; Bossenbroek, *Holland*, pp. 159–63.

45 M. Bois (ed.), *C.A. Lion Cachet, 1864–1945* (Assen 1994).

46 Bossenbroek, *Holland*, pp. 148–52; H. Spanjaard, *Het ideaal van een moderne Indonesische schilderkunst, 1900–1995* (Leiden 1998), pp. 33–64.

47 Bossenbroek, *Holland*, pp. 155–7; Bloembergen, *Colonial Spectacles*, pp. 134, 328 and 334–53.

48 Bloembergen, *Colonial spectacles*, p. 317.

49 Ibid., pp. 321–2.

50 Ibid., pp. 50–105.

51 C. van Dijk, 'Tussen koloniale handel en wetenschap. De volkenkundige musea in Nederland in de negentiende eeuw', *Tijdschrift voor Geschiedenis*, 105 (1992), pp. 346–67. For the Haarlem museum: H. Jans and H. van den Brink, *Tropen in Amsterdam. 70 jaar Koninklijk Instituut voor de Tropen* (Amsterdam 1980), pp. 11–39.

52 Bossenbroek, *Holland*, pp. 289–314.

53 Ibid., pp. 271–8.

54 D. Buur, *Indische jeugdliteratuur. Geannoteerde bibliografie van jeugdboeken over Nederlands-Indië en Indonesië* (Leiden 1992), p. 3; Bossenbroek, *Holland*, pp. 278–81. For girl's books: E.B. Locher-Scholten, 'So close and yet so far: the ambivalence of Dutch colonial rhetoric on Javanese servants in Indonesia, 1900–1942', in Clancy-Smith and Gouda (eds), *Domesticating the Empire*, pp. 141–54, pp. 145–51.

55 G.J. Schutte, *Nederland en de Afrikaners. Adhesie en aversie* (Franeker 1986), pp. 11–22.

56 The following paragraphs are mainly based on: M. Kuitenbrouwer, *Nederland*, pp. 118–29; Schutte, *Nederland*, pp. 22–44; Te Velde, *Gemeenschapszin*, pp. 63–88; Bossenbroek, *Holland*, pp. 243–8.

57 M. Kuitenbrouwer, *Nederland*, p. 130.

58 Te Velde, *Gemeenschapszin*, p. 82; C. Koppen, *De geuzen van de negentiende eeuw. Abraham Kuyper en Zuid-Afrika* (Wormer 1992).

59 M. Kuitenbrouwer, *Nederland*, pp. 129–30; Schutte, *Nederland*, pp. 41–2 and 205.

60 'De Nederlandsch Zuid-Afrikaansche Vereeniging', *De Gids*, 50, 4 (1886), pp. 185–90, p. 185.

61 Schutte, *Nederland*, pp. 101–43.

62 Te Velde, *Gemeenschapszin*, pp. 79–82; also: J.D.F. van Halsema, '"Een ander en beter menschsoort". De Boerenoorlog (1899-1902) in het denken van Albert Verwey', *Voortgang. Jaarboek voor de Neerlandisiek*, 15 (1995), pp. 189–248.

63 S. Huigen, *De Weg naar Monomotapa. Nederlandstalige representaties van geografische, historische en sociale werkelijkheden in Zuid-Afrika* (Amsterdam 1996), p. 113; also: Schutte, *Nederland*, pp. 198–204.

64 This paragraph is based on: M. Kuitenbrouwer, *Nederland*, pp. 173–90.

65 Bossenbroek, *Holland*, pp. 351.

66 U. Kröll, *Die internationale Buren-Agitation 1899–1902* (Münster 1973), p. 324.

67 The following two paragraphs are based on my PhD thesis at the University of Amsterdam: 'A War of Words. Dutch Pro-Boer Propaganda and the South African War (1899–1902)', 2010.

68 Bossenbroek, *Holland*, p. 351.

69 Between 1902 and 1920 this collection (complemented with other donations) was put on display at the Zuid-Afrikaansche Museum in the town of Dordrecht. Afterwards, it was shipped to South Africa and a large part of this collection is still on display at Kruger House Museum in Pretoria.

70 M. Kuitenbrouwer, *Nederland*, p. 143; Te Velde, *Gemeenschapszin*, pp. 171–4; Bossenbroek, *Holland*, p. 252.

71 M. Kuitenbrouwer, *Nederland*, pp. 189–90; Te Velde, *Gemeenschapszin*, p. 16.

72 'gehamerd tot het ras dat Zuid-Afrika ten slotte beschave [sic] en regeeren zal'. *Het Algemeen Handelsblad*, 2 June 1902.

73 Bossenbroek, *Holland*, pp. 348 and 351–2.

74 'onverschilligheid'. Graaff, *'Kalm temidden*, p. 241.

75 Te Velde, *Gemeenschapszin*, pp. 272–3.

76 Bloembergen, *Colonial Spectacles*, p. 23.

77 Graaff, *'Kalm temidden*, pp. 250–2.

78 Bossenbroek, *Holland*, pp. 85–115; M. Kuitenbrouwer and H. Schijf, 'The Dutch colonial business elite at the turn of the century', *Itinerario*, vol. 22, nr. 1 (1998) pp. 61–86.

79 A. Taselaar, *De Nederlandse koloniale lobby. Ondernemers en de Indische politiek 1914–1940* (Leiden 1998), p. 504.

80 Fasseur, *De Indologen*, pp. 412–54; Taselaar, *De Nederlandse*, pp. 319–40.

81 Taselaar, *De Nederlandse*, pp. 165–88; also: H. Jans, *Honderzestig meter Mauritskade* (Amsterdam 1976); Jans and Brink, *Tropen*, pp. 39–81.

82 Gouda, *Dutch Culture*, p. 155; also: Graaff, *'Kalm temidden*, p. 258; Bloembergen, *Colonial Spectacles*, pp. 278–81.

83 Taselaar, *De Nederlandse*, p. xvii; Graaff, *'Kalm temidden*, pp. 243–4.

84 Gouda, *Dutch Culture*, p. 27.

85 Graaff, *'Kalm temidden*, p. 258.

86 Taselaar, *De Nederlandse*, p. 208–9.

87 Ibid., p. 194.

88 Ibid., pp. 344–6; also: Bossenbroek, *Holland*, p. 284.

89 Taselaar, *De Nederlandse*, p. 346.

90 Nieuwenhuys, *Oost-Indische spiegel*, pp. 377–413.

91 J. van Goor, 'Indische reizen in de negentiende en twintigste eeuw. Van verkenning tot journalistiek tourisme', *Tijdschrift voor Geschiedenis*, vol. 105 (1992), pp. 446–65.

92 Buur, *Indische jeugdliteratuur*, p. 3; Bossenbroek, *Holland*, p. 278.

93 H. Vles, *Hallo Bandoeng. Nederlandse radiopioniers* (Zutphen 2008).

94 The most substantial compilation of film from the Indies is: V. Monnickendam, *Moeder Dao: de schildpadgelijkende: een kinomatografische verkenning van Nederlands-Indië 1912 tot ca. 1933* (NPS 1995). More recently, a DVD with a compilation of films from one family was published: F. Steijlen and E. Willems (eds), *Met ons alles goed. Brieven en films uit Nederlands-Indië van de familie Kuyck*, Indische bibliotheek (Zutphen/Leiden 2008).

95 Graaff, *De mythe*, pp. 302–8.

96 'dubbele dekoloniseringsproces van de Afrikaanse taal en cultuur ten opzichte van de Engelse zowel als de Nederlandse culturele dominantie'. I. Glorie, '"...Een reuze taak, die bijna 't onmogelijke vordert...". De Boekzendingen van het Algemeen Nederlands Verbond (1902–1927)', *Tydskrif vir Nederlands & Afrikaans*, 11, 1 (2004), pp. 41–64, p. 42.

97 Graaff, *De mythe*, pp. 221–4; Glorie, '...Een reuze', p. 41.

98 L. van Niekerk, *Kruger se Regterhand: 'n Biografie van dr. W.J. Leyds* (Pretoria 1985), pp. 319–27.

99 Schutte, *Nederland*, pp. 185–6; I. Hofmeyr, 'Building a nation from words: Afrikaans language, literature and ethnic identity, 1902–1924', in S. Marks and S. Trapido (eds),

The Politics of Race, Class and Nationalism in Twentieth-Century South Africa (London/New York 1987), pp. 95–123, p. 111; Huigen, *De weg*, p. 17.

100 F.A. van Jaarsveld, ''N methodologies-kritiese ondersoek naar die werk van Dr. W.J. Leyds', in *Tijdskrif vir Wetenskap en kuns* (1954), pp. 98–107; M. Bossenbroek, 'Geschiedschrijving als hoger beroep. Willem Johannes Leyds, advocaat van de Boeren (1859-1940)', in M. Bossenbroek (ed.), *Historici in de politiek* (Leiden 1996), pp. 191–211.

101 Jonckheere, *Van Mafeking*, pp. 46–54 and 84–96; J. van der Elst, 'Die Anglo-Boereoorlog: 'n vertekende beeld vanuit die vreemde', *Literator*, 20/3 (1999), pp. 147–60.

102 'Hun geschiedenis is een doorloopende strijd voor vrijheid en recht, een machtige kamp van bloed en tranen. Die strijd heeft weerklank gevonden in de harten van ons volk.' L. Penning, *Uit mijn leven* (Zwolle 1927), p. 218.

103 Schutte, *Nederland*, pp. 207–8.

104 S. Hemstra, De culturele betrekkingen tussen Nederland en de Afrikaners in de jaren dertig. Een onderzoek aan de hand van de reis van Pieter Geyl door Zuid-Afrika in 1937. Unpublished MA thesis, University of Leiden, 2007. I thank Barbera Henkes for providing me with this text.

105 G.J. Schutte, 'De organisatie van de Stamverwantschap. Een kanttekening bij 125 jaren Nederlands – Zuid-Afrikaanse betrekkingen', paper at the HASA conference, Pretoria, 26–8 June 2006.

106 The following paragraphs are based on: M. Kuitenbrouwer, *De ontdekking van de derde wereld. Beeldvorming en beleid in Nederland, 1950–1990* (Den Haag 1994), pp. 24–63 and pp. 209–29.

107 'Als iemand in je familie een moord pleegt, trek je je dat meer aan dan wanneer een wildvreemde dat doet.' Quoted in ibid., p. 229.

CHAPTER 4

Learning to love Leopold: Belgian popular imperialism, 1830–1960

Matthew G. Stanard

Leopold II did not long outlive the creation for which he is best known, the *État Indépendant du Congo* (EIC). After years of international and domestic pressure, Leopold ceded his African colony to the European kingdom he ruled, Belgium, on 15 November 1908: Saint Leopold's Day. From that point forward the EIC ceased to exist, having become the Belgian Congo, which it remained until independence in 1960. A year and one month after handing the EIC over to Belgium, Leopold lay dying at the royal palace at Laeken, outside Brussels, after an operation on 14 December.

When he died three days later, few mourned his passing. According to German Ludwig Bauer, who titled his early unsympathetic biography of the king *Leopold the Unloved*, although Leopold's funeral befitted a sovereign, 'No one uttered any words of affection; not a tear was shed; at the gates of the palace and at the doors of the church lampoons and caricatures were sold, heaping abuse upon him'.[1] While Bauer believed he was 'evil' other foreigners saw him as 'a hateful creature' because of the Congo atrocities, brought to light by E.D. Morel and others, that had led to the deaths of millions, often in grisly fashion.[2] At home, he had been unloved by his subjects, as he himself acknowledged. As early as 1886 a royalist magazine described him as 'a funny mummy, but unlikeable'.[3] Newspapers scorned his great constructions in Belgium, calling them 'ruinously expensive extravagances of luxurious works'.[4] Even Jules Wauters, editor of *Mouvement géographique*, the unofficial journal of the EIC, confided to Morel in 1910 that he admired what the Briton had done and called Leopold's Congo 'a nightmare'.[5] Leopold could not even count any royal family member as a friend, not even his successor Albert I. One of the first things Albert did as king was deny Leopold the quiet, private burial he had requested.

A half-century later it seemed as if foreign attitudes toward Belgian colonialism had changed little, as critics vilified imperialism in central Africa and remembered Leopold – if at all – as a rapacious colonial tyrant. What had changed, and remarkably so, were Belgian attitudes. Rather than shy away from the controversial king, officials embraced him as a prescient genius. To one official writing in the 1950s, Leopold's empire had been based not on conquest but on 'peaceful coexistence with the natives', and one could detect Leopold's (and Belgium's) concern for African rights in 'Congo legislation from the very beginning'. This official admitted colonialism had led to abuses but stressed that the same would have occurred under a free enterprise system.[6] Whereas Leopold may have had a difficult relationship with his nephew Albert, his great-grand-nephew Baudouin felt differently, characterising Congo's independence in 1960 as 'the crowning of the work conceived by the genius of King Leopold II undertaken by him with firm courage, and continued by Belgium with perseverance.'[7]

Considering the close ties between the dynasty and the colony it is unsurprising Baudouin would defend Leopold. What was surprising was the level of popular enthusiasm in the 1950s among Belgians generally for the Congo and Leopold. In that decade alone people erected statues to Leopold across the country. Textbooks hailed those who had conquered the Congo despite terrible obstacles like 'hostile tribes ... tropical diseases ... wild beasts', and always reserved the greatest praise for Leopold.[8] Even in the years immediately preceding decolonisation when treatment of Leopold became more 'objective' he 'still was always described with grandiose praise'.[9] Polls conducted in the 1950s reflected a widespread belief in the legitimacy and beneficence of imperial rule, one respondent explaining that the Congo had not been conquered 'by force or violence. We received it from Leopold II to whom it was offered for his humanitarian actions in Africa.'[10] Leopold had gone from worst to first, and imperialism was more popular than ever.

Our understanding of the nature and extent of Belgian 'colonial culture' is limited despite the fact that Belgium ruled one of the largest empires in Africa for most of the 1900s and did so after Leopold ruled the same territory for nearly a quarter century. Both Belgians and historians have argued that Belgians were 'reluctant imperialists'.[11] But considering that the Congo is the size of all of Europe west of the Oder and south of Scandinavia, it seems incredible that rule there could have been established and sustained in the face of popular indifference. A reason not much has been written about Belgian colonial culture is because most attention, scholarly and otherwise, has focused on the Leopoldian period 1885–1908, and only to a lesser extent on the 1908 *reprise* (Belgium's takeover of the colony), the 1959–60 Congo crisis, colonialism's effects on Congolese, and economics. We know much about particular facets of imperialistic culture because of studies of specific media of pro-empire propaganda such as films and expositions, most prominently the 1897 Tervuren exposition.[12]

Even the most recent and stimulating scholarship does little to unveil the extent of popular imperialism beyond the Leopoldian period. Vincent Viaene's 2008 *Journal of Modern History* essay probes colonial culture, yet remains focused on the pre-1905 period.[13] Guy Vanthemsche's recent synthesis about the colony's effects on Belgium deliberately limits itself to politics, international relations and economics. By focusing not only on the Leopoldian era but also the state-rule period and the post-1960 years, Vanthemsche concludes that the colony allowed Belgium to play a bigger role internationally than it would have otherwise, did not have major economic effects, and played only the smallest of roles in domestic politics. His conclusion that empire was primarily about profits is somewhat unexpected considering the Congo's slight economic importance that he himself demonstrates, and the fact that even highly placed officials concluded that free trade – not protected colonial markets – was best. Vanthemsche allows room for the possibility that non-economic reasons drove imperialism, asserting that an *'esprit colonial'* lived on in Belgium after Leopold and that the Congo may have even become, 'the object of a certain interest, perhaps even of a vague pride'.[14]

Like Vanthemsche's work, this chapter avoids an over-emphasis on the Leopoldian period to examine the nature of popular imperialism in Belgium from the EIC epoch to 1960. This broader focus is needed to escape a growing 'exoticisation' of Belgian imperialism in popular culture and in the historiography of modern European empire-building where despite the fact that Leopold ruled the Congo for less than half the time Belgium did, his rule has come to substitute for the whole. A 2009 American Historical Association (AHA) panel typified this synecdoche when Adam Hochschild and others stated that Belgians had had difficulty facing up to their colonial past while meaning they were unable to face up to Leopold's rule. The well-known viciousness of his reign coupled with historians' disregard for the post-1908 period and forgetfulness of violence elsewhere have made Belgian imperialism out as uniquely brutal. Britons have glossed over the hundreds of thousands killed in India at partition in 1947 and brutality in Kenya in the 1950s. It is only recently that France has begun to come to terms with the 1947 crackdown in Madagascar and the innumerable people killed in Vietnam and Algeria, Germany with the genocide in south-west Africa, Portugal its long colonial wars, and the Netherlands with atrocities during their rule in the East Indies.

Empire without enthusiasm

Although he never set foot in the Congo, Leopold II did travel abroad, especially as Duc de Brabant before becoming king. He returned from one trip to Athens in 1860 with a souvenir for future prime minister Walthère Frère-Orban: a block of marble from the Acropolis inscribed with the words, *'Il faut à la Belgique une Colonie'* – 'Belgium needs a colony'. As to which colony and where, any would do. Leopold believed the country needed to acquire some possession from which it could profit, just as the Netherlands benefitted from their East Indies. Leopold was effectively alone in his imperialistic desires because most Belgians were concerned with affairs closer to home, and as late nineteenth-century European expansion into south-east Asia and Africa proceeded apace it seemed unlikely Belgium would take any part. Many in the country might well have still been getting used to being Belgian, since their kingdom had only come into existence in 1830. Divided by language, with Dutch-speaking Flemings in the north and francophone Walloons in the south, the country was united by Catholicism and industrialisation, the latter making it the most industrialised state on the continent only a few years after independence.

It was doubtful industrial power would transform into overseas expansion. Unlike its neighbours, Belgium lacked any substantive colonial tradition or overseas territories upon which to build; if anything it traditionally had been a victim of foreign rule, be it Burgundian, Spanish, Austrian or French. Despite no colonial tradition, in 1908 Belgium suddenly possessed a staggeringly large overseas empire in central Africa. As the late Jean Stengers demonstrated, this was in essence the work of Leopold II.[15] Once king after 1865, Leopold expended huge sums and efforts to make his colonial dreams come true. After repeated failures, including a bid to lease the Philippines, he concentrated on central Africa, hosted a geographical conference on the region, formed purportedly neutral and humanitarian organisations such as the *Association Internationale Africaine*, financed explorations like those of Henry Morton Stanley, surreptitiously staked claims in the Congo River basin, and finally took behind-the-scenes control of those supposedly neutral organisations to make a bid for control over central Africa. Great power rivalries, ingenious if tricky diplomacy, and Leopold's tenacity resulted in recognition of his rule over much of the Congo around the time of the Berlin conference. In July 1885, the EIC was declared, a vast territory eighty times the size of Belgium.

Belgium's monarch achieved all this in the face of indifference among his subjects, and as his schemes unfolded, such as the 1876 Brussels geographical conference, his ambitions kindled virtually zero popular enthusiasm. Bourgeois industrialists, merchants, and financiers remained much more interested in intra-European trade. The military produced few 'excess' soldiers frustrated in their search of advancement, unlike in Italy and Scandinavia. Many were more concerned with the *guerre scolaire* over education in the 1880s and the 'social question' regarding the place of workers in society, an issue intensified by the formation of the *Parti Ouvrier Belge* in 1885. Catholic missionaries were active overseas but took little interest in the Congo. Although the country was likely the most densely populated in the world, few emigrated. The first national geographical society was not founded until the 1876 geographical conference and no Belgian at the time had written a work in the 'tropical' or 'colonial' sciences.[16] The lack of any imperial spirit becomes clearer when the situation is contrasted with what was going on in France, Germany or Britain where in the last quarter of the nineteenth century geographical societies were promoting explorations and organisations like the Primrose League, the *Gesellschaft für deutsche Kolonisation* and the *Union Coloniale Française* were pressuring governments to pursue imperialistic policies. No such small, focused groups or mass organisations accompanied Leopold's drive for empire.

Compounding the lack of an imperial tradition was the nature of the EIC, which did not involve Belgians to the same extent that other empires involved their metropolitan populations. Leopold's colony was legally distinct from his other kingdom, the two linked only by him. Many if not most Europeans who explored, proselytised, conquered and ruled in the Congo were foreigners. A prominent early example is Stanley, a Welsh-American. The colony's administration and its military, the *Force publique*, recruited among non-Belgians, who made up a substantial percentage of officers and administration functionaries. The EIC's first top civil servant, *Administrateur-Général* Francis de Winton, was British. Non-Belgians carried out eighteen of the twenty major scientific expeditions during the Leopoldian period.[17] Most missionaries there in 1885 were British, American or Scandanavian Protestants, and it was only on the urging of Leopold that Belgian orders like the Scheutists became involved. The fact that the author of the first Belgian 'colonial' novel *Udinji* (1905), Charles Cudell, had never been to the Congo was symptomatic: he based his book on letters his brother sent him from central Africa.[18] Likewise in the case of Jules Wauters, editor of *Mouvement géographique* and by the turn of the century one of the foremost Belgian experts on the Congo: he never travelled there.[19] In 1886 only 46 of 254 whites in the Congo were Belgian, rising to only 1,713 among 2,943 by 1908.[20] Because virtually all *colons* were male – the female, white population in central Africa before 1908 was minuscule – entirely half of the population was initially excluded from direct participation in the colonial endeavour. It seemed the vast majority of Belgians would follow Leopold's example and never set foot in the Congo, meaning that if they were to have exposure to the colony it would have to take place in the metropole.

Three things introduced Belgians to the EIC: attempts by imperial enthusiasts to interest them in the Congo; vocal foreign assaults on the EIC administration; and Leopold's propaganda in response to attacks. What did not introduce them to the Congo was Congolese. While few Belgians travelled to central Africa in the late 1800s, even fewer Congolese voyaged to Europe. A number were brought to Europe in the 1890s for education, but the practice quickly stopped.[21] Leopold segregated his European and African subjects to preserve the colony from outside influences and Belgians from supposedly dangerous Congolese, an approach that the post-1908 administration sustained. This contrasts with the situation obtaining in France and Britain, where already by the 1880s individuals such as Blaise Diagne or Mohandas Gandhi could study in the metropole. What this meant was that perhaps more than elsewhere, images of the colony that circulated in Belgium during the colonial period were European creations.

Even if Belgians learnt much about the Congo because of attacks on its administration, discussed below, more significant at first were efforts by Leopold and others to educe an imperialistic spirit to prepare the country to assume control of the colony. Also promoting the Congo was a small but influential group of pro-empire enthusiasts – the 'colonial lobby' – who either collaborated with Leopold or who, like businessman Albert Thys, broke with him and pushed the state to take over the Congo immediately. One scholar has estimated that major pro-Congo periodicals had a total circulation of perhaps as high as 40,000 by the mid-1890s.[22] As the king and the colonial lobby's efforts to promote the Congo increased between 1885 and the First World War, so did 'the resonance of imperialism in Belgian public life', to the point that 'the Congo had clearly struck a chord by the early twentieth century with the upper class and some segments of the middle class in the cities'.[23] Catholics and Liberals were more quickly won over; Socialists, with exceptions, were not.

Among the most spectacular popularisers were ethnographic displays at universal expositions. Antwerp hosted the country's first two World's Fairs in 1885 and 1894, each of which included a major ethnographic exhibit. The 1885 event drew more than 3.5 million visitors and included a Congo pavilion by the *Société Royale Belge de Géographie*. The display comprised Congolese objects as well as a dozen people, including Chief Massola of Vivi, whom Leopold invited to his court at Laeken. The 1894 fair brought a staggering 144 Congolese to Antwerp and attracted around five million visitors, a huge number in a country of six million. Visitors threw coins in swimming ponds to watch the Congolese dive for them, and scientists measured and photographed the African 'specimens'.[24] Brussels hosted a third universal exposition in 1897, this time with the main fairgrounds supplemented by an expansive colonial section in nearby Tervuren where a *Palais des Colonies* showed off colonial goods, Congolese flora and fauna and European-created chryselephantine artwork that 'functioned as both a promotional tool advertising the material riches to be gained from the imperial project, and as a naturalising mechanism employed in order to help efface the controversial nature of King Leopold II's Congo enterprise'.[25] Most striking in 1897 were the *villages nègres* outside that housed more than 260 Congolese behind fences. Because visitors threw food at the people on display organisers put up signs that read, 'Do not feed the blacks – they are already being fed'.[26] Between 1,200,000 and 1,800,000 visitors made their way to Tervuren just to see the colonial exposition, indicating Belgians were beginning to be literally attracted to empire.[27]

Although the Tervuren exposition closed its doors at the end of the year, it left behind the *Palais des Colonies*, which re-opened in 1898 as the *Musée du Congo*. That such a museum came into existence is unsurprising considering all European imperial powers built museums or institutes to educate their populations about overseas empire. The museum's earliest origins are to be found in the country's first significant collection of Congolese objects dating back to the 1894 *wereldtentoonstelling*.[28] Leopold II wanted to promote empire further by also providing a permanent 'window' onto Africa.[29] It took the event of 1897 to make his vision a reality. The Congo museum's development shows how multiple pro-imperialistic media overlapped because its start and later growth resulted in part from ethnographic exhibits at world's fairs in a kind of symbiotic relationship over many years.

The 1897 Tervuren exhibit spurred the creation not only of a museum but also the first colonial cinema by *Optique Belge*, an organisation underwritten by Albert Thys and others connected to the nascent colonial lobby.[30] They recognised the ability of motion pictures to move people, just as others in Europe did, and it was these imperialist enthusiasts who drove this first foray into colonial film propaganda, not Leopold. *Optique Belge* created a pavilion in 1897 called the *Zoographe* to show films to visitors, but because of technical and other difficulties it showed only short films made at the fair itself, such as *Les Congolais à Tervueren* and *L'arrivée d'un train à Tervueren*.[31] These early efforts could not have had much effect because a *Zoographe* ticket cost one franc whereas a worker's daily wage in 1897 did not exceed three francs, making it likely that only the well-to-do could afford to go.[32] In the end

Optique Belge was financially unsuccessful and disbanded immediately after the exposition.[33]

This same period also witnessed the building of commemorative memorials, but in terms of education, literature or drama there was little to no evidence of popular imperialism. The dozen or so colonial monuments built in the 1880s and 1890s manifested characteristics that were to become standard in most such memorials in the decades that followed: they celebrated the military and men.[34] In terms of education, although Leopold II had drawn up plans for an expansive *École mondiale* in Tervuren, of which the Congo museum was to be only part, the government abandoned his plans after his death.[35] Considering the EIC's international nature, Leopold's success at founding it without popular support, and the incipient nature of public schooling in the late 1800s, it would have been surprising had there been mass education about the Congo. This lack of education was paralleled by a lack of literature and theatre about the colony, be it works directed at a literate elite or comic books aimed at a younger readership. Works such as Louis Delmer's 1890s anti-slavery play *L'Esclave* were rare.[36]

A great deal of literature emerged about the Congo outside the country, however, condemning Leopold and his brutal regime of exploitation that had led to atrocities against Congolese peoples and millions of deaths, directly or indirectly. The EIC, funded by the king, drained his personal fortune, leading him to extract maximum resources at minimum cost. This included confiscation of land, concessions to monopoly companies, forced labour and vicious punishments for those who did not or could not comply. By 1895 the first shipments of ivory and rubber reached Europe and by 1900 Leopold was earning a fortune as Congo exports skyrocketed.[37] Antwerp became home to the world's largest ivory market, selling 336,000 kilograms in 1900 compared with the 320,000 sold in London.[38] To many observers the death and destruction in the Congo resulted not in the spread of civilisation but the enrichment of Leopold.

Belgium wins a colony, loses a war

As Leopold's fortune grew, so did foreign criticism. After discovering atrocities in the EIC, Briton E.D. Morel spurred his government into action, persuading Parliament by 1903 to take up the issue. In 1904, Irishman Roger Casement travelled to the Congo and produced a report confirming the worst rumours circulating about the EIC. That same year Morel formed the Congo Reform Association, and then wrote the devastating indictment *Red Rubber* (1906), increasing the momentum for foreign intervention. Although opposition grew in Belgium, foreign calls for reforms elicited hostility there more than anything else. 'The British became unpopular; the Belgian Press attributed the campaign to the spite of "Liverpool traders" who were jealous of the financial prosperity of the Congo State, and to the "English missionaries"' envious of Catholic success.[39] When Leopold fought back by forming his own Commission of Enquiry it misfired, its 1905 report damning his rule. The critical 1906 study *Étude sur la Situation de l'État Indépendant du Congo* by Belgian lawyer Félicien Cattier signalled that Leopold now faced both international and domestic opposition.

Although 1908 represents a key turning point because of Belgium's *reprise* of the Congo that year, 1905 is a more telling moment in the history of attitudes toward empire. As Leopold's Congo rule entered its third decade, open propaganda diminished and efforts began to disassociate him from it. The 1905 Liege World's Fair and the inauguration of the *Arcade du Cinquantenaire* represented this state of affairs. The *Exposition Universelle et Internationale de Liège* celebrated the seventy-fifth anniversary of the country's independence and the fortieth year of Leopold's Belgian reign. Yet the fair's EIC exhibit was decidedly unassuming in contrast to the huge displays at earlier such events, indicating that the colonial administration did not want to call attention to the Congo any more than necessary. The *Arcade du Cinquantenaire*'s unveiling shows something similar. The *Arcade* in Brussels' Cinquantenaire Park had been suggested as early as the 1880s: a triumphal arch joining two massive buildings to form one horseshoe-shaped complex. Although the buildings were built, the arch joining them was not because of lack of funds, and for decades a temporary wooden facade sufficed.[40] Only when Leopold came up with the funds himself was a permanent arch finally built in 1904–05, designed by Frenchman Charles Girault. Rather than celebrate his largesse and revel in another addition to his many architectural bequests to the capital, the king used front men to hide his involvement and thereby his Congo profits.

This attitude toward the colony continued much the same after 1905 through the *reprise* and up to 1914: muted promotion of the colony and a distancing of it from Leopold. This can be seen at the 1910 Brussels World's Fair, which is notable because it led to the inauguration of a new Congo museum in Tervuren that acted as the exposition's colonial section. The same Charles Girault who worked on the Cinquantenaire arch designed it, modelling the building after the Petit Palais he conceived for the 1900 Paris *Exposition Universelle*. But the museum was far from a *'petit' palais*: 175 metres long and 75 metres wide, it covered close to 9,400 square metres and cost 8,700,000 gold francs, of which Leopold paid 8,300,000 before he died.[41] That the new *palais* emerged out of another World's Fair shows again how the permanent colonial museum

4.1   Musée royal de l'Afrique centrale/Koninklijk Museum voor Midden Afrika
(Royal Museum for Central Africa), Tervuren.
(Photo by Matthew G. Stanard)

intersected with more ephemeral expositions. The enormous structure had plenty of space for its display cases, sculptures, and exhibit pieces. One student of Leopold's architectural legacy called it 'one of the most unquestionable successes of the oeuvre of the *Roi-Bâtisseur*'.[42]

King Albert and Minister of Colonies Jules Renkin's speeches at the museum's inauguration conveyed its two-fold mission of scientific research and colonial propaganda, yet also distanced their new regime from the Leopoldian era.[43] Both men were new to their jobs. Leopold II had died without a male heir, making his nephew, Albert, his successor. Unlike his uncle, Albert actually went to the Congo, and during a 1909 trip there struck up a correspondence with Renkin.[44] Thirteen years older than Albert and a lawyer by training, Renkin was a Catholic Party politician who favoured Belgium's takeover of the Congo. In late 1908 he became the first Minister of Colonies, a post he held for a decade. Rather than laud the founder of empire in 1910 both men implied the need to move on, expressing the necessity of a positive propaganda to inform citizens about their empire and civilising mission. As one museum staff member later put it: 'Belgium, which had just taken in hand the destinies of a vast territory offering enormous possibilities, needed to devote itself to bringing its nationals up to speed about African things.'[45] The emphasis on a new era was probably linked to ongoing fears of foreign intervention because despite the 1908 *reprise*, foreign criticisms still were to be heard, and in fact Britain did not recognise the Belgian Congo until 1913.[46] To admit past mistakes and emphasise a new era the Minister of Colonies asserted that both the exposition and the new museum were to eliminate prejudices, foster goodwill and excite people so that they would take part in the great work of civilisation in which the country was engaged in the Congo, 'where Belgium, despite all hardships, will know how to show the profound imprint of her genius'. The king underlined differences between colonial methods of the past and present, the former marked by 'importing arms, liquor and exploiting a country to excess', the latter by Christianity and the sharing of scientific and technological discoveries to the benefit of the colonised.[47] Thus the new king and Renkin took a public opportunity to break with the Leopoldian past.

This distancing from the Leopoldian era continued at the 1913 Ghent World's Fair that emphasised the Belgianness of colonialism in the Congo. As one exposition brochure put it, 'For the first time ... Belgium will reveal itself, to foreign eyes, as a **colonial power**. A **Congo Palace** there [in Ghent] will show the glorious effort realised by the Belgian people in its large African domain.'[48] Fair organisers set the new era off from the old by building an almost outsized *Palais des Colonies* as testimony to 'the rapid progress accomplished in our beautiful colony', thanks to the new Belgian administration.[49] A panorama by Paul Mathieu and Alfred Bastien 'gave a visual lesson in "colonial progress" by means of simplistic contrasts that were supposed to be clear to everyone at first glance: untouched jungles next to Matadi and Leopoldville; vine bridges versus iron overpasses; and huts of natives next to factories of the white people'.[50] The message was that Belgium in just a few years had brought progress to the Congo in myriad ways.

The years after 1905 also saw the first substantive colonial film production and dissemination, much more successful than the short-lived 1897 attempt. Although early films targeted an elite, the rapid growth in the number of theatres in Belgium before 1914 brought the total to around 650, a high density.[51] Exactly how colonial films were distributed, how many people saw them, which ones and how people reacted to them is difficult to gauge. Unfortunately most such early films, like many filmed south of the Sahara, are today lost, making any analysis of them tentative at best.[52] What is clear is that by 1914 films about the Congo and sub-Saharan Africa stopped being rarities and movie theatres were more widespread in Belgium than almost anywhere else. Moreover one group went so far as to set up a film house in 1908 with the sole purpose of showing colonial-themed films. The backers of this effort, called the *Cinéma Colonial*, targeted the 'man in the street' to develop interest in the colony by showing images of progress about 'everything that has to do with our Congo'.[53]

How films, memorials and ethnographic displays reverberated in popular culture varied from medium to medium. For cinema, it is hard to measure the level of demand for colonial films and to say whether pro-imperialists achieved their goals. Although the 1897 *Zoographe* failed, the *Cinéma Colonial* attracted 50,000 paying customers in its first year alone. Local groups hosted smaller screenings, often accompanied by commentary from colonials, a practice that only increased during the inter-war years and beyond. Titles can at least suggest what viewers might have seen, even if early films are no longer available. From 1909–10, film-makers Evenepoel and Reinelt created among others the films *Matadi* and *Le marché de Boma*, suggesting an emphasis on urbanisation and commerce, and *Le fort de Shinkakasa* and *Le défilé de la Force publique*, probably emphasising military control. Other films by the same directors include *Chemin de fer des cataractes*, *L'arrivée du ministre des Colonies à Banana*, *Boma et Matadi* and *Le prince Albert au centre de l'Afrique*, focusing on railways, the new colonial administration and the dynasty, respectively.[54] Other films developed the theme of industry.[55] Rather than showcase Congolese, films focused overwhelmingly on European actions.

The erecting of colonial memorials would seem to signal little enthu-siasm for empire considering that only around two dozen were put up between 1885 and 1914. But if one considers how some were funded and built, it appears some Belgians were warming to empire. An example is the monument built in Antwerp in 1913 to Baron Francis Dhanis, who had played a key role in the conquest of the Congo during the 1890s. When he died in November 1909, Antwerp's *Club Africain-Cercle d'Études coloniales* – of which Dhanis was a founder – began planning a monument to him to be unveiled in 1913 on the twentieth anniversary of an event that helped made him famous, his campaign against so-called Arab slave traders in eastern Congo.[56] The large monument by Frans Joris, surrounded by tropical plants, was located in a prominent position on the Zuiderlei. The *Club Africain* decided to raise the large sums needed to build it by means of a public subscription, and the response was so enthusiastic that the goal was achieved within only a few months.[57]

Reactions to the Congo museum in Tervuren are more difficult to determine, especially since there is no such thing as a typical museum visit, or visitor. It is nonetheless possible to get some sense of the feeling the museum imparted by means of one firsthand account of a 1910 visit. L. Vincart, most probably then or later an official in the government, described the new building to readers of *Onze Kongo*. He wrote that in the museum

the Belgian visitor ... feels his emotions of national pride rising involun-
tarily ... to be part of the people that counts among its sons the heroic
victors over the Arabic slave drivers, and also the numerous fearless heroes
of the work of Evangelisation ... everywhere he is also reminded of the
activity and the daring in the field of trade and industry equally, how the
Belgians in the space of so few years – in only a fourth of a century! – can
have transformed an unknown and unapproachable continent in all
respects.[58]

Here is a panorama of messages: national pride, the spread of
Christianity, the fight against slave traders, and industry and trade.

Just a short time after Vincart described his visit, the halls of the enormous Tervuren museum echoed with only occasional footsteps. By the
end of the decade, the number of annual visitors had dropped precipitously to barely more than 9,000.[59] Museum attendance was, of course,
affected by a global conflict at the centre of which was Belgium itself.
Beginning in August 1914, war physically and mentally cut most Belgians
off from the colony for years. The German army occupied the entire
country, save a tiny sector in its far western corner, and citizens were
preoccupied by more immediate concerns, such as onerous German
requisitions, displacement, or forced labour for the German war effort.[60]
The years of occupation can only have caused a colonial culture caesura
considering that the very existence of the kingdom was at stake. In some
cases signs of popular support literally vanished: there were fewer colonial
monuments at war's end because Germans melted down a number of
them.

The inter-war years

Despite the sudden increase in signs of imperialistic sentiment after 1918
that only accentuated the paucity from 1914–18, for most the Congo
remained peripheral: domestic and European affairs dominated social life
and politics. Nevertheless, an upsurge in imperialistic expressions burst
forth through a variety of media, involving not only an elite but also the
masses, and which only grew and diversified as the inter-war years
unfolded. This included exhibits of empire, from smaller ones to large-
scale universal expositions. The 1930 Antwerp World's Fair and the 1935
universal exposition in Brussels included major Congo pavilions show-
casing the colony that were complemented by almost innumerable
smaller-scale exhibits across the country and abroad. The state was most
active, in particular through the colonial administration's propaganda
office, the *Office Colonial*, followed closely by local pro-empire groups,
colonial veterans and individuals. Less active were missionary groups and
private colonial enterprises, big or small. A major theme was economics

– and this before the financial crisis of 1929 – such as when a 1928 Antwerp colonial fair emphasised the need for Belgium to expand trade with the colony.[61] When administrators spoke in the 1930s of greater *interpénétration* of the metropolitan and colonial economies, they paralleled France's *Conseil économique* of the *Conseil supérieur des colonies* (created 1920), Britain's Empire Marketing Board (created 1926), Italian talk of autarky, and German irredentist claims, all the while building on an idea developed in the 1920s.[62]

Forming a backdrop to temporary expositions was Tervuren's Congo museum, joined by a number of regional or local permanent exhibits of empire. The number of visitors to the Tervuren museum climbed rapidly after the war, reaching 220,000 by 1923, before tapering off.[63] At least six schools founded their own colonial museums that displayed photographs, charts and products from the colony. Local colonial interests groups such as the *Cercle Colonial et Maritime* of Bruges and the *Cercle Africain Charleroi-Thuin* set up their own permanent colonial 'museums' in the provinces, even if the only significant one outside Tervuren was in Namur where a colonial museum in one form or another has existed from 1912 down to the present. Both attendance at Tervuren and a number of smaller museums founded during the inter-war years indicates a certain enthusiasm for the colony.

Education about the colony only really took off after the First World War. Supporters of empire both within and outside the colonial administration decried the ignorance among students and the population at large regarding the Congo.[64] The most targeted effort to redress the situation was the *Université Coloniale* in Antwerp, which was up and running by the end of the war. Colonial pioneer Charles Lemaire initially ran the school, a man better known for his willingness to maim Africans to harvest rubber than for his teaching. But the university represented elite education, graduating only a few hundred students, and it was in primary and secondary school that most learned about the Congo. Textbooks legitimised and popularised the empire by rooting Belgian rule after 1908 within a supposedly national history of imperialism based on the EIC period. Texts hailed Belgians who had worked for Leopold and passed over the many foreigners who had. They also obscured the post-1908 state rule period, even those works published late in the colonial period that had many decades of Belgian colonial history to address. This also de-emphasised African culture and history while conveniently avoiding discussion of recent or current problems such as revolts, Kimbanguism and labour strikes.[65]

Literature, comic books, and radio began to address colonial themes after the war. Beginning in August 1934, radio pioneer and White Father Léon Leloir began to broadcast monthly radio talks [*radio-causeries*] about the colony.[66] Colonial comics of a sort had appeared in Belgium as early as 1910 with the broadsheet *Histoire de Belgique* that praised the work of Leopold II in the Congo, but it was not until the inter-war years that any significant production took place. Not only was Hergé's *Tintin au Congo* the best-selling *bande dessinée* about the colony at the time, but it was the best-selling of the first nine popular black and white Tintin books, reprinted seven times between 1934 and 1944. Its first iteration was obviously colonialist: Hergé depicted Africans as lazy, unable to speak good French, and at one point Tintin enters a white missionary's classroom to teach the Congolese about 'their' country, Belgium. With reprintings, Hergé toned down its overt imperialist attitude. Not all Belgian comic artists portrayed such negative stereotypes, however. The protagonists in *Blondoin et Cirage* (1939) by Jijé (Joseph Gillain) were white and black boys who appeared as equals.[67]

There was a jump in the number of colonial films available in Belgium after 1918 as 'the country was literally submerged by a wave of propaganda. It targeted above all education; it addressed itself very consciously to youth.'[68] Titles such as *Le minerai de cuivre du Katanga, Les tracés du chemin de fer établis pendant la guerre, L'installation d'un colon dans le Kasaï, Le grand centre de Lusambo et son industrie*, all filmed by Ernest Gourdinne between 1917 and 1919, indicated the emphasis on Belgian-led progress, industrial or otherwise. Already by 1919, Gourdinne had projected his films hundreds of times in the metropole.[69] A second wave of post-war colonial film-making followed in 1925–28 with a number of Ernest Genval films financed by, and focusing on, private industry. While understanding its significance, it is equally important to contextualise such production because movies about the Congo comprised only a small fraction of the Belgian film business, which was never a large industry because of the country's small and divided domestic market and foreign competition.[70] Financially successful colonial films, such as Genval's *Le Congo qui s'éveille* (1927), were rare.[71]

The post-war years also witnessed a drastic increase in the building of memorials for colonial heroes. It is possible to over-emphasise the significance of such monuments, especially smaller ones in out-of-the-way places. Yet even if Belgium like other European countries is littered with memorials of all kinds, colonial monuments did play a significant role in everyday life in many locales. An example is a plaque commemorating native sons that a local colonial veterans group erected in 1931 at their own expense near the train station in Verviers. Although small, the plaque attracted throngs on special occasions and served as a meeting spot and backdrop for speeches to celebrate Belgium's *mission civilisatrice*.[72] Inter-war imperialistic memorials indicate that colonial veterans and other enthusiasts were major promoters of empire, some going so far as to worship Leopold and the 'pioneers' who worked for him between 1885 and 1908. Veterans undertook 'pilgrimages' to monuments of Leopold II, such as the one at Brussels' Porte de Namur where they gathered every 15 November on the feast day of Saint Leopold to lower their flags and place wreaths in pious silence.[73] One Minister of Colonies, speaking at the Colonial Monument in the *Parc du Cinquantenaire*, referred to the memorial as an 'altar,' suggesting a holy reverence for the empire and its pioneers.[74]

The embracing of Leopold II and his legacy in monuments, textbooks, expositions, film and elsewhere nationalised and rehabilitated the country's colonial past. It is doubtful this could have occurred had the First World War not intervened, opening up an opportunity to re-write history. Leopold had epitomised rapacious colonialism; Albert I replaced him after 1914 as a wartime monarch whose defiant subjects slowed down the German advance and helped save Paris. Images of 'the Hun' and German atrocities against Edith Cavell, Gabrielle Petit and others replaced those of severed hands and red rubber. This opened a window of opportunity to praise Leopold II, which many people did at a number of *quinzaines coloniales*, or 'colonial fortnights,' which were smaller exhibits that the Ministry of Colonies' *Office Colonial* hosted in the capital between 1925 and 1939. Although the *quinzaines* were supposed to tie metropole and colony closer economically, organisers made particular efforts to target children and get them to attend. These ostensibly economic expositions to promote colonial commerce lauded Leopold when he appeared in brochures or at the exhibits in the form of a bust. Speech givers hailed the king, such as when one notable emphasised, 'We owe the colony to the genius of our great King LEOPOLD II to whom Belgium would never know how to have enough gratitude'.[75] This focus on Leopold was useful because it over-compensated for his terrible actions, and rooted imperialism in the past. If people questioned the legitimacy of their colonial rule, they now could point to an imperial tradition, even if it was invented.[76]

One reason Belgians felt the need to assert the legitimacy of its colonial rule was because Germany appeared to threaten the Congo and their League of Nations Mandates Ruanda-Urundi. Whereas earlier Britain had appeared as the greatest threat, now it was the Weimar Republic. Although the Versailles Treaty stripped Germany of its colonies, it could not control imperialistic sentiment there, and German irredentism began before the treaty's ink had dried.[77] The *Deutsche Kolonialgesellschaft*, which continued to function, was joined by groups such as the *Koloniale Reichsarbeitsgemeinschaft*. Paul von Lettow-Vorbeck became a major hero, groups organised colonial meetings and expositions, and the government formed a colonial section in the Ministry of Foreign Affairs in 1924.[78] The Belgian Chambre's 1925 decision to unify Ruanda-Urundi with the Congo administratively provoked strong German protests.[79]

Although worries about Germany among the population at large might not have specifically focused on its colonial claims, fears of German designs on Africa abounded after 1919 among colonial functionaries and dedicated pro-empire enthusiasts who reacted by 'grasping' the empire to an ever greater extent. At the *Foire Coloniale d'Anvers* in 1932, for instance, *Office Colonial* director Janssen stated that the moment had arrived to 'seize' the Congolese market, to acquire raw materials for Belgium and to manufacture all the colony needed in order to 'remain the masters there after the crisis'.[80] André Van Iseghem, an early convert to imperialism, railed against German claims in a variety of forums such as *L'Essor Colonial Maritime* and organised interest groups to defend the Congo. As an anonymous correspondent to the *Observer* in London, he condemned British appeasement, claiming Germany had 'lost. And has to pay the penalty.' Ignoring foreign contributions to the conquest, administration, and creation of the EIC, Van Iseghem stressed that Belgians had conquered the Congo 'with our blood … and our sweat also'.[81] Other pro-empire enthusiasts with close connections to or within the government echoed Van Iseghem's fear of Germany and were similarly ready to nationalise the history of European involvement in central Africa.[82]

The effort to defend the empire by nationalising the colonial past was nowhere more evident than in the Tervuren museum, whose exhibits made the Congo more 'Belgian'. In 1934, colonial veteran and pro-empire activist Josué Henry de la Lindi drafted a letter of complaint to the Minister of Colonies regarding the representation of history on a wall map of the Congo in the museum. That same year the museum had put up a memorial to 'colonial heroes' inscribed with the names of all 1,508 Belgians who had died in Africa during the Leopoldian period (no Africans), apparently alongside the wall map about which Henry de la Lindi contacted the Ministry. The map, by this time in place for years, represented European knowledge of central Africa circa 1900, and had only two explorers' itineraries mapped out, both by Germans. Henry de la Lindi claimed that it was the (ostensibly Belgian) combatants from the Arab campaigns who first surveyed the area. He wrote, 'As the wall map is in some way the symbol of the works accomplished by our colonial heroes, it would be unfortunate, it seems to me, to leave incomplete this scientific monument raised to their memory, and even more unfortunate to attribute to the Germans works and a glory that are not due to them: the 1,500 names written to the side, instead of being glorified, would be outraged by it'.[83] The museum's administration was favourable to such interpretations. Research has shown that during the colonial period curators deliberately distorted the truth and hid documents in order to control research and produce a more favourable view of Belgium's rule in central Africa.[84]

Inter-war monuments reinforced this nationalisation of the colonial past by paying tribute to the period 1885–1908 and celebrating only Belgian pioneers, not foreigners. A telling example is the monument to Captain Louis Crespel in Ixelles' *Square du Solbosch* whose four-sided stela, topped by a large urn, states: 'Captain CRESPEL, Chief of the 1st Belgian expedition in central Africa. Born at Tournai the 4th of December 1838, Deceased at Zanzibar the 24th of January 1878.' It includes the EIC's motto *'Travail et progrès'*. The monument conflated Crespel's work with that of the EIC and incorrectly made his expedition out as an early exploration into central Africa. When Crespel died, the EIC did not exist, even as a defined vision in Leopold II's mind. Moreover Crespel never stepped foot onto the African mainland, let alone in the area that was to become the Congo: he died only weeks after arriving with his party on Zanzibar in mid-December 1877, to prepare the journey into the interior.[85] By the end of the colonial period at least 150 and as many as 240 'colonial' plaques, busts, memorials and monuments had been built across the country to celebrate missionaries, administrators, Leopold II and above all soldiers who conquered the Congo, many of them highlighting the period 1876/85–1908, that is to say the Leopoldian era. One would be hard put to find among them any of the many American, Swedish, Italian, British, German and other foreign explorers, missionaries, soldiers and administrators who played a key role during that early period or afterward.

The colonial administration and pro-colonialists repeatedly and deliberately targeted youth with these messages in order to cultivate nationalism and pro-empire sentiment. The group *Journées Coloniales*, founded in 1920, organised annual commemorations of the empire called *journées coloniales* or *koloniale dagen*. These events brought school children out to march in commemorative parades or to participate in the inaugurations of monuments, often on the urging of the Ministry of Colonies or local pro-empire groups. Those running the Tervuren museum repeatedly exhibited an intense desire to reach school-aged children, eliciting one foreign observer to admire how schoolchildren from all provinces were brought there to complement their colonial education. As noted, Frans Janssen and others at the *Office Colonial* specifically tracked youth attendance to their *quinzaines coloniales*.

Not only the young, but the masses were targeted as well, showing how Belgians who wanted to develop a popular imperialism aimed to cultivate broad support for empire. An example is the Tervuren museum, which, like colonial material culture museums in Britain and elsewhere, sought to cross class lines to reach all citizens.[87] As a 1920s museum guide put it: 'The goal of the Museum is to instruct, to create the colonial education of the visitors, to create and develop a colonial mentality in Belgium, to completely extirpate that absurd malady, the fear of expatriating, the fear of going to the Congo. The Museum must be a permanent instrument of sound propaganda of the colonial idea; a living and active school.'[88] A Brussels-Tervuren tram line, Belgium's extensive railway system and free and unrestricted entry made sure that citizens of all classes could visit its displays.[89]

The Tervuren museum also shows how Belgians depicted themselves as culturally and racially superior to Africans, and as having brought industrialisation and other advances to the Congo through vigorous action. The museum asserted this in subtle ways. Ostensibly designed to serve as a 'window' onto central Africa, it did not put Congolese artistic production on the same footing as European artwork, instead leaving individual African artists anonymous or relying on traditional ideas of racial 'essence' by identifying pieces only as being typical of a racial 'type'. By contrast curators did name European and American artists; indeed, rare in colonial circles were those like Gaston-Denys Périer who promoted African art as artwork per se.[91] The museum's memorial for colonial heroes and displays of weaponry seized in battle suggested domination over an African foe.[92] Other media reinforced the notion of Belgian superiority: the Congo pavilion at the 1935 World's Fair recycled Mathieu and Bastien's panorama from the 1913 Ghent fair, depicted white officers in charge of the *Force publique*, and showed missionaries tending to sick Africans; colonial novels portrayed the Congo as a field of dynamic Belgian activity with railways, train stations, even house gardens carved out of the bush.[93]

If the view of Africans as inferior was based on anything, it was not based on much interaction with Congolese. The vast majority of Belgians remained isolated from central Africa just as the Congo was cut off from much outside contact because of the administration's segregation of the colony and restriction of Congolese foreign contacts to prevent the spread of subversive ideologies like communism.[94] Restrictions on African travel also resulted from fear, revealed at the time of the 1926 inauguration of the monument to Leopold II at the *Place du Trône*. The main promoter of the monument, Baron Carton de Wiart, wondered in a letter to Brussels' mayor, Adolf Max, whether it would be possible to get a review of Congolese troops for the event:

> The presence of our black soldiers would give a completely special depth to this ceremony and would consecrate the homage rendered to the founder of our African possessions. People have made objections to this suggestion

that appear to me hardly founded. From a hygienic or moral viewpoint, one can respond that the stay of these troops could be limited to the space of time between two steamship departures.[95]

Carton de Wiart's note suggests that Belgians feared Africans for 'hygienic' or 'moral' reasons. (The troops were unavailable in time for the inauguration.) When Congolese were brought to the 1935 World's Fair grounds to be part of the displays that year, their presence elicited anxiousness among officials such as *Office Colonial* director Janssen who warned that organisers needed to 'exercise a serious surveillance on these natives' while they were in Brussels, and that, 'a very strict discipline will have to be observed to avoid any abuse that could happen'.[96]

Although fearful of Congolese, Flemings and Walloons embraced imperialistic messages. In a country of around just several million people, 4,182,500 visitors made their way to the *Pavillon du Congo Belge* at the 1930 Antwerp *Wereldtentoonstelling voor Koloniën, Zeevart en Vlaamsche Kunst* and 3,237,250 visited the colonial pavilion at the 1935 *Exposition de Bruxelles*.[97] More than 65,000 people attended the various *Office Colonial* colonial fortnights from 1925 to 1939.[98] In the year of its inauguration the new Tervuren museum welcomed nearly 200,000 between May and August alone.[99] The number of visits, which dropped precipitously during the First World War, grew to 80,000 by 1922 and then peaked at around 220,000 in 1923. Figures are hard to come by for the 1930s, but it seems likely that the museum welcomed at least 100,000 visitors each year that decade.

This is not to argue there was no indifference or opponents to empire. The Trotskyite *Parti Socialiste Révolutionnaire*'s call for a boycott of a memorial's inauguration in Cuesmes, outside Mons, in 1937 demonstrates there was opposition.[100] If one considers the number of people who left to live in the colony, the growth of imperialistic sentiment appears dubious. The number of Belgian *colons* almost quadrupled from 1917 to 1927 but remained small at 11,898, peaking at only 17,676 in 1930. After economic depression set in and colonial trade plummeted, the Belgian population in the colony dropped by more than a third to 11,423 in 1934. It did not recover for a decade.[101]

But attendance figures and emigration numbers only tell so much, and it remains unclear whether Belgians had developed a visceral attachment to the Congo. Whatever feelings did develop by the 1930s, they were quickly over-shadowed by foreign conquest starting in May 1940 when the German army poured into the Netherlands, Belgium and France, inaugurating a long, four-year occupation.

The Second World War and the post-war years

The Second World War and the German occupation cut Belgians off from the colony and dominated the thinking of even the most ardent imperialists. An example is Norbert Laude, director of the colonial university in Antwerp. Laude was an enthusiastic supporter of the *mission civilisatrice*, dedicating virtually his entire career to educating young men to become *administrateurs territoriaux*. He assumed the directorship of the school after Charles Lemaire died in 1926 and served as director for three decades until age forced him to retire. After Antwerp fell in 1940, Laude's focus shifted from education to resistance, resulting in imprisonment and brutal treatment at the hands of the Gestapo, including torture. He was sentenced to die by shooting on September 6, 1944, only surviving because of the Allied liberation of Antwerp that month.[102]

If war, occupation, and resistance dominated the life of someone like Laude, one can imagine the extent to which the conflict distracted others from colonial issues. Unlike the First World War, Germany occupied the entire country from 1940–44 and a government-in-exile took up residence in London. *Administrateur-général* Albert de Vleeschauwer prevailed over a number of powerful colonial interests ambivalent toward a Nazi-dominated Europe and placed the colony firmly on the side of the Allies, thereby ensuring the kingdom's continued independence.[103] Not only did the Congo sustain Belgian sovereignty, it also provided the government-in-exile with 85 per cent of its resources throughout the conflict.[104] Yet metropole and colony became deeply divided. Administrators had to extend their stays in the colony, sometimes for years, and both functionaries and Congolese were pushed to the breaking point by wartime demands and lack of assistance from the metropole.

Imperialistic propaganda flooded the country after the war in seeming proportion to pro-empire enthusiasts' growing concern that Belgians, in particular young people, did not know enough about the colony.[105] Laude, for instance, lamented the lack of colonial education in primary and secondary schools, noting that students who entered his university demonstrated 'a complete ignorance of the history and the geography of the Belgian Congo,' this despite the fact that after the Second World War messages in favour of empire abounded.[106] Moreover the number of Belgians living in the colony increased rapidly, although it is unclear exactly what drove this increase. It is fair to say that pro-empire propaganda reached an apogee between 1945 and the late 1950s, before dropping off dramatically after Congolese independence in 1960. Although this culmination of years of imperialistic propaganda could not reshape events as they unfolded in 1959–60, they had begun to affect

Belgian feelings toward empire as they developed and deepened a number of key ideas already circulating during the inter-war years.

One of these ideas was more of a feeling, namely fear. Worries about German expansionism were supplanted after the Second World War by fears of takeover by a new power, the United States. For some, US designs on the Congo could be traced back decades to US complicity and participation in attacks on the EIC, such as Mark Twain's scathing *King Leopold's Soliloquy* (1905). Colonial novels such as Léon Debertry's *Kitawala* (1953) expressed fears that the US was destabilising the colony because the Americans were a source of both anti-colonialist pressures and the dangerous Kitawala/Watchtower movement with its origins in the Jehovah's Witnesses.[107] Moreover the US was building a nuclear arsenal and had secured uranium for the atomic bombs used against Japan from the Congo. Responses to a 1950s poll indicating support of more white emigration to central Africa specified that it must be by Belgians, 'if we do not want our colony to fall one day into the hands of the Americans'. In the same poll, fears of US designs on the Congo surfaced repeatedly with a particular focus on the its uranium resources.[108]

Because the post-war years also witnessed a continued desire among imperial enthusiasts to inculcate youth support for empire, the primary school classroom became an ever-more important site of imperialistic propaganda consumption. In the face of perceived indifference, and in the light of limited space in the curriculum to tackle colonial issues, the Ministry of Colonies sent its own Flemish- and French-speaking *conférenciers* into classrooms to show movies and give talks describing the Congo, the value of imperial rule and the greatness of Leopold II. They and the textbooks that students read continued a rooting of the empire in the past that had begun years earlier and which based the right to rule on the foundational period 1885–1908. It was not until the latter half of the 1950s that any doubtful interpretations of Leopold II began to appear, but those were lost among the mountains of praise heaped upon him. The Ministry of Colonies and other groups also continued to target students outside of the classroom by encouraging them to come out to celebrate the *journées coloniales*, participate in the inauguration of monuments or view colonial films.

In fact colonial films multiplied at an unprecedented rate in the late 1940s and 1950s, suggesting a robust colonial culture, although the conclusions one can draw from such production is mixed. The government, private interests, missionaries and colonial corporations produced hundreds of films, answering an apparently booming demand. Missionaries made motion pictures intended for white and black audiences in both Belgium and the Congo, including Father Roger De Vloo's *Feu de brousse* (1947) and *Bizimana* (1951), which extolled missionary activity. The colonial administration, which maintained a tight control over filming rights, promoted the production of films – domestic and foreign – that cast Belgian colonialism in a positive light. All the same, one should not over-state the significance of this steep post-war increase because foreign films continued to dominate the domestic market and movie-making increased dramatically at the time for reasons unrelated to demand for colonial films, strictly speaking. Rare were those colonial films that garnered international acclaim, such as André Cauvin's 1948 *L'Equateur aux cent visages*, which won the Grand Prix international du Documentaire de la Biennale de Venise, or *Les Seigneurs de la Forêt* (Heinz Sielmann and Henry Brandt, 1958), which Twentieth Century Fox distributed around the world in twenty-two languages.[109]

Understanding not only the number but the effects of these films is as difficult to judge in the late 1940s and 1950s as in earlier decades. Unsurprisingly, some local colonialist groups were eager to show them, frequently requesting and screening films from the Ministry of Colonies' collections. One group, the *Société Belge d'Études et d'Expansion*, held 336 film sessions in 1947 alone.[110] *La Revue Colonial Belge* acclaimed Gérard De Boe's film *Etonnante Afrique* (1956) and explained how a packed crowd at the Royale Union Coloniale 'strongly appreciated' the movie.[111] The Ministry of Colonies appears to have encountered little resistance when distributing shorts from its film series 'Visages du Congo' to be shown in cinemas across the country or placing other short films onto television by the 1950s. In that same decade there were several movies that the Ministry of Colonies' *conférenciers* requested repeatedly, indicating their appeal to students, including *Charmant décor* (1952, W. De Boeck), *Le Cuivre* (1951, De Boe), *A la Conquête du Ruwenzori* (1949, G. Félix), *Zwarte landbouwers onder de Tropen* (L. Colleaux, 1951) and *Arts Congolais* (De Boe, 1952), among many others.[112] Although reactions in the press were mixed, some reviewers embraced these films, such as when *La Métropole* characterised a number of 1947 film shorts by De Boe and André Heyman as 'perfectly successful and greatly interesting', going on to state that they were 'superb documentation, teaching us to know our marvellous colony, its rich possibilities and constitute a greatly efficacious medium of propaganda'.[113]

Not only did more and more people see movies about the colony as time wore on, the Congo also became an ever-more strictly Belgian affair. In one sense this was literal because a greater and greater percentage of 'whites' living there were nationals: from 70 per cent in 1945 to 79 per cent in 1959. But in another sense this was figurative as people claimed the Congo in a variety of ways. For the 1949 *Foire Coloniale de Bruxelles*, for instance, one publication gushed that, 'All the products of the Congo and all their characteristics are shown there ... Numerous panels recall

4.2   Poster, 'Notre Congo', Journée Coloniale, designed by Poffé, printed by A
Stevens, Brussels, Belgium. (Courtesy the Wolfsonian, FIU)

that "The Congo is Belgian", "40 billions of capital are invested, of which
almost the totality are Belgian," "300,000 Belgians of the metropole live
from the Congo".'[114] Novels, textbooks and monuments continued to

nationalise the history of European imperialism in central Africa by focusing on the Belgian experience, hailing national colonial heroes and downplaying foreigners. Because the Tervuren museum changed at a glacial pace, visitors continued to be confronted with a positive view of empire, such as when gazing up at the statues of 'Belgium bringing civilisation to the Congo' in its main rotunda. In smaller ways, however, the Congo did not become more Belgian in popular culture. After 1945, francophone comic-strip artists increasingly targeted a broader audience, leading to decreased references to the Congo and an increase in a more generic 'Africa' as a setting.[115] Some comics continued to reinforce ideas of European superiority over so-called inferior Africans and propagate long-standing racist stereotypes, such as Max Bara's comic strips in *Le Soir* in the 1950s that depicted Africans as ape-like and prone to laziness, drunkenness and cannibalism.[116]

One might question the significance of pro-empire rhetoric 'nationalising' the colony and asserting European supremacy considering the paucity of domestic opposition as the government negotiated the Congo's independence in 1960. Yet even if Belgians were unwilling to fight for the empire in 1960, this does not mean they lacked a popular imperial culture. Strong imperialistic sentiment was alive and well among colonial veterans, functionaries, settlers and others. Former governor-general Pierre Ryckmans, for instance, openly and defiantly defended Belgian colonial rule in 1955.[117] More striking by the 1950s and 1960s was the widespread positive view of Leopold II, revealed in the 1956 poll mentioned at the outset of the chapter wherein Belgians affirmed the Congo had not been conquered by force or violence, but rather bequeathed to Leopold because of his humanitarianism. There also was a widespread belief in the legitimacy and beneficence of empire. In response to the same 1956 poll, 80.5 per cent agreed that Belgium's presence in central Africa was rightful, while only 5.4 per cent disagreed; more than 80 per cent believed colonial rule benefitted Congolese. One person legitimised profit-making by Belgians because 'It cost us so much at the beginning'. Young people aged 20–34 years old (born 1922–36) were most enthusiastic about the colony, suggesting that inter-war pro-empire propaganda had worked: when asked as to their interest in the colony, 80.9 per cent indicated they were interested; asked whether colonisation (white settlement) should increase, 59.2 per cent agreed. Polled whether they would be willing to take a job in the colony, almost a third of young people answered yes. Eighty five and 88 per cent, respectively, thought colonial rule good for the indigenous population and for Belgium.[118]

Imperialistic sentiment in Belgium arguably reached a zenith in 1958. Organisers of that year's World's Fair in Brussels created a nineteen-acre Congo section that included seven modern pavilions and a large tropical garden containing a *'village indigène'*. They brought in hundreds of Congolese for the fair, to be displayed, act as guides and perform. A light and video show called *Congorama* enticed hundreds of thousands of viewers and educed ecstatic reviews. The fair was hugely successful with the Belgian public: more than 80 per cent visited it and nearly 70 per cent of those who did went to see the Congo section.[119] Press and television coverage showed Belgians embracing empire and everything that came with it with only rare criticisms, such as the one visitor who complained that the *village indigène*'s Congolese were 'penned in there like livestock and exhibited as strange beasts'.[120] Even the Socialist *Le Peuple* praised the displays and only occasionally critiqued how the empire was being run, signalling the depth of cross-party consensus on the issue.[121]

The 1958 fair's representations of the colony also unveil depictions of an other (Congolese) and self (Belgians) that built on similar practices at earlier expositions, in literature and elsewhere. Belgians continued to depict a Congolese other as inferior and backward, thereby building themselves up as superior and advanced. 'Before and after' depictions in 1958, in print and on the fairgrounds themselves, contrasted African disorder with European development. The atavistic *village indigène* of 1958 dehumanised Africans by bringing in Congolese artisans to be viewed and filmed behind a fence as they went about their everyday affairs. Visitors not only observed the artisans, they also asked to see their teeth and the palms of their hands; some threw food. After weeks of such inhumane treatment the Congolese successfully asked to return home.[122] Many scholars have refuted that the West kept non-Western 'others' – such as the Islamic world – '"silent" and "frozen" in Western discourse'.[123] Yet expositions, culminating in the 1958 fair, show that Belgians were able to keep Africans largely silent and their image frozen right up until the end of the colonial period, in the metropole at least, no doubt in part due to restrictions on Congolese travel.

This control over the Congolese other reflected persistent and deep fears about Africans' presence in the metropole. The colonial administration restricted Congolese travel throughout the colonial period, and the fact that there were a few hundred in Belgium at all was only a result of rule violations: certain returning colonials brought African servants back with them, and some Congolese mariners literally jumped ship. Tervuren museum director Frans Olbrechts, speaking of the hundreds of Congolese organisers would transport to Belgium for the 1958 exposition, warned that,

> It would be very imprudent to unload this thousand Congolese in small hotels, small pensions scattered here and there. In doing so they would escape any control, would be exposed to nefarious and subversive influences

(communism, anti-colonialism, Watch Tower movement, etc.) ... the
Blacks should be gathered in agreeable conditions, but allowing for a certain
control of their activities, of their free time.[124]

The authorities housed most of them at the *Centre d'Accueil pour le
Personnel Africain* (CAPA) in Tervuren, coincidentally only a short
distance from where the *villages indigènes* had been erected for the 1897
exposition. *Le Peuple* indicated the control over Congolese at the CAPA,
whose rules resembled those of a military barracks: 'At ten o'clock [p.m.],
the manageress turns off the lights. If a Black returns after midnight, he
is obliged to alert the management. His passport is held by the centre. He
has to advise the latter of his slightest movements. In brief, it appears to
him that he is considered as a suspect, or at least as a displaced
person.'[125]

The 1958 fair provided another opportunity to praise Leopold II,
demonstrating that if there were negative or ambivalent feelings toward
him when he died, these were long gone as efforts to rehabilitate him had
taken effect. At the entrance to the main Congo pavilion in 1958 organisers put up a bust of him with the quote 'I undertook the work of the
Congo in the interest of civilisation'. Whereas initial post-EIC colonial
displays at the 1910 and 1913 World's Fairs distanced Belgian state rule
from Leopold, inter-war expositions glorified him and connected the
Belgian Congo to the EIC, a practice that accelerated after 1945. There is
no better example than the building of monuments to the empire and its
founder in the years leading up to independence in Namur, Ghent, Hal,
Hasselt and elsewhere. In 1951, the *Cercle Colonial Arlonais* unveiled a
large statue of him with flanking side panels depicting Belgians bringing
progress to a barbarous land wracked by Arab slavery.[126] Because Europeans enjoyed building all kinds of memorials and monuments, it would
be incorrect to argue this is evidence of absolute imperialistic fervor, but
at the very least there was no waning of enthusiasm for empire.

Nonetheless, if one were to judge the strength of imperialistic sentiment by the events of 1960, one would have to conclude that Belgians
had no deep emotional bond with their colony even at that late date. The
Congo achieved its independence rapidly in what Jean Stengers called a
'precipitous decolonisation'.[127] Although independence movements and
nationalist groups were comparatively late to develop in the Congo, they
had grown in force and size by the late 1950s. Largely unrelated riots in
January 1959 in Leopoldville caught authorities by surprise, and within
days King Baudouin gave a speech in which he uttered the word 'independence'. A conference was called for early 1960 that led to independence by the middle of that year, only months after Belgians had put
Congolese on display behind fences. As administrators and the monarchy

hurriedly negotiated Congolese independence they ignored any ardent pro-empire feelings among Belgians in Europe or Africa, yet it also was clear that the population would not fight to retain the Congo. As former governor-general Pierre Ryckmans described the situation in 1955, 'We know that we cannot maintain our position there by sheer force of arms'.[128] The man (and woman) on the street would not countenance armed conflict to thwart Congolese independence that might threaten anything along the lines of the Algerian war in which the country's neighbour, France, was involved at the time.

Belgian popular imperialism

Belgians were certainly more enthusiastic about empire than has been thought. Although many have characterised Belgians as reluctant imperialists because of widespread indifference to Leopold II's imperialism, an over-emphasis on the EIC period has obscured the half century after 1908 during which Belgians not only sustained an empire but in many ways embraced it. It might be true that fervent imperialism only existed among a restricted segment of the population.[129] But there can be no doubt that there was a surprising level of grassroots support for imperialism across the country, led by colonial veterans.

Belgians took in and generated imperialistic messages in diverse forms and few had any doubts as late as the 1950s that empire would continue indefinitely. This is not to say that there was no indifference towards empire, or even outright opposition. One group that was not as affected by the colonial experience or imperialistic culture was women. Women were always a small minority among the population in the colony and were few and far between when it came to representing or promoting the colony in the metropole. There were no pro-empire monuments to women, few female authors of colonial novels, and only one notable female director of colonial films, Hélène Schirren. As noted, there was opposition to empire in the form of calls to boycott the inauguration of colonial monuments and ambivalence toward barbarous displays of Africans in the metropole from the 1897 ethnographic display in Tervuren that had Congolese 'parked as animals are in contests' to six decades later when Africans were 'exhibited as curious beasts' for the Brussels World's Fair.[130] And during the latter event, socialists and communists met clandestinely with Congolese in Brussels to discuss with them the subversive ideas that administrators had feared for so many years. Yet open opponents to colonialism in Belgium were few and far between; more telling was the high turnout for the Congo section in 1958.

To say there was enthusiasm for the central African empire is not to argue that there was a deep emotional attachment to it. Scholars have long debated the efficacy of propaganda, and in this case, pro-empire propaganda from the 1880s seems to have failed in the attempt to establish profound links between Belgium and its colony. No more clear evidence of this could be found than the metropolitan population's acquiescence in the face of the decision to decolonise, or in the fact that the colony had little spillover effects in domestic politics. Although it is true that all parties agreed on the legitimacy of the imperial enterprise, also true is the fact that only in the 1908 election did the Congo play a significant role. Apart from the question of annexation and the years 1940 and 1958–60, 'the influence of the colony on Belgian domestic politics was not really important'.[131]

Nonetheless a kind of popular imperialism did develop, surprising considering the other things demanding attention such as two year-long, devastating foreign occupations. Much of this popular feeling for empire was driven by fears of a takeover of the Congo – first British, then German, later American – and the numerous efforts to increase popular support among young people. Even if pro-empire sentiment dwindled with the trauma of defeat and occupation, propaganda did have effects, successfully transmitting a version of history that shrouded atrocities during Leopold II's rule while simultaneously recasting him as a glorious colonial architect. In fact what sets popular imperialism in Belgium apart from others is the remarkable yet ironic reverence reserved for one individual, Leopold II: remarkable because for veterans, ministers, enthusiasts, and others Leopold took on a holy character, eliciting 'pilgrimages' to his monuments; ironic because it was his dreadful rule that had handed Belgium an empire in the first place. In any case, no other figure achieved such singular status in the other European empires.

A Belgian American Educational Foundation Fellowship and a Berry College Evans School of Humanities, Arts and Social Sciences Travel Grant were important to researching and writing this chapter, and I would like to thank Jonathan Atkins and Kelly Petronis for comments on earlier versions of the essay.

Notes

1 Ludwig Bauer, *Leopold the Unloved*, trans. Eden and Cedar Paul (Boston 1935), p. 335.
2 John Chamberlain, 'Books of the Times', *The New York Times* (8 February 1935), p. 19.
3 *Le Patriote illustré* quoted in Mark van den Wijngaert, Lieve Beullens, and Dana Brants, *Pouvoir & Monarchie: La Belgique et ses rois*, trans. Anne-Laure Vignaux (Brussels 2002), p. 27.
4 Jean Stengers, *Congo: Mythes et réalités* (Brussels 2005), p. 122.
5 Quoted in ibid., p. 157.
6 Pierre Ryckmans, 'Belgian "Colonialism"', *Foreign Affairs* (October 1955), pp. 89–91.

7 Quoted in *The Guardian*, 1 July, 1960.

8 L. Monseur, La Colonisation Belge: Une Certaine Image Officielle (Les Manuels: 1919–1939), Master's thesis, Université de Liège, 1984–85, p. 126.

9 R. De Keyser, 'Belgisch-Kongo in den belgischen Geschichtslehrbüchern', in W. Fürnrohr (ed.), *Afrika im Geschichtsunterricht europäischer Länder* (Munich 1982), p. 164.

10 G. Jacquemyns, 'Le Congo belge devant l'opinion publique', *Institut Universitaire d'Information Sociale et Économique «INSOC»*, nos 2–3, Brussels 1956.

11 Martin Ewans, 'Belgium and the colonial experience', *Journal of Contemporary European Studies*, 11, 2 (November 2003), pp. 167–80.

12 Maurits Wynants, *Des ducs de Brabant aux villages congolais; Tervuren et l'Exposition coloniale 1897*, trans. Chantal Kesteloot (Tervuren 1997).

13 Vincent Viaene, 'King Leopold's imperialism and the origins of the Belgian Colonial Party, 1860–1905', *Journal of Modern History*, 80 (December 2008), pp. 741–90.

14 Guy Vanthemsche, *La Belgique et le Congo: Empreintes d'une colonie 1885–1980* (Brussels 2007), pp. 26, 63, 187–8, passim.

15 See Stengers, *Congo*.

16 Marc Poncelet, *L'invention des sciences coloniales belges* (Paris 2008), p. 39.

17 Ibid., p. 113.

18 Pierre Halen, *Le Petit Belge avait vu grand* (Brussels 1993), p. 45.

19 Poncelet, *L'invention des sciences*, p. 47.

20 Ministère de l'Industrie et du Travail, Commissariat général du Gouvernement, *Exposition universelle et internationale de Bruxelles 1910: Catalogue spécial officiel de la Section Belge* (Brussels 1910), p. 565; Vanthemsche, *La Belgique et le Congo*, p. 353.

21 Barbara Yates, 'Educating Congolese abroad: an historical note on African elites', *The International Journal of African Historical Studies*, 14, 1 (1981), pp. 34–64.

22 Viaene, 'King Leopold's imperialism', pp. 741–90.

23 Ibid., p. 769.

24 V. Jacques, *Les Congolais de l'Exposition Universelle d'Anvers. Communication faite à la société d'anthropologie de Bruxelles, dans la séance du 24 septembre 1894* (Brussels 1894).

25 Tom Flynn, 'Taming the tusk: the revival of Chryselephantine sculpture in Belgium during the 1890s', in Tim Barringer and Tom Flynn (eds), *Colonialism and the Object* (London 1998), p. 188.

26 A. de Burbure, 'Expositions et Sections Congolaises', *Belgique d'Outremer*, 286 (January 1959), pp. 27–8.

27 Brigitte Schroeder-Gudehus and Anne Rasmussen, *Les fastes du progrès: Le guide des Expositions universelles 1851–1992* (Paris 1992), p. 128.

28 Patricia Van Schuylenbergh, 'Découverte et Vie des Arts plastiques du Bassin du Congo dans la Belgique des Années, 1920–1930', in Patricia Van Schuylenbergh and Françoise Morimont (eds), *Rencontres Artistiques Belgique-Congo, 1920–1950*, Enquêtes et Documents d'Histoire Africaine, no. 12 (N.p., 1995), p. 4; Anne-Marie Bouttiaux, 'Des mises en scène de curiosités aux chefs-d'œuvre mis en scène: Le Musée royal de l'Afrique à Tervuren: un siècle de collections', *Cahiers d'Études africaines*, 155–156, 39-3-4 (1999), pp. 595–616.

29 P. Marechal, 'Le Musée royal de l'Afrique centrale', in H. Balthazar and J. Stengers (dirs), *La Dynastie et la Culture en Belgique* (Antwerp 1990), pp. 331–40.

30 G. Onclincx, 'Milieux Coloniaux et cinématographie à l'Exposition internationale de Bruxelles de 1897', *Cahiers Bruxellois; Revue trimestrielle d'histoire urbaine*, 3, 4 (October–December 1958), pp. 300–1; Marianne Thys (ed.), *Belgian cinema; Le cinéma belge; De Belgische film* (Brussels 1999), p. 35.

31 Guido Convents, 'L'apparition du cinéma en Belgique (1885–1918)', *Les Cahiers de la Cinémathèque: Revue d'Histoire du Cinéma*, 41 (winter 1984), p. 17 and *Préhistoire du cinéma en Afrique 1897–1918* (Brussels 1986), pp. 65–6.

32 Convents, 'L'apparition du cinéma', p. 18.

33 Onclincx, 'Milieux Coloniaux', p. 306.

34 Men dominated public life in Belgium and the Congo. L. H. Gann and Peter Duignan, *The Rulers of Belgian Africa, 1884–1914* (Princeton 1979).

35 Liane Ranieri, *Léopold II: Urbaniste* (Brussels 1973), pp. 141–54.

36 Halen, *Le Petit Belge*, pp. 42–3.

37 Félicien Cattier, *Étude sur la Situation de l'État Indépendant du Congo*, 2nd ed. (Brussels 1906), pp. 74–5.

38 George Frederick Kunz, *Ivory and the Elephant in Art, Archaeology, and in Science* (Garden City 1916), p. 467.

39 Ruth Slade, *King Leopold's Congo* (London 1962), p. 200.

40 Ranieri, *Léopold II*, pp. 123–40; Gustave Stinglhamber and Paul Dresse, *Léopold II au Travail* (Brussels 1945), pp. 241–4.

41 L. Vincart, 'Een paar uurtjes in het Koloniaal Museum', *Onze Kongo* 1 (1910–11), p. 374.

42 Ranieri, *Léopold II*, p. 141.

43 Which museum guides reiterated. H. Schouteden, *Guide illustré du Musée du Congo Belge*, 7th ed. (Tervuren 1947), p. 11.

44 van den Wijngaert, Beullens and Brants, *Pouvoir & Monarchie*, p. 340.

45 Marcel Luwel, 'Histoire du Musée royal du Congo belge à Tervuren', *Belgique d'Outremer*, n. 289 (1959), p. 212.

46 Slade, *King Leopold's Congo*, p. 191.

47 Quoted in A. Cockx and J. Lemmens, *Les Expositions Universelles et Internationales en Belgique de 1885 à 1958* (Brussels 1958), pp. 76–7.

48 *Exposition Universelle et Internationale de Gand en 1913. Programme Général. Appel aux Producteurs. Règlement-Classification* (Brussels 1911), p. 6.

49 *Exposition Universelle et Internationale de Gand 1913. Commissariat général du Gouvernement. Section Belge. Appel aux Producteurs. Règlement spécial. Classification/Algemeene Wereldtentoonstelling te Gent in 1913. Algemeen Commissariaat der Regeering. Belgische Afdeeling. Oproep tot de Voortbrengers. Bijzondere Verordering. Klasse-Indeeling* (Brussels 1912), p. 4.

50 André Capiteyn, *Gent in Weelde Herboren: Wereldtentoonstelling 1913* (Ghent 1988), p. 150.

51 Guido Convents, 'Des images non occidentales au cœur de l'Europe avant la Première Guerre mondiale: en Belgique, par example', in Roland Cosandey and François Albera (eds), *Cinéma sans fontières 1896–1918 Images Across Borders: Aspects de l'internationalité dans le cinéma mondial: représentations, marchés, influences et réception/Internationality in World Cinéma* [sic]: *Representations, Markets, Influences and Reception* (Quebec City 1995), p. 54, quoting Convents, 'L'apparition du cinéma', pp. 14–26.

52 Convents, 'Film als politiek instrument: Een medium in handen van kolonialen en katholieken in België, 1896–1914', in Henk Kleijer, Ad Knotter and Frank van Vree (eds), *Tekens en Teksten: Cultuur, communicatieen maatschappelijke veranderingen vanaf de late middeleeuwen* (Amsterdam 1992), p. 134 and 'Documentary and propaganda before 1914', *Framework*, 35 (1988), p. 104.

53 *L'Expansion Belge*, quoted in Convents, *Préhistoire*, p. 95.

54 Thys, *Belgian Cinema*, pp. 65–6.

55 Convents, *Préhistoire*, pp. 77–9.

56 'Inhuldiging van het Gedenkteeken Baron Dhanis te Antwerpen', *Ons Volk Ontwaakt*, 18 October 1913 (15 July 2009) <http://users.skynet.be/ovo/BDhanis.html>.

57 'Le monument à la mémoire du baron Dhanis', *Bulletin de la Société d'Études d'Intérêts Coloniaux de Namur*, 9 (September 1913), pp. 111–12.

58 Vincart, 'Een paar uurtjes', p. 373.

59 Marcel Luwel, 'Histoire du Musée Royal du Congo Belge', *Congo-Tervueren*, VI, 2 (1960), p. 46.

60 Larry Zuckerman, *The Rape of Belgium: The Untold Story of World War I* (New York 2004).

61 'Les Produits du Congo Belge', 'Exportations', and 'L'Exposition des Bois du Congo à la

Foire Coloniale', in *5me Foire Coloniale – 5de Koloniale Jaarbeurs – 5th Colonial Fair of Antwerp. Catalogue Officiel* (Antwerp 1928).

62 E.g., 'Questions Economiques: L'importance des richesses congolaises pour le relève-ment financier de la Belgique', *Congo: Revue générale de la Colonie belge/Algemeen tijdschrift van de Belgische Kolonie*, 1, 4 (April 1924), pp. 560–2, quoting Prime Minister Georges Theunis from Revue Belge, 15 April [1924]; Thomas Geoffrey August, *The Selling of the Empire: British and French Imperialist Propaganda, 1890–1940* (Westport CT 1985), pp. 71–87; John M. MacKenzie, *Propaganda and Empire: The Manipulation of British Public Opinion, 1880–1960* (Manchester 1984), pp. 121–46.

63 Luwel, 'Histoire du Musée Royal du Congo Belge', *Congo-Tervueren*, p. 46.

64 E.g., *L'Illustration Congolaise*, 116 (1 May 1931), mispaginated.

65 Monseur, La Colonisation Belge, pp. 107–8; Benoît Verhaegen, 'La Colonisation et la Décolonisation dans les manuels d'histoire en Belgique', in Marc Quaghebeur and Émile Van Balberghe (eds), *Papier blanc, Encre noire: Cent ans de culture francophone en Afrique centrale (Zaïre, Rwanda et Burundi)*, vol. 2 (Brussels 1992), pp. 333–79.

66 Gilles Routhier and Frédéric Laugrand (eds), *L'espace missionaire: Lieu d'innovations et de rencontres interculturelles* (Paris 2003), p. 131; *Au service des broussards* (Namur 1937) and *Les Grands Ordres missionnaires: Les spécialistes du continent noir* (Paris-Namur 1939), located in Jean Pirotte, 'Les Armes d'une mobilisation. La littérature missionnaire de la fin du XIXe siècle à 1940', in Quaghebeur and Van Balberghe (eds), *Papier blanc*, p. 84.

67 Pascal Lefèvre, 'The Congo drawn in Belgium', in Mark McKinney (ed.), *History and Politics in French-Language Comics and Graphic Novels* (Jackson MS 2008), pp. 166–85.

68 Luc Vints, 'Cinéma et Propagande Coloniale (1895–1960)', trans. Monik Dierckx, in *Zaïre 1885–1985: Cent Ans de Regards Belges* (Brussels 1985), p. 36.

69 Francis Ramirez and Christian Rolot, *Histoire du Cinéma Colonial au Zaïre au Rwanda et au Burundi* (Tervuren 1985), p. 20; Thys, *Belgian Cinema*, p. 95.

70 '"Death to Hollywood": The Politics of Film in the United States, Great Britain, Belgium, and France, 1920–1960', PhD thesis, Harvard University, 1995, p. 451.

71 Thys, *Belgian Cinema*, p. 189.

72 Emails from Léon Nyssen of the Royale Amicale des Anciens d'Afrique de Verviers (RAAAV), 20 March 2003, and letter and photos from Alain Noirfalisse of the RAAAV, 21 March 2003.

73 'La Journée du 15 Novembre', *L'Essor Colonial et Maritime*, 20 November 1930.

74 Edmond Rubbens quoted in *Congo: Revue générale de la Colonie belge/Algemeen tijd-schrift van de Belgische Kolonie*, 2, 1 (June 1937), p. 99.

75 'Discours de M. MOREL, Président de la Fédération Nationale des Chambres de Commerce et d'Industrie de Belgique', liasse *205.812.11. Expositions de Quinzaine. 16) Exposition Produits Alimentaires du 7 au 21 mars 1936*, portefeuille O.C. 416, Ministère des Affaires Étrangères/Ministerie van Buitenlandse Zaken, Archives Africaines (AA).

76 Matthew G. Stanard, 'Selling the empire between the wars: colonial expositions in Belgium 1920–1940', *French Colonial History*, 6 (2005), pp. 159–78.

77 Alan Sharp, 'The colonial settlement', in William R. Keylor (ed.), *The Legacy of the Great War* (Boston 1998), p. 175, originally published in Alan Sharp, *The Versailles Settlement* (London 1991).

78 Eckard Michels, 'Deutschlands bekanntester "Kolonialheld" und sein "Askari": Paul von Lettow-Vorbeck und der Feldzug in Ostafrika im Ersten Weltkrieg', and Chantal Metzger, 'D'une puissance coloniale à un pays sans colonies: l'Allemagne et la ques-tion coloniale (1914–1945)', *Revue d'Allemagne et des Pays de Langue Allemande*, 38, no. 4 (October–December 2006), pp. 541–61.

79 William B. Norton, 'Pierre Ryckmans (1891–1959)', in L.H. Gann and Peter Duignan (eds), *African Proconsuls: European Governors in Africa* (New York 1978), p. 394.

80 'Au Palais du Congo – La 6me Foire Coloniale d'Anvers', *La Métropole* (Antwerp), 4 September 1932.

81 Van Iseghem to Garvin (*The Observer*, London), 21 July 1936, folder 'Publications, Propaganda 1936–1937', Papiers André Van Iseghem, Musée Royal de l'Afrique Centrale Archives Historiques, Tervuren (MRAC).

82 De Lannoy to Van Iseghem, 22 July 1936, folder '1922-1937 L'Essor colonial et maritime', Papiers Van Iseghem, MRAC.

83 Document #62.40.2521, folder 'Lettres de Henry', Papiers Josué Henry de la Lindi, MRAC.

84 Sony Van Hoecke and Jean-Pierre Jacquemin, *Africa Museum Tervuren 1898–1998* (Tervuren 1998), p. 242.

85 Guy Malengreau, 'Crespel', *Biographie Coloniale Belge/Belgische Koloniale Biographie*, 3 (Brussels 1952), columns 171–2.

86 Félix Regnault, 'Une visite au Musée du Congo belge', *Bulletins & mémoires de la Société d'Anthropologie de Paris*, 5 (1924), p. 65.

87 Annie E. Coombes, 'Museums and the Formation of National and Cultural Identities', *The Oxford Art Journal*, 11, 2 (1988), p. 64.

88 J. Maes, *Le Musée du Congo Belge à Tervuren: Guide illustré du visiteur* (Antwerp 1925), p. 11.

89 Vincart, 'Een paar uurtjes', pp. 376–7, n. 1.

90 George W. Stocking, Jr, *Race, Culture, and Evolution: Essays in the History of Anthropology* (Chicago 1968), p. 192.

91 H. Schouteden, *Guide Illustré du Musée du Congo Belge*, 5th ed. (Tervuren 1943), pp. 15, 34, 47, 56, 57, 60, 64; 'Œuvres d'art du Congo à Tervueren', *La Revue Coloniale Belge*, 260 (November 1956), p. 840; 'L'Exposition du Peintre Pierre de Vaucleroy', *La Revue Coloniale Belge*, 256 (1 June 1956), p. 402; Van Schuylenbergh, 'Découverte et Vie', pp. 1–62.

92 Boris Wastiau, 'The violence of collecting: objects, images and people from the colony', unpublished paper, AHA Annual Meeting, 4 Jan. 2009, New York.

93 Envelope 27, box 'Expo. de Brux. 1935 No. 186A, nos. 26-33', Archives de l'Exposition Universelle de Bruxelles 1935, Archives Générales du Royaume/Algemeen Rijksarchief; Halen, *Le Petit Belge*, pp. 247–308.

94 Jean-Luc Vellut, 'Episodes anticommunistes dans l'ordre colonial belge (1924–1932)', in Pascal Delwit and José Gotovitch (eds), *La Peur du Rouge* (Brussels 1996), pp. 183–90.

95 Carton de Wiart to A. Max, 16 October 1926, dossier 235, Fonds Cabinet du Bourgmestre, Archives de la Ville de Bruxelles.

96 '35ème Séance de la Commission du Département pour la Participation du Département à l'Exposition de Bruxelles 1935', 29 March 1935, p. 2, liasse *205.812.22. Expos et foires diverses organisées en Belgique. Expositions universelle et internationale de Bruxelles 1935. 1) organisation 5) Commission du Ministère des Colonies près l'exposition de Bruxelles a) 41 procès verbaux des séances*, portefeuille 433 O.C., AA.

97 Report by L. Castelain, 6 November 1930, liasse *205.812.22. Expos et foires diverses organisées en Belgique. Exposition internationale d'Anvers 1930. 6) Visiteurs, corresp., registres.1930*, portefeuille 425 O.C., AA; undated internal communication, portefeuille 433 O.C., AA; and Directeur Chef du Service to Minister of Colonies, no. 43, 26 June 1935, liasse *205.812.22 Expos et foires diverses organisées en Belgique. Exposition universelle et internationale de Bruxelles 1935. 2) Participation 1) du Département. 4e Direction. Générale*, portefeuille 434 O.C., AA.

98 Matthew G. Stanard, *Selling the Tenth Province: Belgian Colonial Propaganda 1908–1960*, PhD thesis, Indiana University, 2006, p. 328.

99 A. de Haulleville, 'Le Musée du Congo belge à Tervueren', *La Revue congolaise*, 1, 5 (1910), p. 217.

100 Leaflet by Jean Casterman, Cuesmes, 1937, at liasse *205.812.22 Expos et foires diverses organisées en Belgique. Exposition de Cuesmes 24 et 25 juillet 1937*, portefeuille 445 O.C., AA.

101 Vanthemsche, *La Belgique*, pp. 353–4.

102 Fondation Royale des Amis de l'Institut Universitaire des Territoires d'Outre-Mer, *Middelheim*, 35–8.
103 Vanthemsche, *La Belgique*, passim.
104 Anicet Mobé Fansiama, 'Héros méconnus de la seconde guerre mondiale', *Le Monde diplomatique* (June 2007): pp. 34–5.
105 Major Vandevelde, 'L'Ignorance des Belges en ce qui concernent leur colonie', *Les Vétérans Coloniaux*, 3 (March 1946), p. 17.
106 Van Hecke to Laude, quoting Laude, no. 55/Inf., 17 Jan. 1950, portefeuille 23 Infopresse, AA.
107 Halen, *Le Petit Belge*, pp. 104–11.
108 G. Jacquemyns, 'Le Congo belge', pp. 18, 41–2.
109 'Une Expédition cinématographique au Congo Belge', *Courrier d'Afrique* (20 October 1950); Philip Mosley, *Split Screen: Belgian Cinema and Cultural Identity* (Albany 2001), p. 70.
110 Excerpt from *La Gazette de Liège* (18 April 1947), at portefeuille 64 Infopresse, AA; André to Monsieur l'Administrateur, 6 April 1952, portefeuille 67 Infopresse, AA.
111 '«Etonnante Afrique», un film de Gerard De Boe', *La Revue Coloniale Belge*, 262 (December 1956), p. 912.
112 Portefeuille 8-Presse, AA.
113 'Films Congolais', *La Métropole* (Antwerp), 23 April 1947.
114 'La IIe Foire coloniale', *Le Matin* (Antwerp), 13 June 1949.
115 Lefèvre, 'The Congo drawn in Belgium', pp. 166–85.
116 *Le Soir* (Brussels), 5, 17 and 20 June 1958.
117 Ryckmans, 'Belgium "Colonialism"', pp. 89–101.
118 G. Jacquemyns, 'Le Congo belge', pp. 11, 16, 29, 70, 74.
119 G. and E. Jacquemyns, 'L'Exposition de 1958: Son succès auprès des Belges; Opinions et vœux des visiteurs', *Institut Universitaire d'Information Sociale et Économique* «*INSOC*», nos. 1–2. Brussels, 1959, pp. 13, 25, 57.
120 Ibid., p. 43.
121 Vanthemsche, *La Belgique*, p. 70.
122 Matthew G. Stanard, '"Bilan du monde pour un monde plus déshumanisé": The 1958 Brussels World's Fair and Belgian perceptions of the Congo', *European History Quarterly*, 35, 2 (2005), pp. 267–98.
123 Zeynep Çelik, *Displaying the Orient: Architecture of Islam at Nineteenth-Century World's Fairs* (Berkeley 1992), p. 3.
124 Quoted in Wastiau, 'The violence of collecting', p. 22.
125 F.D., 'Le Ghetto Noir', *Le Peuple* (Brussels), 173, 22 July 1958, p. 2.
126 'Erection d'un monument au Roi Léopold II à Arlon', *Revue Congolaise Illustrée*, no. 2 (February 1950), p. 40; author's visit, 2003.
127 Jean Stengers, 'Precipitous decolonization: the case of the Belgian Congo', in Prosser Gifford and Wm. Roger Louis (eds), *The Transfer of Power in Africa: Decolonization 1940–1960* (New Haven CT 1982), pp. 305–35.
128 Ryckmans, 'Belgium "Colonialism"', p. 101.
129 Vanthemsche, *La Belgique*, p. 63.
130 *Le National*, 7 July 1897, quoted in M. Luwel, 'De Congolezen op de Tentoonstelling van 1897', *Revue Congolaise Illustrée*, 4 (1954), p. 44; G. and E. Jacquemyns, 'L'Exposition de 1958', p. 43.
131 Vanthemsche, *La Belgique*, p. 99.

CHAPTER 5

Imagination and beyond:
cultures and geographies of imperialism in Germany, 1848–1918

Bernhard Gissibl

Between August 1903 and January 1904, the Saxon city of Crimmitschau witnessed the largest strike of textile workers in imperial Germany. At its height, 7,500 textile workers had left their factories and spindles to fight for the ten-hour day.[1] When the strike drew to a close in January 1904, the satirical magazine *Simplicissimus* commented on the affair with a caricature that showed a handful of policemen and bourgeois capitalists treading down a mass of hollow-eyed and semi-starved workers. 'We need more policemen', read the subtitle. 'The bastards aren't squashed yet.'[2] The caricature was published as part of a series entitled *Durchs dunkelste Deutschland* ('Through Darkest Germany'), an all-too-obvious allusion to Stanley's best-selling travelogue 'In Darkest Africa'.[3] The suppression of workers' demands by an alliance of state and capital was framed in the cultural language of empire and the civilising mission. Suggesting parallels between the oppression of working-class demands in Crimmitschau and the oppression of colonised peoples in the empire, the caricature portrayed German workers as an oppressed 'other within'. Germany's 'darkness' consisted of glaring deficits of solidarity and civility in a society that assumed the task of civilising others.

Events in Crimmitschau and Germany's colonial empire were also linked through the 'world wide web of cotton production'.[4] At the height of the Crimmitschau layoff, the Dresden-based Association of German Cotton Yarn Consumers approached the German Colonial Department to actively promote cotton cultivation in Germany's colonies.[5] The ultimate cause for strike, social unrest and the instability of the textile industry, it was argued, was a dearth of cotton at reliably low prices. If only employers had a safe and affordable supply, they would not be forced to make cuts on wages or insist on extensive workloads. The aim of stabilising a highly volatile industry in Germany was translated into colonial policies of labour education and agricultural productivity.

5.1 'Through Darkest Germany': policemen and capitalists trampling down starving workers. Caricature from *Simplicissimus*, 1904. The cultural language of empire and of the 'civilising mission' used in the suppression of workers' demands. (*Simplicissimus*)

Most of these schemes of cultivation failed economically. The same could be said of the German colonial project in general. An older school of imperial historiography has, therefore, dismissed colonialism as marginal for German society.[6] The imperial entanglements of the

Crimmitschau strike suggest a different reading. Imperialism did not just happen 'out there', but had become a fundamental part of Germany's self-representation as a 'civilised' nation, providing a cultural language with which to interpret the social and political situation at home. The hopes manufacturers and imperial decision-makers projected onto colonial cotton were part of the 'multiplicity of imaginary colonial investments'[7] that have been a core concern of German colonial studies over the past decade.[8] Many of these fantasies never materialised, but some fed into concrete colonial policies. The social tensions that arose from the capitalist production of textiles in Europe were inextricably linked with the ecological, political and social dimensions of cotton cultivation in extra-European societies. The aim of mitigating social tensions in Germany by turning dependent territories into sources of raw materials provides a striking example of 'social imperialism': not as the Wehlerian elite engineering of popular enthusiasm from above to gloss over social inequalities and the hardships of economic depression,[9] but as the imperial outside of domestic social policy.

Empire: containing the global, transcending the colonial

This essay seeks to trace the impact and repercussions of empire on German society, politics and culture between the middle of the nineteenth century until the First World War. Such an attempt has to cope with considerable conceptual problems. Neither imperialism nor empire, that 'conflict-laden denominator of expansionist, exploitative, missionary, and humanitarian aspirations overseas as well as migration patterns over time and space', are established categories in the interpretation of nineteenth and twentieth century German history.[10] Not only have historians privileged the nation-state as an interpretative framework, but the concept of empire in German history comes burdened with a long continental heritage of a heterogeneous political institution with dynastic appellation. This tradition is still visible in a terminology that distinguishes between 'imperial Germany' as the German *Kaiserreich* and the colonial empire of the *Kolonialreich*. Compared with the transoceanic empires of Britain, France, Portugal or the Netherlands, the geographical and temporal scope as well as the economic performance of Germany's overseas empire was modest. Only between 1884 and 1918 did the country rule formally over territories in Africa and Oceania. While Britain, France and the Netherlands *were* empire-states, Germany, for the most part of the nineteenth and twentieth centuries, only aspired to be one.

Yet, situated within a system of imperial polities 'any serious competitor for geopolitical influence' had to 'think and act like an empire'.[11] Imperialism as the belief in an inherent mission to rule others and the cultural, social, political and economic activities to realise this claim and globalise the nation was not tied to the existence of a polity called empire but aimed at its creation. The fact that Germany was an 'impatient onlooker' for most of the nineteenth century, an imperial late-comer from the 1880s onwards, and an outcast denied participation in the European project of civilising others after 1919 means that for most of the period under discussion, German imperialists were aspiring to something the country did not have. This perceived lack of empire was interpreted as a deficit before 1884, spurred irredentism after 1919, and opened opportunities for allegedly disinterested engagement in Africa and Asia after 1945. In each case, the implications for German society were significant. Also in the absence of a formal political framework, many Germans thought like an empire, and some scholars have even argued that the absence of formal empire assigned a particularly important role to fantasies and cultural productions that expressed a will and desire to empire. These imaginations only produced the according asymmetrical representations of power, difference, space-time and progress on a global scale. Yet, the emphasis on the mental prerequisites and world-views that made imperialist interventions possible should not lead to dissolving imperialism into mere discourse and cultural representation. Representations must be tied to manifest structures of power, economic apprehensions and the social formations and institutions that under-pinned a German *Weltpolitik*.

Imperialism included the establishment of transcontinental connec-tions as well as attempts to control and contain the global circulation of people, commodities, capital and ideas. It transcended boundaries and it drew new ones, and it produced new hierarchies and exclusions. Such an understanding of imperialism provides a concept situated on a level below globalisation (for not all processes and transactions that crossed borders and continents were actually 'globalising') but above colonialism (which is only one form in which empire was realised, albeit an important one).[12] Tracing the impact of 'empire' on German society must encompass both periods of formal colonial rule and imperialism without colonies. It needs to situate the extension of German territoriality between the poles of overseas and continental expansion along Germany's eastern frontier, and it needs to include conscious and unconscious forms of involvement in the exertion of 'Western' domination and governance over the rest of the world. The analysis must also encompass the role other empires played for German imperialism. As much as all European nations re-forged national identities as imperial and aimed at assembling wealth and power for the nation, imperialist competition should not obscure the vital

[161]

part played by the empires of others.[13] They provided role models for emulation and opportunities for the transfer of knowledge, practices and institutions. The possibility of indirect participation in the empires of others highlights that the imperial encounter with the extra-European world was also a key site for producing notions of an imperial cosmopolitanism and what it meant to be 'European'.

This is a bold programme, and what follows is but a tentative and selective attempt to discuss the meaning of imperialism and empire for German society up to the forced formal decolonisation after the First World War. After a discussion of Germany's imperialism without colonies before 1884, German imperiality is analysed along the axes of mobility and migration, 'race' and the sciences, commodities and markets, the missions and imperialist social formations, and the vast field of popular culture.

Imperialism without colonies

Imperialism as the will to create a German empire and exert global influence on a geopolitical par with Britain and France was neither the highest stage of German nationalism nor its redefinition in imperial terms after unification in 1871. Nor did it start with the acquisition of colonies in 1884/85. Core elements of German imperialism had been established by the middle of the nineteenth century. Among these were the desirability of overseas settlement colonies as a destination where the manpower of German emigrants could be retained for the benefit of the nation; the perceived necessity of colonial possessions as a means to secure the interests of German overseas commerce; the agitation for a German navy as a symbol of national unity and for advocating German political and commercial interests overseas; the ambivalent perception of Britain as an imperial role model; and a notion of cultural superiority that included a 'general propensity to universalise the self'.[14] The advances of technology, science and industrialisation provided the 'tools of empire' – steamships, railways, telegraph, medicine and weaponry – that made the globe accessible for Europeans, while the idea of 'race' allowed the distribution of superiority and inferiority along the axes of culture, biology, the nation and the body. Finally, the second half of the nineteenth century witnessed the invention of two imperial traditions that anchored imperialist claims in history: the continental tradition of German colonisation in the marchlands of a 'Slavic wilderness' in the east, and a tradition of overseas colonisation that harked back to the sixteenth- and seventeenth-century colonial ventures of the Great Elector of Brandenburg in West Africa and of the Fugger and Welser merchant houses in South America.

[162]

Perhaps the most influential analyses of German imperialism without empire came from the field of literary and cultural studies. Mining scientific, philosophical and political treatises, but above all various genres of literary fiction dealing with South America, Susanne Zantop has exposed tropes of male conquest and erotic encounters between male European and female 'native'. These 'colonial fantasies' not only amounted to 'occidentalist' representations of the New World but created a 'fictitious German colonial history' that allegedly sedimented in the collective political unconscious of German society. Imperialist imaginations predated actual German colonial rule by over a century, created a 'colonialist predisposition' and entrenched in people's minds the legend of the paternalist, morally superior and hard-working German coloniser. It was exactly the absence of colonial possessions that assigned fantasies such an important function as a substitute and 'imaginary testing ground' for colonial practice. When Germany finally acquired colonies in the 1880s, this was only the realisation of a long-held collective desire.[15]

Others have identified similar tropes of conquest, sexualised desire, strategies of exotic 'othering' and imaginations of empty lands just waiting to be taken by the male German coloniser.[16] As stimulating as this emphasis on the imaginary is, it is fraught with problems. The desires and meanings exposed by careful scholarly analysis are often equated with the meaning contemporary readers derived from this literature, and the cultural productions of intellectuals are taken as expressions of collective fantasies supposedly held by large parts of society. In many instances it remains highly questionable if texts or plays ever reached an audience beyond parts of the educated middle classes. We are on somewhat safer ground with analyses that correlate the imperial imaginary with the structures of an evolving mass market for printed information in the second half of the nineteenth century. One publication that addressed a broad readership in the liberal *Bürgertum* was *Die Gartenlaube*, Germany's most popular liberal family magazine with a peak circulation of 382,000 in 1875. Matthew Fitzpatrick has emphasised the degree to which German claims to colonial imperialism prior to 1884/85 had been popularised in this particular medium. Correcting earlier assumptions that *Die Gartenlaube* largely neglected colonial topics before it burst into a veritable 'colonial obsession' in the mid-1880s,[17] Fitzpatrick distinguished five modes of representation in which Germany's claim to empire was articulated. These representations included the sympathetic coverage of any government policy or private project related to the acquisition of colonial territories or a powerful German navy; reports on German emigrant communities abroad, which were depicted as role models of an already realised national unity where liberal ideas had been put into practice; the moralising and racialising classification of indigenous peoples in articles that could be categorised as popular anthropology; tales of heroic German individuals partaking in the European 'opening up' of Africa through exploration; and a 'vicarious imperialism' that monitored closely the empires of the other European states. Thereby, readers were not only familiarised with the advantages and obligations of having an empire, but also with its potential for violence and genocide. The extermination of indigenous populations in the face of European advance in North America and Australia was taken as inevitable matter-of-fact.[18]

The enormous popularity of *Die Gartenlaube* triggered a wave of other magazines, like *Über Land und Meer* (1858–1925) or *Aus allen Weltteilen* (1870–98) that covered similar topics of geography, popular anthropology, exploration and the exotic. None of them reached the circulation figures of *Die Gartenlaube*, but they marked the birth of a popular press that made the world available and knowable to the educated masses. This fledgling mass market was complemented by more specialised media such as *Petermanns Mitteilungen*, a geographic magazine where the vanishing of the last blanks on the globe was miniaturised in maps and popularised as a transnational European undertaking.

Another defining feature of Germany's imperialism without colonies was a transimperial cult of 'heroic exploration'[19] that extended beyond the German heroes celebrated in *Die Gartenlaube*. Foreign language travelogues on African exploration were almost immediately translated, often in the very year of their original publication. There is no analysis yet of Stanley's reception in Germany, but his fame reached a peak with the Emin Pasha relief expedition of 1889/90. A board game entitled 'The conquest of Africa' allowed the German youth to follow in the footsteps of the explorer, and the Berlin *Victoria-Theater* featured a play entitled *Stanley in Afrika* that was staged at least two hundred times in 1889/90 alone.[20] Yet, vicarious imperialism was not only a matter of discourse and cultural production. Before and after Germany's short-lived colonial empire, the empires of Britain and the Netherlands in particular provided opportunity structures for missionaries, entrepreneurs, mercenaries and experts of science. Several thousand Germans joined the Dutch army for service in the Netherlands East Indies during the nineteenth century, while the number of Germans enrolled in the French Foreign Legion reached new heights after 1945. The important role of German naturalists in the institutions of the British Empire is well established, and both the British and the Dutch recruited German foresters to introduce scientific management into the forests of British India and Java in the second half of the nineteenth century. Some of their experience gathered in the service of other empires was later transferred back to the German colonies.[21]

Germany's imperialism without colonies was not reduced to discursive dreams and imperialism by proxy. Middle-class liberals were the most vocal proponents of a powerful imperialist nation-state to be forged out of the loose German Confederation. Of course, they too thrived upon fantasies. Unsullied by colonial possessions or a unified state, they cast their acquisitive gaze opportunistically over the globe. Hardly a continent was spared from being subjected to fantasies of German colonisation. In the 1830s and 40s, German liberals regarded the American west as the ideal site to establish a 'New-German' settlement,[22] but also the Danube River basin, southern Russia, central America, Chile, Brasil or the Chatham Islands were discussed as possible sites for a *Neu-Deutschland* overseas. The Prussian officer Willibald Huger von der Oelsnitz was among the first to suggest that Africa was only waiting 'for Germany's, for Prussia's forming hand'.[23]

The close association of liberalism, the nation and overseas empire found its most vivid expression in the deliberations of the Frankfurt National Assembly in 1848/49.[24] There, the issues of controlled emigration into settlement colonies and the establishment of a German fleet found almost unanimous support throughout political factions. Advocates of overseas colonisation were convinced that only a strong nation-state led by Prussia could marshal the financial and military means to organise and maintain imperial dependencies overseas. The ultimate failure of the revolutionary Parliament in 1848/49 may have dealt a severe blow to the early colonial movement, but as soon as the oppression of political associations was relieved by the end of the 1850s, the policies of imperial expansion reappeared on the agenda of the foremost liberal lobbying group for national unification, the *Nationalverein*, and its political representatives in the North-German diet, the National Liberals.[25] After the ballot and the nation-state, the foundation of a colonial empire was the third genuinely liberal project that Chancellor Bismarck put into practice when he granted state protection to a handful of randomly acquired African territories in 1884/5.

Mobility and migration

At the heart of the liberal 'imperialism from below' was a discourse of 'migrationist colonialism'[26] that emerged in the 1840s as a response to the waves of emigrants leaving the German states as a consequence of population growth, the capitalisation of land and labour, agrarian crises and pauperism. Around 90 per cent of the six million emigrants who left Germany before the First World War went to the United States, and it was exactly the absence of a German Empire to prevent this drain that made migration so important for German propagandists of empire. The parallels between the ebbs and flows of German emigration and the concern with 'New Germanies' overseas were significant. Public debate increased in intensity whenever the number of Germans leaving their homeland reached a temporal apex, particularly in the 1840s and 1880s. Both decades witnessed the formation of associations advocating the re-organisation of emigration within the confines of a German Empire to be. Twenty-two societies advocating German settlement and colonisation in North America formed in 1848/49 alone, whereas the 1880s saw the emergence of the *Deutsche Kolonialgesellschaft* (DKG) as the *Kaiserreich's* foremost colonialist pressure group.

In the course of the nineteenth century, the discourse of migrationist colonialism was tied up with questions of national identity and social order. Some nationalist-minded liberals saw organised emigration to German colonies as a way to solve the 'social question' and as a 'safety valve' to prevent social unrest; others called for a German Empire to enable emigrants to retain their 'Germanness' and prevent cultural assimilation in host societies abroad. In the wake of 1848, a significant shift in terminology took place. The term *Auswanderer* (emigrants), although not vanishing from German political language, was gradually replaced by the term *Auslandsdeutsche* (Germans abroad). Whereas *Auswanderer* implied dispersal and mobility without return, the reference to diasporic Germans reclaimed them for the imagined national community, suggesting that being German was a timeless cultural and ethnic baggage that could not be lost or corrupted even when separated for generations from the German *Heimat*.[28] Nationhood was thus not only negotiated in terms of inclusion and exclusion within the German territories in Europe. The German diaspora was included within the national imaginary. In the wake of the *völkisch*, racial and geopolitical radicalisation of nationalism around 1900, the figure of the *Auslandsdeutsche* came to underwrite ideas of a pan-German *Volksgemeinschaft* spread around the globe. The fact that only a tiny minority of these diasporic Germans actually ended up in the territories acquired as German colonies provided an additional boost to propagandists calling for the further extension of empire.[29] Above all, the dispersal of millions of German expatriates in Eastern Europe and the New World made the maintenance of national bonds, the propagation of German language and culture and the export of *Deutschtum* a key theme of German cultural policy abroad.[30]

'Race' and science

Migration was not only a one-way movement of Germans spreading outwards over the globe. Research over the last few years has uncovered a considerable presence of migrants from the colonies as well as people of African origin in the *Kaiserreich*, the Weimar Republic and the Third Reich. Some were educated in mission schools, others again worked as language instructors or carved out a niche for themselves as black bit parts in early film. Others became active anti-imperialists, for example in the *League for the Defence of the Negro-Race* founded in Berlin in 1928. Indeed, with a presence of several thousands of colonial migrants mainly from Cameroon, Berlin became a centre for the organisation of anti-colonial resistance, thanks largely to the organising activities of the communist humanitarian Willi Münzenberg. The experiences of these black migrants varied depending on background and on the social and occupational context of their presence. Yet everyday discrimination was pervasive and culminated in the Nazi years when people of colour were subjected to sterilisation, deportation and death in concentration camps.[31] As yet, our knowledge about colonial migrants and the black presence in Germany is still fragmentary. Apart from recovering silenced biographies, further research could also help to assess the evolution and stabilisation of that allegedly natural and 'stubborn white' German identity after forced decolonisation in 1919 and the creation of a virtually homogeneous 'racial state' under National Socialism.[32] In any case, the colonial experience was instrumental in forging the close association of *Deutschtum* with whiteness as it confronted German society directly with issues of racial difference, 'miscegenation' and citizenship. The politics of inclusion and exclusion under conditions of global mobility, imperial expansion and the racial foundation of colonial rule are reflected in the debates about the reform of German citizenship law that lasted from 1898 until the final enactment of the law in 1913.[33] The growing number of *Auslandsdeutsche*, their legal status and their obligations towards the state and vice versa was one issue the law had to deal with, migrant foreign workers another, and a third was a small yet growing number of 'mixed-race' marriages, especially in Germany's foremost settler colony, South-West Africa. According to German citizenship law, citizenship status was inherited from the father, so that any descendant from a relationship between German man and 'native' woman would have been entitled to German citizenship. From 1905 onwards, 'mixed marriages' were banned in South-West Africa, East Africa and Samoa in order to 'protect the white race' and preserve the 'purity' of the German *Volkskörper*.[34] Since this practice neither pertained to all colonies nor to Germany itself, nationalist lobby associations like the DKG and the

Pan-German League were quick to link the issue with the ongoing metro-politan debate about citizenship. They advocated a legal definition of German citizenship on racial and biological grounds to the explicit exclu-sion of non-Whites, and their identification of nationality with whiteness found adherents among the colonial administration, civil servants, scien-tists and conservative politicians. Social Democrats and the Catholic Centre Party were opposed to a legal ban of mixed marriages in Parliament. However, they were less motivated by an anti-racialist stand than because such a ban would promote promiscuity and prostitution and curb the sovereign rights of individual men. Ultimately, the revised citizenship law was not organised along the 'eugenicist concept of racialised citizenship' (Pascal Grosse) proposed by the *völkisch* right-wing. But the very fact of the debates about miscegenation in the colonies matters, for even those who opted for the patriarchal right of the white father hardly questioned the racial basis of German nationhood. In any case, citizenship law was redefined to bind the German diaspora back to their homeland: whereas earlier, citizenship expired ten years after the person had left the country, the reformed law in 1913 foresaw the reten-tion of citizenship and, thanks to the *ius sanguinis*, allowed it to be passed on to descendants who had never set foot on German territory.[35]

Although German citizenship law was not racialised in 1913, colonial rule proved nonetheless important for the biopolitics of race in Germany. On the one hand, colonial rule can be interpreted as a laboratory for a social order that rested upon a biological and eugenicist understanding of society.[36] On the other hand, the colonial empire provided 'material' – including skulls and corpses of Herero killed in the Namibian War – and, after the turn of the century, a 'field' for the sciences concerned with study of man, such as ethnology and anthropology. Only a small number of German anthropologists tried to make their discipline directly relevant to colonial rule, yet, as Andrew Zimmerman has argued, anthropology was the way in which the human sciences tried to come to terms with the world order imperialism created. While the discipline's anti-humanism, the emergence of 'racial hygiene' and Eugen Fischer's application of the Mendelian laws of heredity to human genetics prepared the ground for Nazi racial policies, the writings on African culture by the ethnologist Leo Frobenius inspired anti-imperialist intellectuals like Léopold Sédar Senghor, the first president of independent Senegal.[37]

Anthropology and ethnology show that empire provided an important framework for the development and institutionalisation of several scien-tific disciplines. Tropical medicine was indispensable for European settle-ment, but also for the conservation of an African labour force, at least in Germany's tropical colonies. The discipline had also a powerful appeal to German society after the loss of the colonies when the research of the bacteriologist Robert Koch and the discovery of an effective drug to treat human sleeping sickness were glorified as proofs of German scientific humanitarianism. The myth of the Germans as benign colonisers was continued after the Second World War in the cult around the Alsatian-born missionary doctor Albert Schweitzer and his hospital in Lambarene (situated in today's Gabon).[38] Geography, botany and veterinary science helped to rationalise resource extraction and determine to what uses the land could be put, while ethnographic museums and their natural history counterparts collected and ordered the colonial world for metropolitan audiences.[39] Geography in particular was wedded to imperialism in a symbiotic relationship. As early as the 1870s, geographers and ethnologists had formed a *German Society for the Exploration of Equatorial Africa*. Merging with the German branch of the Belgian King Leopold II's *Association Internationale Africaine*, the society's expeditions not only served the production of geographical knowledge, but pursued the explicit aim of opening up the continent for 'culture, trade and traffic'.[40] From the turn of the century onwards, geographers provided the ideological background for imperialist territoriality with their notions of space as *Lebensraum* and the associated naturalisation of conquest and colonisation.[41]

Botany was another field of science that benefited from empire. Countless diplomats and *Auslandsdeutsche* were mobilised to report on tropical cash crops, and naturalists of diverse scientific backgrounds swarmed to East Asia and the Americas to study plants that might be suitable for introduction into Germany's tropical colonies. Institutions based in Berlin were instrumental in coordinating around 300 such expeditions between 1884 and 1914. The Berlin Botanical Garden was officially declared the centre of colonial botany in 1891 and quickly developed into a node of complex transimperial networks of seeds and knowledge. There are no studies yet that analyse its situation at the intersection of political ecology, colonial rule and scientific endeavour, but the institution provides a prime example of transnational cooperation as a viable strategy for the imperial latecomer to make up for deficits in funding and knowledge.[42]

Commodities and markets

Empire as an attempt to organise global mobility during the nineteenth and twentieth centuries to the benefit of the nation was not restricted to people but also pertained to commodities and raw materials. The classic theories of imperialism saw the globalisation of markets and the dynamics of industrialist capitalism as the actual driving forces behind

European expansion in the late nineteenth century. Hans-Ulrich Wehler understood imperial expansion as an anti-cyclical policy of state intervention upon ample evidence from contemporary economists who regarded colonies as indispensable extensions of national markets. Imperialism comprised neo-mercantilist efforts of the advanced industrial economies to dominate 'undeveloped' areas, secure markets and raw materials in order to re-territorialise the control over people and resources on a global scale. This aspect of imperialism as attempted economic re-territorialisation has been somewhat eclipsed since globalisation has become the dominant interpretative framework for economic developments prior to the First World War;[43] whereas the post-colonial re-interpretation of relationships between 'metropole and colony' has hardly dealt with manifest structures of economic exploitation and the modification of social and political structures in those societies turned into markets by European capital.

Contemporaries such as the Leipzig geographer Kurt Hassert were convinced that, thanks to 'mental superiority, the power of capital and his keen entrepreneurial spirit' the tradesman was best qualified for pioneering *Kulturarbeit* abroad.[44] Hassert's praise of the imperial businessman was part of his campaign to extend the teaching of geography in schools and the foundation of further commercial and economic colleges in Germany. Between 1898 and 1910, *Wirtschaftshochschulen* were founded in Leipzig, Aachen, Frankfurt, Berlin, Cologne, Mannheim and Munich, and economists with close ties to the colonial movement were often instrumental in their foundation. Curricula made sure that students were educated broadly in international trade, economic geography, the study of commodities and colonial policy, sometimes even including a field trip to a German colony.[45] The mindset thus conveyed structured the world into resources, markets and exploitable values. In cities that could not offer academic training in applied economics, such as Stuttgart or Bremen, local industrialists established *Export-* or *Handelsmuseen* to give manufacturers an impression of possible markets, foreign tastes and how to design commodities for overseas export. The initial emphasis on economic geography in these museums soon gave way to the more general aim of ethnographic representations of the colonial world.

The European overseas empires provided an opportunity for capitalists, tradesmen and enterprising individuals. Investment in overseas ventures affected thousands of European shareholders, and important segments of the German economy, like the textile industry, came to depend on raw materials imported from either colonial territories under direct European rule, or states where the Western powers used their diplomatic, military or economic leverage to impose their interests. The industrial production of soap needed palm-oil; car manufacturers demanded oil and rubber. In 1907, Germany imported 15,809 tons of rubber to supply a fledgling automobile industry. Roughly one-third of this was imported from the Brazilian Amazon, around 20 per cent from the Congo Free State, where European enterprises not only procured rubber under conditions of slavery, oppression and brutal violence, but also produced their own forms of 'commodity racism'. An inferior variety of South American rubber was dealt on the market under the label 'Negroheads'.[46]

The territories Germany actually acquired as colonies played only a minor part in German foreign investment. Still, German enterprises tried to render the colonies productive for cash crops and raw materials, and individual companies managed to make a sound profit from them. Colonial administrations could open markets, provide infrastructure or exclude competitors, and there were many cases in which companies and enterprising individuals turned to the state to receive diplomatic support or protection for their commercial ventures. The state also cooperated with banks and enterprises to pursue geostrategic interests, as in the case of the Baghdad Railway, or in the informal establishment of a strong German economic foothold in the African colonies of Portugal.[47] Banks and capitalists followed the flag or framed their economic and financial objectives in the national interest if this promised to pay. But generally, economic and nationalist aims and rationalities were not necessarily congruent and the structures of empire were but one opportunity for capitalist enterprises: the empires of others and zones of informal influence were, at least in the German case, more important. The arms manufacturers Krupp and Mauser, for example, were engaged in stiff competition with British, French and Austrian competitors and could rely on the help of German consulates and the Foreign Office when they capitalised on political tensions to gain war orders in Latin America or modernise the weaponry of Russia or the Ottoman Empire.[48]

Probably the most marked connection between German society and the transformation of nature into exploitable resources in colonial territories was established by the imperialism of consumption. European consumers acted as 'absent-minded imperialists' who played a major part in turning the 'new Imperialism' since the 1880s into a vast project of resource extraction and commoditisation. The global political ecology of consumption, especially of German society, has, until recently, been a neglected field of historical research.[49] Ebbs and flows notwithstanding, the 'ghost acreage' and environmental transformation induced by the German consumption of tropical products only increased in the course of the twentieth century. *Kolonialwaren* (colonial groceries) like sugar, cocoa, coffee or spices became accessible to wider strata of society; new ones, like bananas, were added. Some 'exotic' commodities retained their exclusive tinge of social distinction. Such was the case, for example, with the colourful plumage of exotic egrets and birds of paradise that became fashionable among aristocratic and middle-class women around the turn of the century. The moral outrage caused by the killing of rare species resulted in a campaign that linked the preservation of birds in colonial New Guinea with feminism and female suffrage in Wilhelmine Society. Male conservationists framed the feather fashion in a language of anti-feminism, while female activists condemned plumage as offending the innate female care for the living and thereby women's stake in society.[50] Exotic feathers were not the only instance of moralised consumption: there were also protests against the 'Arab' slave trade, the near-extinction of African elephants for their ivory, and the atrocities associated with rubber extraction in central Africa or Putumayo.[51] Activist networks in European societies embraced these cases to different degrees and at different times, often with Britain in the lead. Further research could examine how far these differences resulted from diverging structures of attention and information towards imperial matters, or if they also reflect national differences in the perception of humanitarian duties to the distant.[52]

The consumption of exotic plumage remained exclusive, whereas other commodities imported from colonial settings, like cocoa or coffee, percolated down the social scale to become products of mass consumption. If contemporary statistics are to be believed, the consumption of bean coffee per head in Germany rose from 30 litres in the 1870s to over 50 litres in 1911 – a demand that spurred the colonisation of tropical landscapes through coffee monocultures, particularly in German East Africa and Cameroon, but also in Guatemala. By 1913, there were 170 German-owned coffee farms in the country which produced more than a third of Guatemala's coffee. German consumption not only induced widespread landscape change, but also turned Guatemala into a theatre of trade rivalries between Germany and the United States.[53]

The imperialism of consumption led to ever-more refined marketing strategies through which colonial commodities promoted European ideas of race, gender and the colonial order.[54] Although procured from Brazil or Guatemala, the marketing of coffee associated the product almost exclusively with the more popular exoticism of Africa.[55] Adverts and labels depicted the black population as servants or plantation workers and featured images of African flora and fauna, effacing the ecological transformation of a plantation-based economy through stereotypes of exotic paradise. According to David Ciarlo, the exoticism of advertising was increasingly complemented by an outright colonialist imagery from 1900 onwards, and the older, paternalist trope of the 'Moor' was gradually replaced by the racialist and inferior 'Native'.[56] Capitalist marketing strategies reified global asymmetries of race and power, while race and empire helped to sell products and stir the desire for the exotic. The reach of these commodities was not only extended socially, but also geographically. *Kolonialwarenläden* were mushrooming throughout the country and linked the exotic lure of the colonial world with the everyday life of ordinary people even in the provinces.[57]

Missions

The nineteenth century witnessed a considerable religious revival in European societies and it was the century when Christianity became a 'world religion' in the sense of actual global presence. The relationship between imperialism and Christian missions is complex and contradictory, ranging from outright anti-imperialism and criticism of colonial rule to complicity and cooperation.[58] In many instances, missions were 'on the spot' before the colonisers came, and they remained there when the colonisers left again. With their knowledge of local structures, they lent invaluable service to official colonialism as interpreters, as in the case of the Rhenish Missionary Society that preceded German colonialism in Namibia for half a century.[59] Germany's acquisition of colonies in 1884/85 provided an enormous boost for missionary activities: there was an influential pro-colonial wing among the missions, several new societies were founded with the explicit aim to evangelise the German colonies, and the context of anti-slavery agitation that accompanied the establishment of colonial rule in East Africa provided Catholic missionary societies with an opportunity to convince official authorities of their national reliability after decades of *Kulturkampf*. There are good reasons to qualify the impact of Christian missions as cultural imperialism and 'colonisation of consciousness', as the Comaroffs did,[60] but equally good reasons to point to the manifold ways in which the evangelised appropriated the opportunities of the missions for their own ends. Missions shared with imperialism a Manichean worldview and the 'propensity to universalise the self'. They cultivated a self-perception of the missionary as heroic bearer of salvation and civilisation, yet the missionaries' abstinence of violence, their theological anthropology, their often mediating role in conflicts, and their organisational autonomy set them apart from political empire.[61]

In the context of this discussion, the transnational and transcontinental networks established by Christian missionary societies are relevant for at least three reasons. First, the religious revival in Europe motivated an unprecedented increase in Christian missionary activity both overseas and within Europe. The number of Protestant missionary societies, for example, increased from a mere five around 1800 to more than 550 a century later.[62] The explosion of missionary activity propelled thousands of men and women of an often humble rural background to Africa, Asia and Latin America. Missionaries produced knowledge and representations of indigenous societies that were spread through sermons and Christian newspapers. Missions forged links between the internal periphery of villages that were home to missionary societies, like St Ottilien or Neuendettelsau, with the external periphery of villages in Asia, Africa and Latin America. Missionary societies also established connections across borders in Europe. The revival of the Catholic mission in the first half of the nineteenth century originated in France, whereas the infrastructure of British missionary societies provided an opportunity for German Protestants to enter overseas service. Especially in the early years of the London-based Church Missionary Society (CMS), the number of Germans far outweighed missionaries recruited in Britain itself.[63]

Second, overseas missions were supported by a growing infrastructure of local associations that participated in the networks of missionary societies through donations and prayer, but also as recipients of missionary images, exhibitions and slide-shows. The global divide between Christians and pagans was inscribed into the routines of individual religiosity. A local study of religious culture in the south-western diocese of Rottenburg, for example, shows how associations like the Catholic *Franziskus-Xaverius-Missionsverein*, founded in Aachen in the early 1840s, became rooted at the parish level. From the 1860s onwards, the *Missionsverein* established local branches in several village parishes with the intention to support the work of catholic missionaries overseas by alms and daily prayer.[64] Unlike the Colonial Society or Navy League, whose social constituency was largely urban, commodities and the church also reached people in the country. As late as the 1960s, German churches featured collecting boxes called *Nickneger* which nodded thankfully whenever a coin was inserted in support of the mission.[65]

Finally, recent research has drawn attention to the entanglements of *innere* and *äußere Mission* and the analogies between a civilising mission at home and overseas.[66] The Catholic evangelisation of the rural masses and the evangelisation of 'heathens' both emanated from the religious revival in the 1830s. Towards the end of the century, Protestant missionaries like Friedrich von Bodelschwingh advocated 'education for labour' as a programmatic cure for the ills of the social question at home and the colonial question abroad. Language and metaphors used to describe a proletariat in need of salvation and education 'within' and primitive *Naturvölker* abroad were strikingly similar, and probably so were the social constituencies of social work within Germany and missionary work abroad: deaconesses originally trained for social work in Germany were often sent abroad.[67] However, more empirical research is needed to determine the degree to which mission established tangible reciprocal entanglements between 'metropole' and 'colony'.

Imperialism as social formation

If the mission's relationship towards empires was ambivalent and at times contradictory, the societies and associations that were formed to support and promote German *Welt-* and colonial policies provide safer ground for tracing the impact of empire on German society. The *Kolonialgesellschaft* was the *Kaiserreich*'s foremost pressure group and government-leaning think-tank in colonial matters and developed its own consultative commissions for government and business.[68] The Pan-German League separated from the DKG in 1891 with a broader and more radical agenda of developing a racially defined Germany into a cultural and political world power. The anti-Polish *Ostmarkenverein* (German Association for the Eastern Provinces) propagated the Germanisation of Prussia's Eastern Provinces, whereas the *Deutsche Flottenverein* (Navy League, DFV) was the one association that managed to attract a mass membership of close to 350,000 individual members by 1914.[69] This figure does not include the considerable corporate membership in the Navy League, such as by veterans' associations, sailing clubs or student fraternities.

The role of these nationalist pressure groups in 'reshaping the German right', side-stepping parliamentary dispute, professional organisation and the popularisation of an uncompromisingly racialist and expansionist nationalism has been rightly emphasised. Their propaganda took politics to the streets, for example during the so-called 'Hottentot elections' in 1907 when controversies over financing the costly war in Namibia brought the empire home to dominate parliamentary elections. Their objectives, although propagated with varying emphasis, crystallised around ideas of Germanness rooted in race and *Volk*, colonial expansion and a strong fleet. In order to determine the degree to which these associations popularised empire and imperial expansion in German society, four aspects need to be assessed: the social reach of these associations in terms of membership and social background, the role of women, the geographical spread of societies, and the resonance of their activities in the local context.

As Geoff Eley has observed, the nationalist pressure groups 'shared a common sociology' of recruiting among the professions, businessmen, entrepreneurs, academics and civil servants: an educated middle class. Despite the DKG's explicit aim to popularise the German colonies among vast swathes of society, its bourgeois bias against the working classes restricted its social reach and accounts partially for the association's comparative weakness in numbers: after thirty years of colonial rule, the DKG comprised slightly over 40,000 members. Ultimately, the society's emphasis was on effective lobbying of political decision-makers and the practical concern to make the colonies work economically rather than the creation of a popular mass movement.

Its impressive membership numbers notwithstanding, the Navy League found few supporters among factory and other industrial workers. Membership figures should, therefore, not be too readily equated with social impact. Not everybody sympathising with the views of the agitationist groups expressed their support by payment of a membership fee, whereas multiple membership in the various agitational associations was a common feature at the local level. Internal structure and the geographical reach of local and regional sections were equally important. The Navy League's structure after the turn of the century was marked by an 'effective blend of centralisation of resources and participation by regional activists in the central organs' that allowed for concerted nationwide agitation and a feeling of 'grassroot' participation. The top-down organisation of the DKG, on the other hand, assigned the local branches little impact beyond suggesting motions for discussion at the annual meetings of the society. Both associations remained urban phenomena. By 1914, the DKG was organised in 462 local sections in cities all over Germany, the colonies and among Germans abroad, whereas the *Flottenverein* featured roughly 3,000 local branches in 1906. In most cases the local establishment of DFV-branches was unthinkable without the help of state bureaucracy, and, the ruling Princes of the German states usually served as honorary patrons.[70]

Membership in the imperialist associations was essentially, but by no means exclusively, male. The *Ostmarkenverein* was the first to introduce a separate branch for women, which amounted to 3,400 female members in 1914. The *Flottenverein* followed suit in 1905, mobilising the most women among the imperialist organisations with a membership of 60,000 by 1914, while the female branch of the DKG, founded in 1907, featured 18,700 women members and boasted its own publication entitled *Kolonie und Heimat*. Its activities often rivalled those of the Women's Red Cross Association for the Colonies, a slightly larger and older society dedicated to promote nursing and schooling as the 'cultural tasks' of women in the colonies. These societies may have shared the general objectives of the male associations they sprang from, but they mixed them with aspirations for a less restrained social role of women.

[176]

The importance of empire for the Women's League of the DKG, for example, lay in the possibility for framing the traditional roles of women – marriage, motherhood and reproduction – as essential for the mainte-nance of the racial and social order in a colonial society that first and fore-most consisted of men. The debates about 'miscegenation', fears of racial degeneration and men 'going native' without the civilising influence of white women assigned the German woman, in the Eastern Marches as well as in the overseas colonies, a pivotal place as the bearer of German culture. This elevation of the women's role as indispensible border guards of race and family was appealing to conservative nationalists, but the 'female cultural imperialism' also provided a framework in which an extension of female participation in politics and society could be articu-lated.[71] However, it remains to be determined how far the colonial expe-rience actually transcended the imperial public sphere and gained relevance for the overall structuring of gender dynamics in German society.

On a practical level, the Women's League of the DKG engaged in the mediation of jobs for women in the colonies, institutionalised prepara-tory colonial education for women, acquired books for the establishment of libraries in the colonies, and organised the migration of women willing to wed German farmers (561 between 1908 and 1914). The eagerness of German women to emigrate far outstripped the capacities of the League: between 1907 and 1914, the League allegedly received up to fifty enquiries per day.[72] In the context of the local branches in Germany, female engagement took on the form of raffles, charity events, meetings, fundraising, lecture series and other forms of colonial propaganda and information sharing. In these activities, they differed little from the male chapters, which also organised lecture series, exhibitions, plays and cele-brations, touted for new members and, in bigger cities, entertained libraries and club rooms. Unfortunately, these activities and their embed-ding in municipal society have been a neglected aspect of scholarly treat-ment so far.[73] Further research is vital to assess the regional geography of imperialist agitation and the degree to which not only nation and *Heimat*,[74] but also *Kolonie* and *Heimat* were implicated in each other.

Imperial representations in popular culture

In any case, the nation-wide organisations were by no means the only transmitters of global political aspirations to the respective localities. Local chapters rivaled and co-operated with other formations of civil society that shared an imperial world-view, such as economic and geographic societies. Equally, spectacles and celebrations of the fleet were not promoted by the *Flottenverein* alone. Jan Rüger has underlined the 'local factor' of municipal self-representation and imperial self-fashioning that motivated the celebration of the navy in the German port cities.[75] Moreover, as suggestive as the number of local branches may sound, not every *Ortsverein* burst into frantic activity. Complaints about feeble public responses to lectures, patriotic celebrations and recruitment initiatives may well have been the rule rather than the exception.[76]

An assessment of the provincial geography of imperialism at the 'grassroot' level is essential to determine the geographical and social reach of colonial discourses and images, and their many manifestations in a mass popular culture that emerged in the last quarter of the nineteenth century. Cinemas, zoos, variety shows, fairs, popular theatres and a literary mass market enabled people to encounter the colonial world as adventure, danger and exotic spectacle. Recent research has shown that colonial literature not only shaped and corroborated the world-view of a middle-class readership, but was also received among those that were usually not represented in the social formations of organised imperialism in Germany. In a case study of working-class reading cultures in Leipzig between 1890 and 1914, John Phillip Short has shown how working-class readers gained access to travelogues, war stories, ethnographic accounts, pulp fiction and other colonial literature. The organised colonial movement and its reading rooms played a minor part in the distribution of colonial literature among working-class readers, who could access such works through colportage dealers as well as in public and even socialist libraries. An occasional study of a Dresden public librarian in 1910 established that out of fifty proletarian library users, ten read books on African exploration and colonisation. Working-class reading habits constitute yet another variety of social imperialism: not inculcated as ideology from above, but embraced and imagined from below.[77]

Short's observations on the reading habits of Leipzig workers confirm the limited appeal of institutionalised imperialism to workers, but they should also warn against too neat an equation of a fascination with exoticism, adventure and colonial fantasies with support for the ways German imperialism was acted out politically. The reports about dock workers' conversations compiled by the Hamburg police in the *Kaiserreich*, for example, contain compelling evidence for workers' criticism of the theatricality and brutality of German *Weltpolitik*.[78] Moreover, the books preferred by workers also substantiate Susanne Zantop's thesis that German imperiality was hardly contained within the framework of the colonial empire. The events in Karl May's best-selling adventure novels – the number of volumes sold in German has been estimated at 50 million since 1892 – may have been situated at the American frontier and in a Middle Eastern 'Orient', but his peculiar blend of fact, fiction and the imaginary brimmed with colonialist attitudes and a 'nonoccupational imperialism' that shaped its readers' assumptions about non-Western peoples.[79] The popularity of May's novels proves that even after the acquisition of colonies, imperialist values and claims to German superiority continued to be negotiated in arenas that had no direct relation to the colonial empire. Such fantasies exerted their influence alongside a colonial literature inspired by the German colonial encounter. The genocidal war against the Herero in South-West Africa inspired Gustav Frenssen's bestselling *Peter Moors Fahrt nach Südwest*, an instant success that was translated into several languages and remained a popular read for German youth until 1945.[80] An author often overlooked but utterly influential beyond the borders of Germany, was the hunter-naturalist Carl Georg Schillings. His travelogues of hunting and wildlife conservation developed into one of Germany's best-selling publications in the field of colonial literature.[81] His books, which were also translated into English and Dutch, combined the thrill and heroism of big-game hunting with urgent calls for wildlife preservation and a melancholic regret for a wilderness passing away under the march of civilisation. What earned the books their outstanding reception was their lavish illustration with photographs of Africa's wildlife. Schillings had supplemented rifle with camera in order to document a wilderness he believed to be irretrievably doomed. The result was a visual archive of roughly two thousand photographs, most of which showed live animals in their natural surroundings. These pictures not only turned the books into best-sellers, but made Schillings' lantern-slide lectures a popular success in Germany and beyond. Wherever Schillings turned up with his pictures, lecture halls were packed. His use of the latest technology enabled him to visualise Africa as a timeless paradise of wildlife which became one of the most persistent misrepresentations of the continent's ecology. The heterotopia of Africa as an original wilderness animated by primeval game not only naturalised the alleged backwardness of the continent and legitimised colonial intervention. It also motivated European engagement in wildlife conservation and established a powerful myth on which a growing industry of hunting and wildlife tourism could thrive throughout the twentieth century.[82]

The new media of photography and film played a generally vital part in the popularisation of imperial themes and values. Recent research has drawn attention to the pervasive reach of imperial images in the medium of postcards,[83] and cinematography lent itself perfectly to the communication of 'progress' and the worth of colonies. The DKG and the *Flottenverein* were quick to embrace this fledgling medium.[84] Between 1905 and 1908, the DKG provided its local branches with short films to arouse support and interest in Germany's colonies. The films juxtaposed the exoticism of African dances with the visual proof of German colonial achievement. In many instances, free admission and co-operation with trade associations, the Navy League and school parties followed by evening screenings for adults, were used to enhance the popular appeal of the early colonial films. Wolfgang Fuhrmann has been able to confirm forty-five screenings in German cities, including metropoles such as Berlin and Frankfurt as well as provincial cities such as Calbe or Sigmaringen. In some cities, the screenings were an undeniable success – 8,000 school children were alleged to have seen colonial films in February 1907 – but there are also reports about extremely poor turnouts. The varying attendance was surely influenced by ticket prices, yet middle-class domination of the local branches may also have played a role. So did competition from the spread of commercial travelling cinematographers. Significantly, the DKG only occasionally published the number of viewers of its film screenings, and in early 1909, the Colonial Society abandoned the circulation of colonial films among its local branches. Attendance figures of the DKG were nowhere near the numbers the *Flottenverein* managed to mobilise by its visualisations of the fleet as imperial icon: in its peak year, the Navy League attracted an attendance of over 870,000 for 512 screenings in 1905 alone. Comparing the cinematographic campaigns of *Flottenverein* and *Kolonialgesellschaft* indicates that sea and fleet were probably the more appealing medium through which impe-rialist aspirations were articulated before the First World War.[86] The failure of the DKG also shows that the empire of meaning and images had its limits, although film increased significantly in importance as a medium to negotiate 'race', articulate imperial claims and boost colonial revisionism after the loss of the colonies.[87]

The medium of film is a good example of how the popular culture of empire, though brimming with jingoist zeal and rivalry, was decidedly transimperial in character. In the early 1900s, cinematographic material from the European colonies was still a rare treasure and quickly became a commodity that circulated on transimperial markets. The film 'Progress of civilisation in German East Africa', for example, was shot and distrib-uted by the French company *Pathè frères* before it was screened in Germany in 1911. In many respects, the visual language of colonialism was exchangeable unless nationalised by contextualising information: the heroic white male in bright tropical suit surrounded by half-naked natives was an icon that circulated throughout Europe. There is no dearth of further examples. The 'Anglo-German naval theatre' (Jan Rüger) was a stage shared by both nations, its spectacles characterised equally by antagonism and transfer. Instilling imperial values into young people through scouting was a striking example of transimperial exchange. Published in a climate of anxiety about degenerating imperial vigour and masculinity in Britain, Sir Robert Baden-Powell's *Scouting for Boys* was enthusiastically received by two German officers plagued by similar concerns after the experience of the Namibian War. They translated the English original within a year and popularised scouting as *Jungdeutschlands Pfadfinderbuch* in 1909. The first edition was heavily criticised for its enthusiastic embrace of a foreign idea, so that further editions subsequently 'Germanised' the concept of scouting.[88]

Another institution that transmitted and reinforced imperial values was the cultural displacement of indigenous people for commercial spectacle in the form of travelling exhibitions. These shows accompanied the heyday of European imperialism between the 1870s and 1930s and became more or less synonymous with the Hamburg animal trader Carl Hagenbeck, who included *Völkerschauen* ('shows of peoples') in his business portfolio from the 1870s onwards. Hagenbeck was certainly not the only impresario of such displays – there were around 400 exhibitions between 1875 and 1930 – but he was by far the most important one. At least one hundred *Völkerschauen* were organised by his company which became a popular brand throughout Europe and the United States. Hagenbeck's troupes ranged from a handful of 'Laplanders' or a glamorous 'Ceylon caravan' of seventy craftsmen accompanied by twenty-five elephants in 1886, to the colossal *Völkerschau* of 'India' in 1911.[89] The commercial ethnographic exhibitions were mass events in their day. A group of 'Nubians' presented by Hagenbeck in the Berlin Zoological Garden in 1878 attracted 62,000 visitors on one single Sunday, while the Ceylonese exhibition that toured Europe in 1886 was visited by over a million people during the ten weeks it performed in Paris.

It has been argued that the *Völkerschauen* are best understood not as colonial propaganda, but within the logic and competition of contemporary commercial spectacles.[90] This is surely adequate: the shows' foremost aim was to attract the masses and earn money, and the exoticising reach of the shows constantly transcended the borders of Germany's colonial empire. The exhibited people had to be spectacular, novel and needed to conform to clichés. Ultimately, European heads, not the indigenous performers, defined what counted as authentic cultural expressions of indigeneity. Within this framework of spectacle, references to the 'colonial' and/or 'scientific' were strategies to arouse interest. Members of the German colonial society saw the exhibition of colonial subjects as a powerful means to bring empire to the 'man on the street'[91] and impresarios did not miss out on the opportunity to familiarise metropolitan audiences with people from the newly acquired colonial territories. Hagenbeck imported a troupe from Cameroon in 1885, and the great Berlin commercial exhibition of 1896 featured over 100 people from the German colonies, rendering even the commercial civilisation of the

Swahili on the East African Coast a 'tribe'. Such 'tribalisation' of African societies and the reduction of their complexity to the performance of an allegedly authentic primitivism was powerfully underwritten by the contemporary standing of *Völkerschauen* as 'anthropological' or 'commercial ethnographic exhibitions' where representative foreign peoples 'performed' either their ethnic group or country of origin 'for the satisfaction of visual pleasure and the dissemination of anthropological knowledge'.[92] Indeed, armchair anthropologists sometimes measured the bodies of people on display as objects of science. This framing as 'scientific' vanished in the late 1890s with increasing middle-class criticism of proletarian audiences and mounting concern about the precarious ethics and potentially disruptive implications of the shows. In 1901, the import of people from the German colonies for purposes of display in *Völkerschauen* was prohibited, as leading members of the DKG feared that the behaviour of the European audience might compromise the respect of the colonial subjects for their self-acclaimed masters.

Völkerschauen may not have been a straightforward means of colonial propaganda, but they were definitely expressions of an imperial mindset. The shows made remote places accessible through the bodily presence of dislocated people. They framed the arbitrary categorisations of these people as authentic; they visualised cultural difference as inferiority and underwrote the fundamental Western dichotomy of a world split into 'civilised' and 'native' peoples. It was more than mere coincidence that the preferred places of the exhibitions were zoological gardens: *Wild und Wilde, Natur und Naturvölker*, place and people were closely associated in late nineteenth and early twentieth century European evolutionary thinking. Finally, the techniques and practices of display of the *Völkerschauen* influenced other contemporary forms of themed environments. Three years after Hagenbeck's Ceylonese exhibition had attracted the masses of the French capital, 'human showcases' from the French colonies were included in the universal exhibition in Paris in 1889.[93] Commercial and colonial exhibitions in Germany also borrowed from the *Völkerschauen* to add some spectacle to their presentations of goods and commodities. Between 1896 and 1940, about forty colonial exhibitions propagated the colonial idea, connecting the empire overseas with cities throughout Germany. They were a particularly popular instrument after 1918 to keep the memory of the colonies alive: in the 1930s, there was a standardised set of displays that toured through various German cities, combining the staple message of the necessity of colonies for a *Volk ohne Raum* with local exhibitors interested in associating themselves with the colonial cause. However, public attention never reached the popularity of the *Völkerschauen* and attendance was estimated at around 880,000 for all colonial exhibitions between 1936 and 1938.[94]

5.2 The Colonial Monument, Bremen, erected 1931–32.
(Courtesy German Colonial Society collection, Frankfurt University Library)

Conclusion: imperialism without colonies after 1919

German imperialism did not end with the forced decolonisation of the Versailles treaties. Indeed, German society was never as unanimously pro-colonial as in the years immediately after the country was officially excluded from Europe's civilising project in Africa and Oceania in 1919. Colonial literature and novels flourished, and the activities of the imperialist associations continued, perhaps even increased as the social reach and appeal of the DKG eroded over the years. Klaus Hildebrand's voluminous analysis of the colonial question between 1919 and 1945 has revealed the extent of propaganda and popularisation through literature, exhibitions, radio and film in the 1920s and 1930s, decades that witnessed the mushrooming of monuments to communicate Germany's claim to its lost colonial empire.[95] The loss of the colonies was certainly no interruption in the realm of phantasies, projects and projections. The arguments that Germany needed colonial territories for their resource as markets and for settlement continued unabated, at times demanding the restitution of the former colonies, at times unleashed from concrete geographies. Authors of popular non-fiction like Herman Soergel, Anton Zischka, Colin Ross or Hans Dominik reframed the *mise en valeur* and development of Africa as a joint European task that would enable

Germany's re-entry among the civilising nations. The loss of empire ushered in a new round of geo-political phantasies that rendered whole continents, if not the globe, as objects of German technology and engineering. In this sense, important continuities persisted after imperialism was transformed into ideologies of 'development' after the Second World War.[96]

However, there is also consensus among historians that the restoration of the former colonial empire was hardly a core issue in Nazi ideology, whose politics of imperial expansion focused primarily on the 'German East'.[97] Recent research has tried to integrate overseas and continental imperialism into one analytical field, essentially in two ways.[98] One approach extends concepts and terminology applied to understand exterminatory Nazi politics back into Germany's colonial past. Controversies have centered around two issues: possible continuities in the bureaucratic practice of racial segregation and miscegenation; and an archaeology of 'genocide' that linked the exterminatory warfare against the Herero and Nama between 1904 and 1907 with the Holocaust and the war of annihilation at the Eastern Front of the Second World War.[99] As yet, many of the arguments put forward in support of the continuity thesis are based upon structural analogies rather than an empirically grounded discussion of causalities or research into the biographical and institutional transmission of genocidal ideas and practices. Birthe Kundrus has exposed structural similarities, but also important differences between the 'anthropological racism' based upon skin colour and anti-Semitism as the racialist radicalisation of older religious prejudices to stigmatise the Jews as outsiders within German society.[100] On a conceptual level, the analytical purchase of a concept like 'genocide' is questionable for its stress on intentionality obscures decisive differences in the respective contexts of excessive colonial violence and the Nazi genocide.[101] Finally, reservations have been registered concerning the alleged exceptionality of German colonial practices compared with the excessive violence of Western colonialism in general. The second approach has proceeded the other way round. Scholars have applied the terminology of colonial studies to German racialist expansion and hegemony in Eastern Europe in order to trace possible transfers and similarities between Eastern Africa and the Eastern Marches of Prussia. Are there identifiable avenues of transfer through which the colonial experience overseas was transferred to Eastern Europe during the First World War and after? And how 'colonial' was Nazi settlement policy in Eastern Europe?[102] Indeed, terminology suggests that contemporaries might have seen Africa and the 'German east' as two related frontiers of German territoriality: whereas *innere Kolonisation* referred to the governmental attempt to encourage German settlement in Prussia's eastern provinces in order to strengthen the

German (and Protestant) element vis-à-vis the Polish majority, *äußere Kolonisation* denoted the German claim to territory overseas. Both terms are based upon an ideology of settlement and a colonial gaze that discerned nothing but unused and undeveloped land inhabited by an inferior race that needed the German colonist to be transformed into a proper *Kulturlandschaft*.[103] The German claim to land in the Eastern Marches was historically anchored in the *Ostkolonisation* of the Middle Ages and was powerfully underwritten by a literature brimming with civilised superiority and racialist othering.[104] Yet, the analytical 'colonisation' of Germany's 'Eastern frontier' also runs the risk of over-stretching the analytical potential of the colonial terminology and thereby over-looking important differences between empire-building overseas and continental empire-building. The perpetration of violence on the Eastern front by hundreds of thousands of German soldiers in the First World War was probably more significant for the brutalisation of German military culture than the experience of a few thousand in South-West Africa. As yet, these questions are still unresolved, but they draw scholarly attention to hitherto neglected fields of analysis. In order to assess similarities and differences between the 'internal' and 'external' forms of racial discrimination, scholars need to explore the relationship between Jews and the German colonial project. While figures like colonial secretary Bernhard Dernburg or the botanist Otto Warburg suggest that the bourgeois integration of Jewish Germans was also visible in the administration of the colonial empire, the Zionist quest for a Jewish homeland was in complex ways tied in with Europe's imperial colonialism. Theodor Herzl's *Jewish State* drew inspiration from Theodor Hertzka's socialist colonial utopia *Freeland*, and leading Zionists tapped the knowledge and networks of German and British colonialism to facilitate Jewish colonisation. This was true not only for settlement in Palestine but also for plans to establish a Jewish colony in East Africa, the so-called 'Uganda Plan' that was much debated and ultimately abandoned in the first decade of the twentieth century. Jewish participation in German colonialism as well as the Zionists' inscription of Jews into a European discourse of whiteness, civilisation, and colonisation should caution against overstressing the colonial roots of European genocide or too ready equations of 'internal' and 'external' discourses of racialist discrimination.[105] They also invite further investigations into the peculiar postcoloniality of German society after 1918. Brought about by forced decolonisation, it was on the one hand marked by the absence of a drawn-out struggle of colonial subjects who asserted their equality and independence and by the creation of a homogeneous 'racial state' under Nazi rule on the other. The effects of both on German attitudes towards 'racial' difference before and after 1945 are yet to be fully explored.[106]

***

This study has argued that the impact of empire upon German social, cultural and political life was pervasive, despite but also because of the short period of formal colonial rule. However, it has also elucidated some of the limits and problems associated with the assessment of the impact of empire on the German metropole. This metropole was hardly as homogeneous as the term suggests. The entanglements created by missions, commodities, pressure groups, literature and popular culture affected different strata of German society, and their impact also varied geographically. Analyses of colonial discourse and cultural figurations need, therefore, to be anchored in their geographical as well as in their social reach and reflect the existence of fragmented public spheres. Their translation into the structures and institutions through which imperial power has been exercised also needs to be determined if the claim to the close association of culture, power and knowledge is to have any concrete meaning.[107]

German imperial expansion was accompanied by several forms of social as well as popular imperialism – economic policies in the colony to protect German labour at home, workers' access to colonial literature, colonialism as a social formation and the popular spectacles of *Völkerschauen* – all of which were different from the manipulative idea of social imperialism described by Hans-Ulrich Wehler. Yet, they substantiate his claim of the existence of a widespread 'ideological consensus' in German society as well as the social importance of imperialism. Ironically, it was Wehler who has recently disputed the importance of the German colonial empire on German society. That empire, he argued, was so short-lived and diasporic that it could not reasonably be compared with the empires of France and Britain.[108] Yet, exactly such a comparative approach is necessary, combined with a sensitivity to transfer. In their competition to territorialise and control the mobility of people, resources and commodities, imperialists constantly learned from each other. Concepts, people and practices transcended the boundaries of empire, particularly in economy and the sciences, but also in imperial folklore. The transfer of knowledge and practices especially from the British Empire was a central characteristic of a German imperiality that constantly oscillated between rivalry and emulation. The psychological consequences of this double bind have yet to be explored, and so have the implications of these transfers for the making of a 'European' culture of imperialism. A comparative approach is also vital to allow for balanced assessments of the peculiarities as well as the commonalities of the social and cultural impact of empire on German society. A comparative study of students in Tübingen and Cambridge in the first three decades of the twentieth century has exposed the differing importance of the colonial empire in the self-perception of students.[109] Whereas the Cambridge students excluded the few students from India and constantly debated the power and position of the British Empire, the German colonies did not matter for students in Tübingen. Non-white students were no problem for they did not exist, and racialised identities were forged by excluding Jewish fellow students. For all the recovery of colonial traces, representations and repercussions in the German metropole, future research should be equally wary not to colonise history with concepts that ultimately obscure more than they reveal.

Notes

1 Brigitte Rauer, Volker Ullrich, 'Textilarbeiterstreik in Crimmitschau 1903/04', *Geschichtsdidaktik* 1983, pp. 126–51; Kathleen Canning, *Languages of Labor and Gender. Female Factory Work in Germany, 1850—1914* (Ithaca 1996), pp. 195f., 261–8.

2 Thomas Theodor Heine, 'Durchs dunkelste Deutschland. 13. Crimmitschau', *Simplicissimus*, 8/2 (19th January 1904), p. 337.

3 Henry Morton Stanley, *In Darkest Africa, or the Quest, Rescue and Retreat of Emin, Governor of Equatoria* (London 1890). (German translation: *Im dunkelsten Afrika. Aufsuchung, Rettung und Rückzug Emin Pascha's, Gouverneurs der Aequatorialprovinz* [Leipzig 1890]).

4 Sven Beckert, 'Emancipation and empire: reconstructing the worldwide web of cotton production in the age of the American Civil War', *American Historical Review*, 109 (2004), pp. 1405–38.

5 Thaddeus Sunseri, '"The Baumwollfrage". Cotton colonialism in German East Africa', *Central European History*, 34 (2001), pp. 31–51, and *Vilimani. Labor Migration and Rural Change in Early Colonial Tanzania* (Portsmouth 2002).

6 Especially Lewis H. Gann, 'Marginal colonialism: the German case', in Arthur J. Knoll and Lewis H. Gann (eds), *Germans in the Tropics. Essays in German Colonial History* (New York, Westport, London 1987), pp. 1–17.

7 Uta G. Poiger, 'Imperialism and empire in twentieth-century Germany', *History and Memory*, 17 (2005), pp. 117–43, p. 123.

8 For a survey, see the 'Forum: the German colonial imagination', *German History*, 26 (2008), pp. 251–71.

9 Hans-Ulrich Wehler, 'Bismarck's imperialism 1862–1890', *Past & Present*, 48 (1970), pp. 119–55.

10 Pascal Grosse, 'What does German colonialism have to do with National Socialism?', in Eric Ames, Marcia Klotz and Lora Wildenthal (eds), *Germany's Colonial Pasts* (Lincoln NE 2005), pp. 115–34, p. 116. Poiger, 'Imperialism and empire', pp. 117–24. See, however, Dirk van Laak, *Über alles in der Welt. Deutscher Imperialismus im 19. und 20. Jahrhundert* (Munich 2005).

11 Frederick Cooper, *Colonialism in Question: Theory, Knowledge, History* (Berkeley LA, London 2005), p. 154.

12 Sebastian Conrad, *Globalisierung und Nation im Deutschen Kaiserreich* (Munich 2006), pp. 316–36.

13 John M. MacKenzie, '"Mutual goodwill and admiration" or "jealous ill-will"? Empire and popular culture', in Dominik Geppert and Robert Gerwarth (eds), *Wilhelmine Germany and Edwardian Britain: Essays on Cultural Affinity* (Oxford 2008), pp. 91–114; David Blackbourn, "As dependent on each other as man and wife': cultural contacts and transfers', in ibid., pp. 15–40.

14 Jürgen Osterhammel, *Europe, the 'West' and the Civilizing Mission. The 2005 Annual Lecture* (London 2006).

15 Susanne M. Zantop, *Colonial Fantasies: Conquest, Family and Nation in Precolonial Germany (1770–1870)* (Durham 1997); Sara Friedrichsmeyer, Sara Lennox and Susanne Zantop, 'Introduction', in their *The Imperialist Imagination: German Colonialism and Its Legacy* (Ann Arbor 1998), pp. 1–32.

16 Gabriele Dürbeck, *Stereotype Paradiese. Ozeanismus in der deutschen Südseeliteratur 1815–1914* (Tübingen 2007); Axel Dunker (ed.) *(Post-)Kolonialismus und deutsche Literatur* (Bielefeld 2005).

17 Kirsten Belgum, *Popularizing the Nation. Audience, Representation, and the Production of Identity in Die Gartenlaube, 1853–1900* (Lincoln NE, London 1998), pp. 143–82.

18 Matthew Fitzpatrick, *Liberal Imperialism in Germany: Expansionism and Nationalism, 1848–1884* (New York, Oxford 2008), pp. 177–204.

19 Felix Driver, *Geography Militant: Cultures of Exploration and Empire* (Oxford 2001).

20 Nic Leonhardt, *Piktorial-Dramaturgie. Visuelle Kultur und Theater im 19. Jahrhundert (1869–1899)* (Bielefeld 2007), pp. 257–78.

21 Martin Bossenbroek, '"Dickköpfe" und "Leichtfüße". Deutsche im niederländischen Kolonialdienst des 19. Jahrhunderts', in Klaus J. Bade (ed.), *Deutsche im Ausland – Fremde in Deutschland. Migration in Geschichte und Gegenwart* (Munich 1993), pp. 249–54; Eckard Michels, *Deutsche in der Fremdenlegion 1870–1965. Mythen und Realitäten* (Paderborn 1999); Ulrike Kirchberger, 'German scientists in the Indian forest service: a German contribution to the Raj?', *Journal of Imperial and Commonwealth History*, 29 (2001), pp. 1–26; Peter Boomgaard, 'Colonial forest policy in Java in transition, 1865–1916', in Robert Cribb (ed.), *The Late Colonial State in Indonesia: Political and Economic Foundations of the Netherlands Indies 1880–1942* (Leiden 1994), pp. 117–37.

22 Stefan von Senger and Etterlin, *Neu-Deutschland in Nordamerika. Massenauswanderung, nationale Gruppenansiedlungen und liberale Kolonialbewegung, 1815–1860* (Baden-Baden 1991).

23 Willibald Huger von der Oelsnitz, *Denkschrift zur Erhebung Preußens zu einer See-, Kolonial- und Weltmacht ersten Ranges* (Berlin 1847), pp. 8, 33f.

24 Frank Lorenz Müller, 'Imperialist ambitions in Vormärz and revolutionary Germany: the agitation for German settlement colonies overseas, 1840–1849', *German History*, 17 (1999), pp. 346–88, Fitzpatrick, *Liberal Imperialism*; but see already and Hans Fenske, 'Imperialistische Tendenzen in Deutschland vor 1866', *Historisches Jahrbuch*, 97/98 (1978), pp. 336–83.

25 Fitzpatrick, '"A fall from grace?" National unity and the search for naval power and colonial possessions 1848–1884', *German History*, 25 (2007), pp. 135–61, p. 152–6.

26 Woodruff D. Smith, *The Ideological Origins of Nazi Imperialism* (Oxford 1986), p. 21.

27 Von Senger and Etterlin, *Neu-Deutschland*, pp. 459–61.

28 Bradley D. Naranch, 'Inventing the *Auslandsdeutsche*: emigration, colonial fantasy, and German national identity 1848–71', in Ames, Klotz and Wildenthal (eds), *Germany's Colonial Pasts*, pp. 21–40; Sebastian Conrad, 'Globalization effects: mobility and nation in Imperial Germany, 1880–1914', *Journal of Global History*, 3 (2008), pp. 43–66.

29 Philippa Söldenwagner, *Spaces of Negotiation. European Settlement and Settlers in German East Africa, 1900–1914* (Munich 2006); Daniel J. Walther, *Creating Germans Abroad: Cultural Policies and Settler Identities in Namibia* (Ohio 2002).

30 Rüdiger vom Bruch, *Weltpolitik als Kulturmission. Auswärtige Kulturpolitik und Bildungsbürgertum in Deutschland am Vorabend des Ersten Weltkrieges* (Paderborn 1982); Jürgen Kloosterhuis, *'Friedliche Imperialisten': Deutsche Auslandsvereine und auswärtige Kulturpolitik.* (Frankfurt 1994).

31 Marianne Bechhaus-Gerst, Reinhard Klein-Arendt (eds), *AfrikanerInnen in Deutschland und schwarze Deutsche – Geschichte und Gegenwart* (Münster 2004); Peter Martin, 'Schwarze Sowjets an Elbe und Spree?', in Martin and Christine Alonzo (eds), *Zwischen Charleston und Stechschritt. Schwarze im Nationalsozialismus* (Munich 2004), pp. 178-193; Patricia Mazon, Reinhild Steingrover (eds), *Not so Plain as Black and White: Afro-German Culture and History, 1890–2000* (Rochester 2005).

32 Lora Wildenthal, 'Notes on a history of "imperial turns" in German history', in Antoinette Burton (ed.), *After the Imperial Turn: Thinking with and through the Nation* (Durham, London 2003), pp. 144–56, p. 151.
33 Howard Sargent, 'Diasporic citizens: Germans abroad in the framing of German citizenship law', in Krista O'Donnell, Nancy Ruth Reagin and Renate Bridenthal (eds), *The Heimat Abroad: The Boundaries of Germanness* (Ann Arbor MI 2005), pp. 17–39; Dieter Gosewinkel, *Einbürgern und Ausschließen. Die Nationalisierung der Staatsangehörigkeit vom Deutschen Bund bis zur Bundesrepublik Deutschland* (Göttingen 2001).
34 Lora Wildenthal, *German Women for Empire, 1884–1945* (Durham 2001), pp. 79–130; Birthe Kundrus, *Moderne Imperialisten. Das Kaiserreich im Spiegel seiner Kolonien* (Köln, Weimar, Wien 2003); Frank Becker (ed.), *Rassenmischehen – Mischlinge – Rassentrennung. Zur Politik der Rasse im deutschen Kolonialreich* (Stuttgart 2004); Krista O'Donnell, 'Home, nation, empire: domestic Germanness and colonial citizenship', in O'Donnell, Reagin and Bridenthal (eds) *The Heimat Abroad,* pp. 40–57.
35 Sargent, *Diasporic Citizens,* p. 30.
36 Pascal Grosse, *Kolonialismus, Eugenik und bürgerliche Gesellschaft in Deutschland 1850–1918* (Frankfurt 2000).
37 Andrew Zimmerman, *Anthropology and Antihumanism in Imperial Germany* (Chicago, London 2001); Anja Laukötter, *Von der 'Kultur' zur 'Rasse' – vom Objekt zum Körper? Völkerkundemuseen und ihre Wissenschaften zu Beginn des 20. Jahrhunderts* (Bielefeld 2007).
38 Wolfgang U. Eckart, *Medizin und Kolonialimperialismus. Deutschland 1884–1945* (Paderborn 1997); Nina Berman, *Impossible Missions? German Economic, Military, and Humanitarian Efforts in Africa* (Lincoln 2004), pp. 63–82.
39 Hugh Glenn Penny, *Objects of Culture: Ethnology and Ethnographic Museums in Imperial Germany* (Chapel Hill NJ, London 2002); Susanne Köstering, *Natur zum Anschauen. Das Naturkundemuseum des deutschen Kaiserreichs 1871–1914* (Köln, Weimar, Wien 2003).
40 *Mittheilungen der afrikanischen Gesellschaft in Deutschland,* 1 (1878), p. 3.
41 Jürgen Zimmerer, 'Im Dienste des Imperiums. Die Geographen der Berliner Universität zwischen Kolonialwissenschaften und Ostforschung', *Jahrbuch für Universitätsgeschichte,* 7 (2004), pp. 73–99; Smith, *Ideological Origins of Nazi Imperialism;* David Thomas Murphy, *The Heroic Earth: Geopolitical Thought in Weimar Germany, 1918–1933* (Kent 1997).
42 Eugene Cittadino, *Nature as the Laboratory: Darwinian Plant Ecology in the German Empire, 1880–1900* (Cambridge 1990); Michael Flitner, *Sammler, Räuber und Gelehrte. Die politischen Interessen an pflanzengenetischen Ressourcen 1895–1995* (Frankfurt, New York 1995), pp. 21–50; Christopher Conte, 'Imperial science, tropical ecology, and indigenous history: tropical research stations in northeastern German East Africa, 1896 to the present', in Gregory Blue (ed.), *Colonialism and the Modern World: Selected Studies* (Armonk, London 2002), pp. 246–61.
43 Cornelius Torp, *Die Herausforderung der Globalisierung. Wirtschaft und Politik in Deutschland 1860–1914* (Göttingen 2005).
44 Kurt Hassert, 'Die geographische Bildung des Kaufmanns', in *Zu Friedrich Ratzels Gedächtnis* (Leipzig 1904), pp. 153–68, p. 167.
45 Gunther Herbert Zander, *Gründung der Handelshochschulen im deutschen Kaiserreich* (1898–1919), PhD thesis, Cologne 2004; Keith Tribe, 'Business education at the Mannheim Handelshochschule', *Minerva,* 32 (1994), pp. 158–85, p. 165; Ulrich Soénius, *Koloniale Begeisterung im Rheinland während des Kaiserreichs* (Cologne 1992), pp. 91–3.
46 C. Freyer, 'Uebersicht über Gummi', *Jahrbücher für Nationalökonomie und Statistik,* 93 (1909), pp. 777–800; Michael Edward Stanfield, *Red Rubber, Bleeding Trees. Violence, Slavery, and Empire in Northwest Amazonia, 1850–1933* (Albuquerque 1998); Martin Ewans, *European Atrocity, African Catastrophe: Leopold II, the Congo Free State and its Aftermath* (London, New York 2002).

[189]

47 Gregory P. Nowell, *Mercantile States and the World Oil Cartel, 1900–1939* (Ithaca 1994), pp. 64f.; Dietrich Eichholtz, *Die Bagdadbahn, Mesopotamien und die deutsche Ölpolitik bis 1918. Aufhaltsamer Übergang ins Erdölzeitalter* (Leipzig 2007); Boris Barth, *Die deutsche Hochfinanz und die Imperialismen. Banken und Außenpolitik vor 1914* (Stuttgart 1995).

48 Jonathan A. Grant, *Rulers, Guns and Money: The Global Arms Trade in the Age of Imperialism* (Harvard 2007), pp. 128f.

49 For Britain, see Joanna de Groot, 'Metropolitan desires and colonial connections: reflections on consumption and empire', in Catherine Hall and Sonya O. Rose (eds), *At Home with the Empire: Metropolitan Culture and the Imperial World* (Cambridge 2006), pp. 166–274. Excellent for the US: Richard P. Tucker, *Insatiable Appetite: The United States and the Ecological Degradation of the Tropical World* (Lanham 2007).

50 Bernhard Gissibl, 'Paradiesvögel: Kolonialer Naturschutz und die Mode der deutschen Frau am Anfang des 20. Jahrhunderts', in Johannes Paulmann (ed.), *Ritual Macht Natur. Europäisch-ozeanische Beziehungswelten in der Neuzeit* (Bremen 2005), pp. 131–54.

51 Klaus J. Bade, 'Antisklavereibewegung in Deutschland und Kolonialkrieg in Deutsch-Ostafrika 1888–1890. Bismarck und Friedrich Fabri', *Geschichte und Gesellschaft*, 3 (1977), pp. 31–58; A.W. Schreiber, 'Die Deutsche Kongo-Liga', *Koloniale Rundschau* (1911), pp. 753–70.

52 For a comparative approach of the social responses to the Armenian atrocities see Margaret L. Anderson, '"Down in Turkey, far away": human rights, the Armenian massacres, and Orientalism in Wilhelmine Germany', *Journal of Modern History*, 79 (2007), pp. 80–111.

53 Andreas Eckert, 'Comparing coffee production in Cameroon and Tanganyika, c. 1900 to 1960s: land, labor, and politics', in William Gervase Clarence-Smith and Steven Topik (eds), *The Global Coffee Economy in Africa, Asia, and Latin America, 1500–1989* (Cambridge 2003), pp. 286–311; Volker Wünderich, 'Die Kolonialware Kaffee von der Erzeugung in Guatemala bis zum Verbrauch in Deutschland. Aus der transatlantischen Biographie eines "produktiven" Genußmittels (1860–1895), *Jahrbuch für Wirtschaftsgeschichte* (1994), pp. 37–60; Robert G. Williams, *States and Social Evolution: Coffee and the Rise of National Governments in Central America* (Chapel Hill, London 1994), pp. 164–74.

54 Angelika Epple, 'Das Auge schmeckt Stollwerck. Die Bildsprache einer "Weltmarke" zwischen Imperialismus und Globalisierung', *Werkstatt Geschichte*, 45 (2007), pp. 13–32; Stefanie Wolter, *Die Vermarktung des Fremden. Exotismus und die Anfänge des Massenkonsums* (Frankfurt, New York 2005); Poiger, *Imperialism and Empire*; and David Ciarlo, *Advertising Empire, Consuming Race: Colonialism, Commerce and Visual Culture in Germany, 1887–1914* (forthcoming).

55 Laura Rischbieter, 'Globalisierungsprozesse vor Ort. Die Interdependenz von Produktion, Handel und Konsum am Beispiel "Kaffee" zur Zeit des Kaiserreichs', *Comparativ*, 17 (2007), pp. 28–45.

56 David Ciarlo, Globalizing German colonialism', *German History*, 26 (2008), pp. 285–98, and 'Rasse konsumieren. Von der exotischen zur kolonialen Imagination in der Bildreklame des Wilhelminischen Kaiserreichs', in Birthe Kundrus (ed.), *Phantasiereiche: Zur Kulturgeschichte des deutschen Kolonialismus* (Frankfurt, New York 2003), pp. 135–79; Joachim Zeller, *Bilderschule der Herrenmenschen. Koloniale Reklamesammelbilder* (Berlin 2009).

57 Michael Kamp, 'Zwischen Alltag und Exotik. Kolonialwaren in München', in Helmut Zedelmaier and Anne Dreesbach (eds), *'Gleich hinterm Hofbräuhaus Waschechte Amazonen'. Exotik in München um 1900* (Munich, Hamburg 2003), pp. 99–115.

58 Rebekka Habermas, 'Mission im 19. Jahrhundert. Globale Netze des Religiösen', *Historische Zeitschrift*, 287 (2008), pp. 629–79; Klaus J. Bade (ed.), *Imperialismus und Kolonialmission. Kaiserliches Deutschland und koloniales Imperium* (Wiesbaden 1982); Horst Gründer, *Christliche Heilsbotschaft und weltliche Macht. Studien zum Verhältnis von Mission und Kolonialismus* (Münster 2004), Artur Bogner, Bernd

Holtwick and Hartmann Tyrell (eds), *Weltmission und religiöse Organisationen. Protestantische Missionsgesellschaften im 19. und 20. Jahrhundert* (Würzburg 2004).

59 Nils Ole Oermann, *Mission, Church and State Relations in South West Africa under German Rule (1884–1915)* (Stuttgart 1999).

60 John L. and Jean Comaroff, *Of Revelation and Revolution: Christianity, Colonialism, and Consciousness in South Africa* (Chicago 1991).

61 Tyrell, 'Weltgesellschaft, Weltmission und religiöse Organisationen', in Bogner, Holtwick and Tyrell (eds), *Weltmission*, pp. 13–134; Thorsten Altena, *'Ein Häuflein Christen mitten in der Heidenwelt des dunklen Erdteils'. Zum Selbst- und Fremdverständnis protestantischer Missionare im kolonialen Afrika 1884–1918* (New York, Munich, Berlin 2003).

62 Gerald Faschingeder, 'Missionsgeschichte als Beziehungsgeschichte. Die Genese des europäischen Missionseifers als Gegenstand der Historischen Anthropologie, *Historische Anthropologie*, 10 (2002), pp. 1–30, p. 15.

63 Ulrike Kirchberger, *Aspekte deutsch-britischer Expansion. Die Überseeinteressen der deutschen Migranten in Grossbritannien in der Mitte des 19. Jahrhunderts* (Stuttgart 1999), pp. 247–77; Paul Jenkins, 'The Church Missionary Society and the Basel Mission: an early experiment in Inter-European cooperation', in Kevin Ward and Brian Stanley (eds), *The Church Mission Society and World Christianity, 1799–1999* (Grand Rapids, Richmond 2000), pp. 43–65.

64 Henning Pahl, *Die Kirche im Dorf. Religiöse Wissenskulturen im gesellschaftlichen Wandel des 19. Jahrhunderts* (Berlin 2006), p. 187.

65 Jan Nederveen Pieterse, *White on Black: Images of Africa and Blacks in Western Popular Culture* (New Haven CT, London 1992), p. 71.

66 Alexa Geisthövel, Ute Siebert and Sonja Finkbeiner, '"Menschenfischer". Über die Parallelen von innerer und äußerer Mission um 1900', in Rolf Lindner (ed.), *'Wer in den Osten geht, geht in ein anderes Land'. Die Settlementbewegung in Berlin zwischen Kaiserreich und Weimarer Republik* (Berlin 1997), pp. 27–47; Conrad, *Globalisierung und Nation*, pp. 74–123; Habermas, *Mission im 19. Jahrhundert*.

67 Christine Keim, *Frauenmission und Frauenemanzipation. Eine Diskussion in der Basler Mission im Kontext der frühen ökumenischen Bewegung (1901–1928)* (Münster 2005), pp. 90–2.

68 Richard V. Pierard, The German Colonial Society, 1892–1914. PhD thesis, University of Iowa, 1964; Imre Josef Demhardt, *Die deutsche Kolonialgesellschaft 1888–1918. Ein Beitrag zur Organisationsgeschichte der deutschen Kolonialbewegung* (Wiesbaden 2002).

69 For the latest survey, see Peter Walkenhorst, *Nation, Volk, Rasse: Radikaler Nationalismus im Deutschen Kaiserreich, 1890–1914* (Göttingen 2007). Influential studies include Rainer Hering, *Konstruierte Nation. Der Alldeutsche Verband 1890–1939* (Hamburg 2003); Roger Chickering, *We Men who feel most German: A Cultural Study of the Pan-German League, 1886–1914* (Boston MA 1984); Geoff Eley, *Reshaping the German Right: Radical Nationalism and Political Change after Bismarck*, 2nd ed. (Michigan MI 1991); Jens Oldenburg, *Der deutsche Ostmarkenverein 1894–1934* (Berlin 2002). A brief comparison between German and British agitationist groups is included in Daniel K.W. Trepsdorf, *Afrikanisches Alter Ego und europäischer Egoismus. Eine komparative Studie zur Selbst- und Fremdperzeption im Wilhelminischen Deutschland und Spätviktorianischen Großbritannien (1884–1914)* (Dresden 2006).

70 Eley, *Reshaping the German Right*, pp. 121f.

71 See Birthe Kundrus, 'Empire, colonies, and ethnic identities in modern German history', in Karen Hagemann and Jean H. Quataert (eds), *Gendering Modern German History: Rewriting Historiography* (London, New York 2007), pp. 86–106; Wildenthal, *German Women for Empire*; Katharina Walgenbach, *Die weiße Frau als Trägerin deutscher Kultur. Koloniale Diskurse über Geschlecht, Rasse und Klasse im Kaiserreich* (Frankfurt, New York 2005); Anette Dietrich, *Weiße Weiblichkeiten. Konstruktionen von „Rasse' und Geschlecht im deutschen Kolonialismus* (Bielefeld 2007).

72 Wildenthal, *German Women for Empire*, p. 163.

[191]

73 See, however, Soénius, *Koloniale Begeisterung*, and several contributions in Ulrich van der Heyden and Joachim Zeller, *Kolonialismus hierzulande. Eine Spurensuche in Deutschland* (Erfurt 2007).

74 Alon Confino, *The Nation as a Local Metaphor: Württemberg, Imperial Germany and National Memory, 1871–1918* (Chapel Hill 1997); Celia Applegate, *A Nation of Provincials: The German Idea of Heimat* (Berkeley 1990).

75 Jan Rüger, *The Great Naval Game: Britain and Germany in the Age of Empire* (Cambridge 2007), pp. 96–103.

76 Anne Dreesbach and Michael Kamp, 'Kolonialismus in München', in Van der Heyden and Zeller, *Kolonialismus hierzulande*, pp. 68-74.

77 John Phillip Short, 'Everyman's colonial library: imperialism and working-class readers in Leipzig, 1890–1914', *German History*, 21 (2003), pp. 445–75.

78 Richard J. Evans (ed.), *Kneipengespräche im Kaiserreich. Die Stimmungsberichte der Hamburger politischen Polizei 1892–1914* (Reinbek 1989), pp. 360, 396f.

79 Nina Berman, 'Orientalism, imperialism, and nationalism: Karl May's "Orientzyklus"', in Friedrichsmeyer, Lennox and Zantop (eds), *The Imperialist Imagination*, pp. 51–67.

80 Medardus Brehl, *Vernichtung der Herero. Diskurse der Gewalt in der deutschen Kolonialliteratur* (Munich 2007).

81 Carl Georg Schillings, *Mit Blitzlicht und Büchse. Neue Beobachtungen in der Wildnis inmitten der Tierwelt von Äquatorial-Ostafrika* (Leipzig, 1905), and *Der Zauber des Elelescho* (Leipzig 1906).

82 Bernhard Gissibl, 'The Nature of Colonialism: Hunting, Conservation and the Politics of Wildlife in the German Colonial Empire', PhD thesis, University of Mannheim, 2009.

83 Volker M. Langbehn (ed.), *German Colonialism, Visual Culture, and Modern Memory* (London 2009).

84 See Wolfgang Fuhrmann, 'Locating early film audiences: voluntary associations and colonial film', *Historical Journal of Film, Radio and Television*, 22 (2002), pp. 291–304; and his unpublished PhD thesis on Propaganda, Science and Entertainment. Early Colonial Cinematography: A Case Study in the History of Early Nonfiction Cinema, Utrecht, 2003.

85 Martin Loiperdinger, 'The beginnings of German film propaganda: the Navy League as traveling exhibitor, 1901–1907', *Historical Journal of Film, Radio and Television*, 22 (2002), pp. 305–13.

86 Patrick Ramponi, 'Weltpolitik maritim. Meer und Flotte als Medien des Globalen im Kaiserreich', in Silvia Marosi et al. (eds), *Globales Denken: Kulturwissenschaftliche Perspektiven auf Gobalisierungsprozesse* (Frankfurt 2006), pp. 99–120.

87 See Tobias Nagl, *Die unheimliche Maschine. Rasse und Repräsentation im Weimarer Kino* (Munich 2009); Wolfgang Struck, 'Die Geburt des Abenteuers aus dem Geist des Kolonialismus. Exotistische Filme in Deutschland nach dem Ersten Weltkrieg', in Kundrus (ed.), *Phantasiereiche*, pp. 263–81.

88 Alexander Lion, *Maximilian Bayer, Jungdeutschlands Pfadfinderbuch* (Leipzig 1909; 1911, 1912, 1914).

89 Eric Ames, *Carl Hagenbeck's Empire of Entertainments* (Seattle, London 2008); Sierra A. Bruckner, 'Spectacles of (human) nature: commercial ethnography between leisure, learning, and schaulust', in Hugh Glenn Penny and Matti Bunzl (eds), *Worldly Provincialism: German Anthropology in the Age of Empire* (Ann Arbor 2003), pp. 127–55; Nigel Rothfels, *Savages and Beasts: The Birth of the Modern Zoo* (Baltimore MD, London 2002).

90 Anne Dreesbach, *Gezähmte Wilde. Die Zurschaustellung 'exotischer' Menschen in Deutschland 1870–1940* (Frankfurt, New York 2005).

91 Grosse, 'Zwischen Privatheit und Öffentlichkeit. Kolonialmigration in Deutschland, 1900–1940', in Kundrus (ed.), *Phantasiereiche*, pp. 91–109, pp. 96f.

92 *Meyers Konversations-Lexicon* (1893), quoted after Ames, *Empire of Entertainments*, p. 65.

93 See Paul Greenhalgh, *Ephemeral Vistas: The Expositions Universelles, Great Exhibitions and World's Fairs, 1851–1939* (Manchester 1988), pp. 82–111.
94 Stefan Arnold, 'Propaganda mit Menschen aus Übersee. Kolonialausstellungen in Deutschland, 1896–1940', in Robert Debusmann and János Riesz (eds), *Kolonialausstellungen – Begegnungen mit Afrika?* (Frankfurt 1995), pp. 1–24; Klaus Hildebrand, *Hitler, NSDAP und koloniale Frage (1919–1945)* (Munich 1969), pp. 428f.
95 Joachim Zeller, *Kolonialdenkmäler und Geschichtsbewußtsein. Eine Untersuchung der kolonialdeutschen Erinnerungskultur* (Frankfurt 2000).
96 Dirk van Laak, *Imperiale Infrastruktur. Deutsche Planungen für eine Erschließung Afrikas 1880 bis 1960* (Paderborn 2004).
97 Karsten Linne, *Deutschland jenseits des Äquators. Die NS-Kolonialplanungen für Afrika* (Berlin 2008); Mark Mazower, *Hitler's Empire: Nazi Rule in Occupied Europe* (London 2008).
98 Philipp Ther, 'Imperial instead of national history: positioning modern German history on the map of European empires', in Alexei Miller and Alfred Rieber (eds), *Imperial Rule* (Budapest 2004), pp. 47–68.
99 See e.g. Jürgen Zimmerer, 'The birth of the *Ostland* out of the spirit of colonialism: a postcolonial perspective on the Nazi policy of conquest and extermination', *Patterns of Prejudice*, 39 (2005), pp. 197–219; Benjamin Madley, 'From Africa to Auschwitz: how German South West Africa incubated ideas and methods adopted and developed by the Nazis in Eastern Europe', *European History Quarterly*, 35 (2005), pp. 429–64.
100 Birthe Kundrus, 'Von Windhoek nach Nürnberg? Koloniale 'Mischehenverbote' und die nationalsozialistische Rassengesetzgebung', in Kundrus (ed.), *Phantasiereiche*, pp. 110–31.
101 Isabel V. Hull, *Absolute Destruction: Military Culture and Practices of War in Imperial Germany* (Ithaca, London 2005); Birthe Kundrus, 'Kontinuitäten, Parallelen, Rezeptionen. Überlegungen zur "Kolonialisierung" des Nationalsozialismus', *Werkstatt Geschichte*, 43 (2006), pp. 45–62; Robert Gerwarth and Stephan Malinowski: 'Der Holocaust als "kolonialer Genozid"? Europäische Kolonialgewalt und nationalsozialistischer Vernichtungskrieg', *Geschichte und Gesellschaft*, 33 (2007), pp. 439–66.
102 See Vejas G. Liulevicius, *War Land on the Eastern Front: Culture, National Identity and German Occupation in World War I* (Cambridge 2000); Wendy Lower, *Nazi Empire-Building and the Holocaust in Ukraine* (Chapel Hill 2005); Robert L. Nelson (ed.), *Germans, Poland, and Colonial Expansion to the East 1850 through the Present* (New York 2009).
103 On the ideology of Germans' singular ability to rationalize and tame the 'wild East' see David Blackbourn, *The Conquest of Nature: Water, Landscape, and the Making of Modern Germany* (New York, London 2006), pp. 251–309.
104 Kristin Kopp, 'Constructing racial difference in colonial Poland', in Ames, Klotz and Wildenthal (eds), *Germany's Colonial Pasts*, pp. 78–96; Elizabeth A. Drummond, *Protecting Poznania. Germans, Poles, and the Conflict over National Identity, 1886–1914* (Ann Arbor 2007); Liulevicius, 'The languages of occupation: vocabularies of German rule in Eastern Europe in the world wars', in Nelson (ed.), *Germans, Poland, and Colonial Expansion to the East*, pp. 121–39.
105 Mark Levene, 'Herzl, the Scramble, and a meeting that never happened: revisiting the notion of an African Zion', in Eitan Bar-Yosef and Nadia Valman (eds), *'The Jew' in Late-Victorian and Edwardian Culture: Between the East End and East Africa* (Houndmills, New York 2009), pp. 201–20; Shalom Reichman and Shlomo Hasson, 'A cross-cultural diffusion of colonization: from Posen to Palestine', *Annals of the Association of American Geographers*, 74 (1984), pp. 57–70; Derek J. Penslar, 'Zionism, colonialism, and technocracy: Otto Warburg and the Commission for the Exploration of Palestine, 1903–7', *Journal of Contemporary History*, 25 (1990), pp. 143–60.
106 See Heide Fehrenbach, *Race after Hitler: Black Occupation Children in Postwar Germany and America* (Princeton 2005).

107 Birthe Kundrus, 'Von der Peripherie ins Zentrum. Zur Bedeutung des Kolonialismus für das Deutsche Kaiserreich', in Sven Oliver Müller and Cornelius Torp (eds.), *Das Deutsche Kaiserreich in der Kontroverse* (Göttingen 2009), pp. 359–73.
108 Hans-Ulrich Wehler, 'Transnationale Geschichte – der neue Königsweg historischer Forschung?', in Gunilla Budde, Sebastian Conrad and Oliver Janz (eds), *Transnationale Geschichte. Themen, Tendenzen, Theorien* (Göttingen 2006), pp. 161–74.
109 Sonja Levsen, *Elite, Männlichkeit und Krieg. Tübinger und Cambridger Studenten 1900–1929* (Göttingen 2006), pp. 150–71.

CHAPTER 6

'The peasants did not think of Africa': empire and the Italian state's pursuit of legitimacy, 1871–1945

Giuseppe Finaldi

Introduction

In the summer of 1935 Carlo Levi, wealthy liberal-republican and anti-Fascist from Turin, was sent into 'internal exile' in a hill-top town in the deep south of Italy. During his relatively benign captivity there he was forced into an unusual encounter for a man of his education and class; deprived of the literate and politically aware with whom he was accustomed to spend his time, his gaze was turned for the first time in his life on the 'Italian' peasantry. The months in which Levi was banished from the Italy that mattered coincided with that country's war with and conquest of Ethiopia. According to this refined scholar, artist, doctor and cosmopolitan (he had lived in Paris, the Mecca of all aspiring Italian intellectuals), the trumpet blowing associated with Italy's imperial ambitions was greeted with stony-faced indifference by the dour and fatalistic peasants whom he witnessed scratching out a precarious living on the rocky slopes of southern Italy's treeless mountains. For them, Levi asserted, the Italian Empire was yet another of nature's slings and arrows against which and indeed for which they could and would do nothing. For this convinced anti-Fascist, that empire had reached the inhabitants of this remote village when, as the peasants were wont to say, even Christ had passed it by, would have been an intolerable sign that Fascism was capable of getting into the minds of even Italy's most impervious and opaque citizens. These dark-eyed peasants were not what was usually referred to as the 'Italian people'; the latter, according to Levi, were 'the schoolchildren and their teachers, Fascist Scouts, Red Cross ladies, the widows and mothers of Milanese veterans, women of fashion in Florence, grocers, shopkeepers, pensioners, journalists, policemen and government employees in Rome'. These may have been 'swept off their feet by a wave of glory and enthusiasm'[1] but no such emotions perturbed the inscrutable

Italy 'beyond the mountains'. Imperial propaganda, when it encountered this bedrock of the uncontaminated people evaporated away in the puff of rhetorical whimsy. As they 'descended the vale of the Agri', Levi assures us, 'the peasants did not think of Africa'.

Yet this artist from the cultured north was also a witness to the surprising fact that Mussolini's imperialism had washed over even this proverbially peripheral locality: loudspeakers had been set up in the piazzas to keep radioless villagers abreast of Italy's advancing armies, the local school teacher had drummed his pupils with *Faccetta Nera*, a song celebrating Italian conquest, and at least he and his classes turned up at all the ceremonies marking some event in distant Africa; at the announcement of Italy's capture of Addis Ababa, Levi and other 'exiles' held in the village were amnestied, a clear sign that in this 'Italy over the mountains' the Fascist regime's imperial victory was meant to really matter to the people, including those who lived in places that for the rest could only be regarded as fitting locations for banishment.

If empire mattered to the 'people' is clearly not just of import to contemporary academics battling it out over semantics, disciplinary boundaries or what should or should not be considered plausible expressions of 'imperial' culture. For Levi in the 1930s it was a pressing political issue. During those months of exile he had been relieved that the 'people' had failed to be convinced by what proved to be Mussolini's 'finest hour', but he had also thereby stumbled across the nub of how and why colonialism mattered not only to the Fascist but also to the previous liberal regimes. In the Italian case, forging a connection between empire and 'people' was absolutely fundamental; in fact I want to suggest that the very *raison d'être* of Italian imperialism was none other than an attempt to connect the 'people' to Italy's various and what were in fact fragile regimes. I use the word *regime* not just in the sense of government and state but much more broadly to include civil society and in particular written texts that sought to resonate with state agendas. I want to suggest that far from it being a matter of dragging the 'people' into 'cheering on' an empire possessing its own self-sustaining momentum, in the Italy of the late nineteenth to the mid-twentieth centuries it was that very 'cheering on' which drove Italy to empire. The *primary* reason for which Italy turned its gaze and grasp to Africa was not for the benefits bestowed (be they strategic, military, financial or whatever) by the conquest and maintenance of palm and pine (or just palm in the Italian case) but as a search to establish the country's various regimes with a consensual and 'cheering on' Italian people. Without involving (or at least attempting to involve) the 'people', the Italian Empire would simply not have been. For Levi the stubborn refusal of his peasants to be moved by empire meant not that empire did not matter but that Fascism's general claim to legit-imacy had fallen on deaf ears.

In this context Bernard Porter's 2004 study on how much (or, as he tries to show, how little) empire mattered to the British in the nineteenth and twentieth centuries is of significance. Porter argues that notwith-standing the British Empire's size, it does not follow that its acquisition, its maintenance and even expansion required the involvement of a corre-spondingly large number of people back home, not only for the empire's day to day running but also to 'cheer it on'. With some discrepancies (the period of the 'New Imperialism' at the end of the nineteenth century for example requiring more), the British Empire was in fact run on a cultural shoestring and with only a bare minimum of (British) human capital, or at least with a lot less than has come to be accepted over the last few decades. Porter secondly draws attention to what he considers to be Britain's unique class system; there was, he suggests, no need for mass engagement with the British Empire at home because it was an institution almost entirely run by members of the middle-class, and not many of them at that. Lacking a unified national identity at home (to be British meant completely different things depending on one's class) the empire and what it stood for never became a fundamental ingredient of working-class 'Britishness' and even middle class identity need not have been 'steeped' in imperial ideology for the empire to function. According to this interpretation of British culture and society, in the homeland of the greatest empire the world had ever known, the 'people' were not required to think very much about it at all as long as significant minori-ties did.[2]

Can such an argument be transposed to Italy? It is difficult not to be persuaded by the implications Porter ascribes to the class system for the British case. So much about British culture (until recently, as Porter points out) is explained by it: the absence of regional accents in the diction of the upper-classes, the compartmentalised tastes for different sports, food, drink, newspapers, schools etc. According to Porter the nationalising process, which we all presume aimed at creating a common sense of citizenship, never did so in Britain; partly because the 'ruling class' had established its hegemony so successfully at a very early stage compared with other European countries the two (or three?) social classes lived out what 'being British' (or English) meant in uniquely closed boxes, or more precisely like the two rails of a railway line, both following the same route and connected by sleepers but neither ever meeting. In normal times only one rail was required to run the empire, or as Porter argues, until the end of the nineteenth century 'the working class … was not encouraged to be patriotic'. In the absence of a British notion of 'common citizenship' the empire did not have to be shared (with the working class) or even passed off as democratic (for the benefit of Liberals and Labourites); it was generally hushed up.[3]

That empire may have been 'hushed up' in the imperial society *par excellence* comes as a great surprise. Since the early 1980s so much capital has been invested by historians and cultural theorists to prove the opposite that the terms of comparison for anyone dealing with other empires have perforce become slippery indeed. It has been a painstaking task for historians of other ex-imperial countries to begin to examine non-British 'imperial cultures', but when they did so the lessons of Edward Said and John MacKenzie have always been at their elbow.[4] What then to do with Porter's view of things? The making or breaking of this revisionist's argument rests in the end on his analysis of the way class worked in the British context. When John MacKenzie famously stated that empire had the power to 'regenerate … the British themselves … and by creating a national purpose with a high moral content lead to class conciliation',[5] he was ascribing to empire something that his magisterial archaeological work on British culture only supported indirectly. It was a thesis based on circumstantial evidence that presumed class conflict. For Porter, the British class system was inert and therefore required no 'getting over' an inherently conflictual and potentially explosive ordering. In his model, classes exist but they do not clash, or at least they did not do so in Britain. It was on the French Revolution-impacted European continent (and across the Atlantic) that the state's ambition to create a 'common citizenry' with shared values and culture was evident, but Britain's idiosyncratic nature survived well into the age of the New Imperialism, rendering MacKenzie's ascription of consequence to imperial 'propaganda' superfluous. What is left of MacKenzie's thesis, as Porter knows very well, is a mountain of circumstantial evidence lacking a motive and without a motive the suspect must be acquitted. So what 'motive' may there have been for harnessing 'the people' to Italy's colonial ventures from the late nineteenth century, when it was indeed the state which consistently led the way?

The premises of Italian colonial expansion

According to Roberto Battaglia, left-wing historian of Italy's 'First African War', by 1887, 'the majority of the country had already demonstrated that it wanted nothing to do with [the Italian government's colonial politics]'.[6] Angelo Del Boca, who like Battaglia had been an anti-Fascist partisan between 1943 and 1945, and who painstakingly reconstructed the history of Italian Empire in six volumes published between the 1970s and 1990s, reinforced his anti-Fascist colleague's conclusion:

In [Liberal] Italy ... sixty per cent of the population was illiterate, there were little over fifteen thousand university students and readers of daily newspapers numbered no more than a few hundred thousand ... Italy was an underdeveloped country, beset by new and chronic problems, but its ruling class searched for diversions due to its incapacity to resolve internal problems more than because it was firmly convinced that 'colonies are an absolute necessity for modern life' (Francesco Crispi).[7]

Francesco Crispi was, on and off, Italian prime minister in the 1880s and 1890s. In Del Boca's view, Italian Empire failed to resonate among the people and remained little more than the personal obsession of, in this case, maverick nationalists such as politician Francesco Crispi. Yet, as Christopher Duggan has so cogently shown, it was a desire to give to the *Risorgimento* the flesh of popular participation that inspired Crispi to thrust Italy into the colonial fray[8] and in this venture he was not merely acting on personal impulse but within the framework of the fraught and complicated process of 'nationalisation' that lay at the very heart of Italy's recasting after unification.

While this chapter may not be the place to re-tell the story of Italy's difficult path into the twentieth century,[9] it is worth reiterating that the conditions of the peninsula and its new political superstructure were hardly such as to inspire a sense of confidence in the 'ruling class' or a feeling of ease in the Italian population. As Del Boca rightly points out, widespread illiteracy, poverty, struggling new institutions (the construction of the new state school system, for example, was encountering enormous difficulties), endemic violence, rebellion and Catholic hostility to the new state made consensus politics on the British model well nigh impossible. In the 1880s and 90s only about 6 per cent of the population were given the vote and parliament was still bereft of the aura of sacredness that might have gone some way to establish it as the primary locus of popular representation and debate. Rather, corruption, elitism and the 'adaptability', if not to say the downright dishonesty of its members ensured, as a prominent newspaper put it, that parliament had an 'anaemic, pointless and pernicious existence'.[10] Broadening the electorate, reluctantly regarded by many of Italy's ruling Liberals as the only means to ensure the long-term viability of the new national state, was feared as all too likely to introduce a Trojan horse (in which lurked the insidious forces of recalcitrant popular Catholicism or the unknown quantity of Socialism) into the heart of the nation. Before 1900 there were no mass political parties in Italy. The reading public was infinitesimally smaller than Britain's or France's. Furthermore, extraordinarily fractious regionalism, in many places the people of one valley could hardly understand the dialect of those in the next, without considering the huge cultural and economic discrepancies between Italy's north and south, meant that the prospect of true unification was unfailingly daunting.[11]

In the years of the Scramble for Africa Italy did not possess, as Porter argues was the case for Britain, two distinct and established 'rails' but rather heaps of twisted metal, rusted sidings and scattered debris of razor sharp fragments with which the reproduction of a class system on the British model was all too likely to come to grief. In the Italian nation-making process the only choice available was one of state-sponsored 'common citizenship' in which much of the clutter of old identities could be cast away. The character of the relationship between Italian imperialism and 'the people', it will be argued, was no more therefore than one facet of this process at work.

The signing of the Uccialli Treaty, which gave Italy a paper protectorate over Ethiopia in 1889, was hailed by Crispi as having 'secured the [necessary] air for Italy's lungs.'[12] The Sicilian statesman was certainly not alone in regarding the acquisition of territory in Africa as providing 'air' for 'Italian lungs'; the forbidding consequences of Italy's lack of activity, as other European nations claimed vast tracts of territory overseas, worried, for example Baron Leopoldo Franchetti.

In the 1870s, as Carlo Levi was to do in much more restricted circumstances half a century later, this wealthy Jewish landowner journeyed to the south of Italy with his fellow Tuscan Sidney Sonnino, uncovering for Italy's small literate public the seriousness of the peninsula's 'social question'.[13] As Franchetti and Sonnino, young and adventurous gentlemen who, as Levi was to do three generations later, had studied in and travelled on many occasions to London or Paris, picked their way along mule tracks into the rugged interior of Sicily, a world opened up before their eyes they described as 'having remained outside the current of European civilisation' for hundreds of years, leaving a society similar to that which had been universal in Europe 'four centuries before'.[14] Poverty, disease, ignorance, crime and obscurantism cast a pall over the deceptively sunny island and it seemed all too likely that these failings would eventually undermine those parts of northern and central Italy whose health had been assured by participation in the progressive development of modern Europe. For Franchetti, the Liberal state had the duty to attempt to cure the Sicilian extremity by bestowing upon it the benefits of the superior civilisation of the north and, should this fail, cut the island permanently adrift, avoiding thus the contamination of the whole.

The state was to be crucial in designating and applying an appropriate therapy and along with mass arrests, land redistribution and the freedom to emigrate, Franchetti envisaged also that the state would 'provide Italian colonies to which the flow of emigrants could be redirected'.[15] This particular 'solution' to the Italian social question had the enormous advantage of requiring no tampering with the social order at home and by the 1890s it had already become apparent to Franchetti and many others that draconian remedies in Italy (such as the breaking up of the South's great estates, and coerced expropriations of land in favour of the peasantry, or the exclusion of the South's elites from control of their territory) were all too likely to have explosive and undesirable consequences. The 'Brigandage'[16] of the 1860s, which had prompted Franchetti's enquiries into the ills of the south in the first place, was clearly understood to have been partly caused by the *Risorgimento*'s unbalancing of the old regime in those regions. In many ways the lesson learned by the young Franchetti in his travels in Italy's south and in his mulling over a variety of models for Italian development hinged on a particular interpretation of Italy possessing a soiled and contaminated past which reached forward time and again to trip up the young nation. How to improve things without arousing the spectre of peasant insurgence (in the early 1890s the *Fasci Siciliani* movement had organised peasant discontent to the point that Crispi declared martial law throughout the island), and without simply allowing Italians to lose themselves in the torrent heading across the Atlantic, was a vexing problem for Italy's political class, and one to which colonialism, the Tuscan baron felt, offered the most auspicious solution. By the 1890s Italy's possession of a colony, Eritrea in East Africa, was seen by Franchetti (he was now a parliamentary deputy and able to influence policy directly to a degree) to be of great significance, indeed a vital necessity for Italy's uncertain future. There in Africa, a *terra nullius* could make up for the oppressive weight of Italy's long history, its antiquated norms and the diehard traditionalism which hampered social, economic and cultural progress. He looked with envy at those countries (Britain, France and the USA) which had left behind their own pasts, or indeed had had none: 'Those new and young societies', he wrote in 1891,

> free of the slag heaps and servitudes of the old political and social order are far stronger, vigorous and ready for battle than are we ... it is a great fortune that we can create a new society of the Italian race overseas ... a truly democratic society based on land-holding peasants ... A time will come when those old societies, if they are unable to find a place on which to lean in their distant, their greener and more dynamic colonies, will be crushed by the greater vigour of more fortunate competitors.[17]

Franchetti is clear: only an aggressive and dynamic position in the international arena aiming to take possession of land before competitors acquired it would ensure the future of the 'old society' by rendering the upheavals brought about by modernisation innocuous. The imperial model envisaged was one where a landholding peasantry would be free even of the share-cropping shackles of the baron's native Tuscany (at his death Franchetti was to bequeath to his own tenants the ownership of the land they cultivated),[18] let alone the horrors of the southern Italian *latifondo* (Hacienda). In the colonies there would be the opportunity of copying the bringing under the plough via the planting of state-granted *homesteads* (left in English in the original Italian) of the vast expanses of the American west and in general 'all those countries occupied by the Anglo-Saxon race'.[19] These sturdy and satisfied peasants (now to be called farmers) would be natural propagators of the kind of democratic spirit Franchetti saw at work in the United States: universal suffrage that did not entail an immediate exasperation of the contradictions of the old and decrepit social order that the baron was sure were the root cause of the bleak condition of the Italian south. The colonies would escape from the original sin that marked the homeland and in so doing remake the homeland itself. Franchetti was capable of stirring visions:

> Come, come here [to Italy's colony], peasant of Italy … Come, yourself alone. You who still conserve purity of heart and mind. You will fertilize this land, and from the generations that will issue from you, the new Italy will arise … yours will be a labour of salvation without which the weary nation will crumble.[20]

For Franchetti then, colonialism was to be the deliverance of a straight-jacketed homeland. This reasoning pointed in one direction, and one direction only: the Italian state had to guarantee its population living space. Although Franchetti was at first content with the small colony of Eritrea, he felt Italy should be much more ambitious. During the First World War, disappointed with what had been achieved so far, he claimed most of Anatolia for Italy, further expansion in Africa and in parts of the Balkans too, and he clearly spelled out the reasoning that had made him such a strenuous advocate of Italian colonialism over the previous twenty years:

> [halting] Italian expansion … would prevent the healthy employment of the exuberance of Italy's energy and its people; it would be the same as condemning those energies to being wasted for the benefit of other nations or spent in the fruitlessness of internecine class warfare at home.[21]

The relationship between 'people' and Empire, certainly in the visions of this conscientious mandarin of Italian late nineteenth-century politics, was of absolute vitality for Italy's future.

The desire to acquire colonies became bound up with a forthright and self-conscious need to legitimise the new Liberal regime. Rome (and in 1861 this meant the Papacy, not Liberal Italy) had its apostles all over the world and when the decision was made that the capital of the new kingdom was to be the Eternal City and not modern but provincial Turin (where the new king of Italy had previously dwelled as ruler of Piedmont), there could be no question of Italy not espousing some form of *Weltpolitik*, within its means perhaps, naturally. Rome exuded empire, power and international significance and the nationlet born of defeat at the hands of the Austrians, which punctured the Eternal City's two thousand-year-old walls in 1870, had acquired an inheritance of unimaginable and possibly unmanageable proportions. For the men who ordered the breaching of the Aurelian Walls a juncture had been reached: the choice ahead was to preside over a heritage museum in which foreigners dawdled away the time and money gained by *their* invested stocks, *their* smoking factories and *their* trading ships or to look ahead and to make Italy a competitive, viable and modern concern beholden to none, 'feared' by others, as King Victor Emmanuel II had put it. As has been mentioned, for men like Franchetti the choice was in reality only an illusory one; the seething masses, their poverty, their discontent and pent-up rage meant that Italy could not simply look on as other Europe nations marched forward and took what they needed to satisfy their desires and to placate their own internal contradictions.

In his seminal analysis of Italian culture in the Liberal era, historian Silvio Lanaro caught the mood; very quickly after unification the new Italian ruling class, he argues, realised that it was only through the industrialisation and commercial expansion of Italy that the gains it had conquered at unification could be made permanent. Its privileged role in the new state could only be guaranteed by a culture of 'greatness', by unifying the population behind the ideal of what Emilio Gentile has called 'La Grande Italia':

> From the 1870s on the ruling classes eliminated the last vestiges of their civil liberalism as they steadily made a series of valuable discoveries ... [they realised] that an authoritarian activation of 'national' resources required a corresponding 'nationalist' and demagogic ideology which – resting on values accepted by broad strata of the population – would allow the unequal distribution of the sacrifices required by accumulation.[22]

In the 1880s 'Liberal' commentator Attilio Brunialti bewailed the plight of the ruling class 'if the exhausted ideals of 1870 were not replaced by others able to keep the mind and the imagination of the majority (educated or non-educated) fired and alert'.[23] In his masterly and still highly usable path through the ideas that underlay Italy's foreign policy in the years between 1870 and 1896, Federico Chabod stated that for many Italians the years after unification were 'luckier than they were great ...' and Italians 'a youthful people ... desiring the pursuit of military glory and the consecration of the young nation'.[24]

A 'common citizenship', as understood by Italy's elites, could only be forged on the anvil of popular participation in the nation's expansionist aims. In the late nineteenth century colonialism was espoused with the same logic as Italy's later joining of the First World War in 1915, its assailing of Ethiopia in 1935 and even Mussolini's uniting his country's forces with the Third Reich in the late 1930s. The Italian state, in its various regimes, needed to speak to the people and to show them that a programme of expansion and the 'authoritarian activation of national resources' was embarked upon for their benefit. In so doing the people and the nation-state would come together and clinch the prize of social peace, class conciliation and economic development. Were 'the people' prepared to abide by such logic?

The first African War, 1880–96

On 1 November 1895 the Socialist journal *Critica Sociale* rued that

> this Africa, so cursed and maligned, is, after macaroni, the most popular thing in Italy. Italians don't read books or newspapers ... but when it comes to Africa ... they are willing to pay their penny for the gazette and want to know everything.[25]

That the skirmishes, battles and personalities of Italy's first colonial adventure in East Africa in the 1880s and 90s were known of at the popular level appears to be beyond doubt. While rudimentary compared with Britain or France, the means of communication available in Italy in the 1880s and 90s were nevertheless sufficient to tell a broad swathe of the people that 'their' nation was fighting a war in Africa in the hope of conquering colonial possessions for their benefit. The question *Critica Sociale* was discussing in 1895 was the same as that which was to trouble Carlo Levi many decades later: that is, did what the 'Regime' was doing in far away Africa actually resonate among the people?

In a barely literate Italy the broadsheet ballad might assist in shedding light on this issue. The Palatine Library of Parma possesses a collection of Pennaroli broadsheets from the late nineteenth and early twentieth century. Pennaroli was a publisher operating out of the small town of Fiorenzuola D'Arda in the province of Piacenza. Its cheap and rudimentary printed sheets were distributed across Italy by travelling salesmen known colloquially as *Pontremolesi*. In the second half of the nineteenth century the countryside around Pontremoli, a town not far from Fiorenzuola, became specialised in supplying the poor end of the book market with underemployed peasants who took to Italy's roads selling cheap books and broadsheets. Although the origin of the *Pontremolesi* goes back to Early Modern times,[26] the wicker baskets they carried on their backs as they trudged their way up the highways and byways of late

6.1 Typical broadsheet of the 1890s illustrating Italy's colonial wars for a popular audience. Published by Salani, Florence 1896.
(Courtesy Giuseppe Finaldi and Biblioteca Centrale Nazionale, Florence)

nineteenth-century Italy were filled with material recent printing innovations had made cheaper than ever before. In Britain it may have been the
modern sales methods of Charles Mudie and W.H. Smith which got
books to readers in the late nineteenth century, but in Italy the wandering
chapbook seller was still an essential and effective way to distribute
written culture.[27]

The subject matter of Pennaroli's broadsheets was varied but Italy's
wars in Africa in the 1880s and 90s appear to have been quickly inserted
among the publisher's staple of brigand stories, love affairs and crime
thrillers. In the Parma collection for 1888, out of twenty broadsheets
held, three refer to events in Africa. *A' retirata* (Call to Duty) was a piece
which did well at the Piedigrotta Neapolitan song festival of 1888 and
referred to the expedition to Ethiopia to avenge the Italian troops who had
died at Dogali. Another song glorified the men who participated in the
Combattimento di Saganeiti in Africa (Battle of Saganeiti), and the third,
the *Tarantella degli Italiani in Africa* (Tarantella of Italians in Africa)
spoke of a popular desire for vengeance on Ras Alula, leader of the
Ethiopian troops at Dogali. In 1889 Pennaroli brought out *Il ritorno delle
nostre truppe dall'Africa* (The Return of Our Troops from Africa) and *La
ritirata degli abissini ed il suo re* (The Retreat of the Abyssinians and their
King) which the sheet informs runs to the same tune as *Il prigioniero
d'Africa* (The Prisoner in Africa). In 1890 a ditty celebrates *La morte del
Negus* (The Death of the Negus); we also have an *Inno dei soldati in
Africa* (Hymn of Soldiers in Africa) as well as *La strage d'il nostrì soldà,
ossia la guerra d'Africa* (The Massacre of our Soldiers, or the African War).
In 1891 we have *Il milite italiano che parte per l'Africa* (The Italian
Soldier who leaves for Africa), *Il bersagliere che parte per l'Africa* (The
Bersagliare leaves for Africa), *La partenza del coscritto per l'Africa* (The
Conscript who goes to Africa), and *Il Militare italiano prigioniero in Africa*
(The Italian Soldier, Prisoner in Africa) and the really suggestive
*Canzonetta nuovissima sopra la riccia bionda figlia del marinaio la quale
fugge partendo per l'Africa* (New Song on the Curly Haired Blonde,
Daughter of the Sailor who Runs Away to Africa). In 1892 arguments
between Italy and France over East African ambitions led to the dialect
broadsheet *Italia e Franssa*. The broadsheet *Il combattimento di Sahati*
(The Battle of Sahati) was also published in 1892 and notwithstanding it
referred to a battle fought five years earlier, publishing a new broadsheet
recounting previous events must have still been a worthwhile economic
venture. In the same year a report on *L'orribile disastro avvenuto in Africa
nelle vicinanze di Massaua e Moncullo* (The Terrible Disaster that
Occurred in Africa near Massaua and Moncullo) was also turned into a
broadsheet. In 1893 the song *Il marinaio che parte per l'Africa* (The Sailor
who Leaves for Africa) joins the many others referring to soldiers leaving

behind their lovers to go to the 'Dark Continent'. And so, year by year, the baskets of the *Pontremolesi* were refilled.

Pennaroli broadsheets were also potted 'histories' of the wars in Africa. One, printed in 1897 (and republished in 1901), attempted to chronicle all the most important events that had made headlines in the previous decade by concentrating the war into four key moments and figures. De Cristoforis at Dogali, Toselli at Amba Alage, Galliano at Makalé and Baratieri at Adowa. This is a version of the African War narrated as a clichéd set of heroic poses. Pietro Toselli 'bears his chest to the enemy', Giuseppe Galliano leaves the fort at Makelè because of thirst, the ring of soldiers around Colonel De Cristoforis 'presents arms to fallen comrades'. The broadsheet ballad's final verse reads as follows (Antonio Baldissera was the general who replaced the defeated Oreste Baratieri as Italian commander in East Africa in 1896):

> Whoever says Italy cannot fight
> Was surely born an ass.
> Now we've sent Baldissera down there
> He will open the road for our citizens.
> Having struggled so hard
> The tricolour flag will always point Italy forward
> She is as always anxious to make war.[28]

Broadsheets were merely the cheapest of a variety of published artefacts that recounted the African War. Novels and plays were also widely available. A significant number, in particular, of new publishers focused on the doings in Italy's colony and brought out special issues dealing with salient events there or accepted quickly written novels focusing on the Dark Continent.

Edoardo Perino was typical of this new brand of publishing entrepreneur who concocted Italy's vicissitudes in Africa into a brew of patriotism, adventure and melodrama (reinforced by liberal doses of Orientalist titillation) guaranteed to attract the attention of the country's growing popular readership. Originally a working-class typographer, Perino set up shop in Rome in 1860. By the 1880s he was publishing low cost series such as *La Biblioteca Patriottica* (Patriotic Library), *La Biblioteca Popolare Romantica* (Popular Romantic Library), an *Enciclopedia Popolare Illustrata* (Popular Illustrated Encyclopaedia) and a *Biblioteca di Viaggi* (Travel Library) focusing on international African exploration literature. His illustrated works on Italy's doings in Africa were successful publishing ventures. Maffeo Savelli's *Italiani in Africa* (3 illustrated volumes) came out in 1885; Giuseppe Piccinini's *La Guerra d'Africa* in 1888 (1,000 plus pages) and Oreste Gorra's *Guerra d'Africa*

(500 pages) in 1895. The two volumes of Silvio Ghelli's *Guerra d'Africa 1895–6* appeared as events unfolded in Ethiopia.[29]

Piccinini's *La Guerra D'Africa* was the centrepiece of Perino's 'African' oeuvre. Published in 1887–88, *La Guerra D'Africa* has been called by Battaglia '... among the most significant examples of popular colonial literature [published during the *Prima Guerra*]'[30] and by Labanca a successful 'popular publication'.[31] *La Guerra d'Africa* was issued by instalment, a method that was to become an enormously successful tradition in Italian book publishing to the present day. Four numbers came out every week, eventually totting up to 150; each had eight pages, making the whole work 1,200 pages long. The price of a single instalment was five *centesimi*. This was cheap, little more expensive than a daily newspaper. That *Guerra d'Africa* aroused interest and sold successfully appears to be beyond doubt. According to their own advertisement Perino at first intended to publish no more than fifty issues but '... the rapid evolution of events, the exceptional gravity of the situation and the unexpected conditions of our African possessions persuaded us to increase the number of instalments to one hundred.' With Italy's determination to make war on Ethiopia and to avenge Dogali, even one hundred did not suffice. Only 150 instalments would do justice to

> the incredible number of copies sold so far which, apart from flattering us, will spur us to continue to do better and to merit the favour bestowed upon us by the public. We will make *Guerra d'Africa* absolutely indispensable to all those who have an interest in the future of the Fatherland.

Whoever renewed a subscription for a further hundred instalments would also receive, free of charge, the eighteen volumes of Perino's *Biblioteca Patriottica* (containing ' ... everything patriotic that has been done in Italy from Medieval times to our *Risorgimento*'), a map of the fortifications around Massaua, and a coloured print representing 'The Battle of Dogali'.[32] If their own advertisement is to be believed, *Guerra D'Africa* had a real impact; it was a concrete source of information for anyone discussing the subject of Italy's prospects in the colonial struggle and a source for imagining and locating Italy in the world. Perino's representation of the 'Battle of Dogali' must have been put on the wall by many a proud owner and have been a constant reminder to friends and family of the bravery and selfless devotion of the Italian soldier. Its most potent message was surely that the new Italy was actively engaged in claiming a role on the international stage and fighting for a resolution to the challenges of the modern world. That such an agenda claimed the lives of so many of Italy's 'brave young men' was always depicted as the consecration in blood of what the new Italy was purported to stand for.

Before turning to the 1911 Italian conquest of Libya it is worth evaluating one other form of communication that reached the 'people' of the peninsula. After the 1887 defeat of an Italian detachment of 500 troops at Dogali an extraordinarily large number of commemorative services honouring the dead took place throughout Italy.[33] Evidence gleaned from hundreds of publications associated with these services and research based on local newspapers and surviving posters advertising commemorative events shows that even in the tiniest mountain village a ceremony was likely to have been held where sermons (many took place in churches) or speeches extolling the virtues of Italians fighting in Africa were the order of the day. One example, taken from a poster advertising a commemoration held by the town council of the small town of Pieve di Soligo in the province of Treviso, sums up wonderfully the importance of empire in connecting people to the new national state. Affixed to the town council chambers in mid-March 1887, the poster read as follows:

> The Mayor of Pieve di Soligo announces:
>
> The heroic deeds of our soldiers at Dogali have enthused the whole nation ... They died without turning their face from the enemy, to save the honour of the flag on which they had taken an oath of loyalty to King and Country. The latter have both proclaimed them heroes and are proud that on the African continent they have shown the entire world how ITALIANS can fight and die in the call of duty. We invite all citizens to flock to the commemoration ceremony to be held ... in the Parish Church on Wednesday 16 of the current month. There we may testify the affection that ties all Italians to the vicissitudes of the Fatherland. Let us honour the memory of our soldiers fighting on African soil and we may take from their action the evidence that our pride, the Italian Army, will be able to defend the Fatherland from any enemy that dares to attack its unity and independence of which the first guardian is the glorious DYNASTY of SAVOY
>
> Long live the King – Long live the Army[34]

On all this talk and high hopes the catastrophic defeat of Adowa came crashing down or, as Labanca puts it, 'the news of Adowa fell like a millstone on any of the bewitching capabilities that the hex of war in Africa may have had'.[35] While Dogali had seen the 'heroic' death of 'the five hundred' (as they came to be called with Thermopylaen overtones),[36] the almost 5,000 who died in 1896 and the Italian soldiers (and their commander) who took to their heels in the face of Emperor Menelik's huge Ethiopian host could not so easily be passed off as having done their duty to a man. More than a thousand were taken into shameful captivity in Addis Ababa and there was little Italy could do about it short of renewing an already prohibitively expensive colonial campaign. Attacking a 'weak' and impoverished African nation in search of the chrism the new Italy was so desperately in need of had backfired calamitously. While people rioted in the streets and train tracks were torn up to prevent more conscripts being sent to the killing fields of the Dark Continent, Crispi could hear his windows being pelted with stones as he was hounded from office.[37] A new governor for Italy's tiny remaining colony was rustled up (playwright and journalist Ferdinando Martini) and was given orders to go down there to Africa to preserve the colony (Eritrea) 'by making Italians cease to remember it'.[38]

Such a bizarre idea was within the logic of why Italy had turned to colonialism in the first place. The 'people' had been told to hope in empire and thereby to confirm the efforts of the new Liberal regime in its quest for legitimisation before them; they were now expected to forget it lest they realise that Victor Emanuel's expectation that the new Italy would be 'feared' as well as united[39] had been as hollow as the many promises which had been delivered to all 'Italians' at the moment of Unification itself. Crispi's politics of a restricted franchise, martial law and repression allied to glory on the battlefields of Africa may have paid off had that glory been consistently attained. Defeat highlighted the shoddiness of a violent and petty State whose ambition to bypass the aspirations of the people through 'authoritarian activation' had only revealed its hypocrisy. When Italy turned to Africa once again the terms and conditions with which it crossed the Mediterranean needed to be different.

Tripoli 1911–12: 'the proletarian nation stirs'

In his 1925 highly influential history of Italy the Neapolitan philosopher Benedetto Croce wrote that

> …Italy went to Tripoli because it would have been intolerable that upon no stretch of the African coast that lay before her was the Italian flag flying. Because it would have been intolerable for Italy not to participate in the European project for the Europeanization of Africa, or to pronounce that the setback of Abyssinia under Crispi had been final. Italy was not the same as it had been fifteen years before; it desired and knew that it could undertake a military campaign and pursue it until victory had been achieved. In other words Italy went to Tripoli for reasons of sentiment which are as real as all the others.[40]

The years between Adowa and the 1911–12 conquest of the last Ottoman territory in North Africa that was to become the Italian colony of Libya were, according to Croce, extraordinarily important. As Italy prepared to celebrate its fiftieth anniversary, what better present could the Fatherland bestow on its coming-of-age children than a colony that Eritrea (and the hardly noticed Somalia) could never become. Italy's 'Fourth Shore', as propaganda was to call it, was to be a kind of confirmation that notwithstanding all its teething and then teenage problems, the 'people' had reconciled itself to be wedded to Liberal Italy; a 'proper' colony was provided as dowry.

Such metaphors may have been hard to square with reality for many Italians, especially for the almost ten million who had left the country in search of a better life across the Atlantic in precisely the years since Adowa. Yet Croce's 'reasons of sentiment' need to be taken seriously as once again this colonial conquest cannot be put down to the needs of pre-existing trade and influence.[41] To Crispi's Italy further complications had been added; industrialisation was rapidly transforming the north-west of the country and the Liberal order was now under the expanding shadow of what have been called the 'subversive' forces of Socialism and political Catholicism.[42]

Significantly, the first decade of the twentieth century had also witnessed the rise of a new and challenging Right: the Italian Nationalist Association had only coalesced into a political grouping in 1910 but its loose conglomeration of sympathisers and flankers had been growing in importance since the last decade of the nineteenth century. Enrico Corradini, chief spokesman of this new movement, had, or at least he liked to think he had, experienced the news of the battle of Adowa as a kind of conversion of Saul. Defeat at the hands of Ethiopia, or more specifically Italy's decision to accept that defeat as final, could only mean that there was a deeply ingrained canker at the heart of liberalism's project to 'make Italians'. The energies of the nation had to be harnessed in an authoritarian new synthesis that welded the dynamic ideas of Socialism's rejection of top-hat and tails bourgeois society with an outward thrust for territory and international prestige. Corradini considered Crispi to have been the one politician who had guided the fortunes of the nation with virility. But the Sicilian statesman's bad luck was due to his having been far ahead of the toadies, bureaucrats and corrupt money-grabbers who dragged him in the mud to the gloating cheers of the stone-throwing *canaille*, and all while the heaps of bodies in Africa remained unburied and unavenged.[43] War and charismatic leadership would break the undermining and pernicious forces of democracy and the liberal pluralism which had tolerated the cries of 'Long live Menelik' in the streets of Italy's cities. The notion of class struggle was reified into the sphere of international relations. Italy, Corradini maintained, was the 'proletarian nation' of Europe. To break its shackles of poverty, underdevelopment and 'mediocrity' it needed a new moral consciousness. Enlightenment democracy was to be replaced by a new 'equality according to worth'. The Tuscan intellectual stated in the founding article of his journal *il Regno*:

> In founding this journal, my friends and I will be a voice among all those who despair and are enraged by the cowardice of the present moment... with our voice we will raise the old statues that glorify man and the nation before the eyes of those who will rise up.[45]

The tense climate of the first decade of the twentieth century did not stop Croce from asserting that Italy had changed, and much for the better compared with the years of the First African War. It was Giovanni Giolitti (prime minister at different times through the decade) who was to remain the hero of the Neapolitan philosopher. Giolitti's period of rule should be considered as the coming to maturity of the Liberal state before the shockwaves of the Great War knocked things out of kilter (this at least is how Croce saw it). The question of whether Italy would follow the path of Britain and France and be able to make its parliament and its representative institutions the loci of political and social conflict, as opposed to leaving the latter in the streets to be dealt with summarily by the police and the army (as had happened so often under Crispi) came to the fore. The parliamentary Socialists, for example, Giolitti considered, were only a threat if the Liberals remained cerebrally over-rigid. Crispi's implacable hostility to Socialism as the irredeemable enemy of everything Italy, as he understood it, stood for had succeeded only in rendering their intransigence towards the post-unification set up all the more rigid. Social legislation and a more tempered approach in the State's handling of industrial relations as well as a slow expansion of the suffrage would leave Socialists (or for that matter political Catholicism) no choice but to work within the system for fear of being excluded from the body politic altogether. Giolitti had stated in a circular in 1906:

> I remind all State officials that in this period of profound social transformation, government action must be inspired both by absolute neutrality in the struggles between capital and labour, and by the affectionate concern for the legitimate concerns of the working classes. And it must be the government's special task to persuade everybody that the struggles for progress can only be fruitful when they are peaceful, disciplined and non-violent.[46]

The exchange in Giolitti's terms was to be a fair one. The leadership of the nation would remain in the hands of the post-unification Liberals and the 'people' would be granted their 'legitimate' aspirations. The re-ignition of imperial dreams more than a decade after Adowa was part of the elaborate brokering package with which Giolitti (who was personally lukewarm towards colonial expansionism) sought to legitimise the new direction the Italian state was taking vis-à-vis the 'people'. It is no coincidence that it was precisely when the new wave of imperial enthusiasm was sweeping the country that universal male suffrage was finally granted to the Italian population.

This logic can best be understood through an appeal made to Giolitti just before the Italian invasion by the extraordinarily jingoistic journalist Giuseppe Bevione. Through his 'open letters' and editorials in the Turinese newspaper *La Stampa*, Bevione had for months not only been singing the praises of Libya's 'fabulous wealth' and its enormous potential (he suggested that a rock melon grown in Libya would weigh 'twenty to thirty kilograms'[47]) to solve many of Italy's problems, but had challenged the government to trust the Italian 'people' in bringing a colonial campaign to the felicitous conclusion it had not been capable of at the time of Crispi. In an open letter to Giolitti dated 30 July 1911 he defied the cautious prime minister to refute the fact that 'the Italy of 1911 is no longer the Italy of 1896. Its moral worth had increased to the point that a defeat by an African people would no longer be tolerated' Not long after, and even more pointedly he wrote:

> Should we renounce to [Libya], this great gift destined to the Italian nation due to lack of preparation [on the part of the government]? Because up till now all Italian governments have demonstrated a lack of vitality ... should we *eternally* believe our people to be incapable of any grand endeavour? Logic does not oblige us to answer in the affirmative; a faith in the virtues of our race permits us rather to answer in the negative.[49]

For all Bevione's exaggerated claims about the fertility of the Libyan desert allowing for the absorption of 'one million' Italian peasants, it was the kind of challenge he posed to the Italian state in 1911 that lay at the heart of the re-activation of colonialism during Giolitti's 'regime'. The people had to prove their capacity to serve their nation and the nation (as represented by the Italian state) had to trust in the virtues and abilities of the people themselves. In a relationship of mutual respect and trust, Italians would be transformed in the process whose final outcome would be the 'common citizenry' Bernard Porter sees so markedly absent in the imperial aspirations of Great Britain.

That such an idea remained exclusive to elite newspapers, the conferences of the Nationalist Association, or indeed the bridge tables of the Italian diplomatic service need not detain us for long. The Socialist Party, for example, so worried about the 'popularity of Africa' in 1896, was as concerned as Bevione (but for the opposite reason) that a relationship of trust between people and state be forged on the anvil of colonial war. The insidiousness and downright attractiveness of the message contained in nationalist discourse concerning colonialism was recognised but confronted confusedly. Many prominent Socialists could see no harm in Italy providing 'living space' for its downtrodden peasantry,[50] but even for those who considered a war, any war, to be a tool to hoodwink the Italian proletariat, or to raise the levels of repression in the country, the challenge of the Libyan adventure being interpreted very widely as a government bowing to the needs of its poorest citizens was met with great disconcert. The most prominent voice in the Left's anti-war campaign proved to be a young radical of the Romagna region who accused the Socialist leadership of failing to understand Giolitti's game for what it was: cheap war to divert the 'people' from their real interests. Benito Mussolini, still a firebrand on the far left of the Socialist Party in 1911, wrote in his newspaper *La lotta di classe* (Class Struggle):

> If the Fatherland, which is itself a fictitious invention that has no future, demands sacrifices of blood and money, the proletariat that follows the orders of the Socialists, will respond with a general strike. War between nations will therefore become war between classes.[51]

But the future 'Founder of the Italian Empire' (an official title bestowed by Mussolini on himself in 1936), as Del Boca laments,[52] remained an isolated voice in 1911. The enthusiasm for the war, when it broke out in September 1911, was well nigh universal. Filippo Turati, leader of the Socialist Party, could only rue that, for all its posturing, Socialism had failed to stem the tide of jingoism engulfing the country. The only thing to do, he argued wanly in October 1911, was to 'wait patiently while the songs quieten themselves and this drunken binge draws to a close'.[53]

There were others who instead placed great weight on Turati's 'drunken binge', if such it was, and loaded it with enormous significance. For prominent poet Giovanni Pascoli, the reasoning put forward by the Nationalists was greeted with enthusiasm. In that euphoric autumn of 1911 he delivered a widely reported speech in the small town of Barga high in the Apuan Alps between Tuscany and Liguria. The choice of this town was apt because it was so representative, in the first decade of the twentieth century, of the great haemorrhage of Italian emigration. Pascoli had moved to this rugged but beautiful setting more than ten years before, partly as a kind of self-imposed desire to connect with the 'true' Italian peasantry and to witness what he regarded as its immemorial, eternal and enormously dignified labour of love with the harsh contours of the Italian landscape. But during his years there he instead observed the disintegration of a world which he had thought to be everlasting. Under Pascoli's eyes tens of thousands abandoned the lands their forefathers had painstakingly transformed over centuries and took the high road to the New World and the punishing streets of Chicago, New York or Buenos Aires; there, the Italian peasantry's millennial culture Pascoli so admired was as chaff. Corradini's idea of a 'Proletarian Nation' enslaved by the unequal distribution of the world's resources was being confirmed on the doorstep of his farmhouse. As Italian troops prepared to cross the Mediterranean in September 1911 Pascoli jumped at the opportunity to give a speech in their honour.[54]

Its title set the tone: by taking Libya the 'Great Proletarian Nation had Stirred'; as Gian Luigi Ruggio argues, the speech narrated an 'ideal history of Italy running from ancient Rome' to the 'miracle' of the *Risorgimento*.[55] Pascoli had absorbed enough Socialism to understand its appeal as well as some of its fundamental truths. Large numbers of Italians were transferring their loyalties to this political creed for altogether understandable reasons; but the capitalism they so inveighed against was hardly to be seen in Italy. The 'Proletarian Nation's' poverty, its exclusion from the banquets of world diplomacy, made it a loser, a have-not, a pariah of the international order. Its people

> were set to work, paid a pittance and labelled as Carcamanos! Gringos! Cincali! Degos! In all but name they had become Negroes. In America, the citizens of the country of the man who had discovered it, were placed outside the law and outside humanity.[56]

Pascoli did not mention that there had been a spate of killings of Italian workers in the USA but also in Europe. *Aigues Mortes* had been the most infamous. Nine Italians had been lynched in 1893 and the cries of their murderers had been *Mort a les Italians!* Yet, Pascoli continues, these were the heirs of the Romans, the children of those who civilised the world and it was the labour of these men which was now reconstructing the earth. The Italian state, the Italy that had come together only fifty years before, had (until now argued Pascoli) abandoned them to their fate and had failed to marshal their huge potential. Bereft of a state capable of sustaining them, Pascoli believed that it had become

> shameful to say 'Si' as had Dante, to say 'Land', as had Columbus, to say 'Forward', as had Garibaldi ... Dante? [They say of us] But you are a country of illiterates! Columbus? But yours is the honoured society of the Camorra and the Black Hand! Garibaldi? But yours is the army that was defeated and destroyed by barefoot Africans! Long live Menelik!

In a sweeping flourish of rhetoric Pascoli looked to the troops invading North Africa and sustained that all was now changing. Henceforward the labour of Italy's 'huddling masses' would benefit Italy and Italians. The Italian state was finally at the service of its population and the conquest of colonies was proof that the interests of Italy's most humble citizens, those forced to abandon the land of their forefathers, was of the greatest concern to the Italian state and its most treasured institution, the national army. For Pascoli this was proof that in the fifty years since Unification (and the fifteen since Adowa) Italy had come a very long way. Giolitti's democratisation, the rise of popular political representation, the modernisation of the Italian economy, the creation of a railway network spanning the peninsula, the establishing of a national school system and so much more were signs that 'Italy' was now able to successfully turn to colonialism and thus recast the relationship with its people.

> Blessed are you, o fallen for your country! You do not know what you are for us and for history itself! You do not know what Italy owes you! Italy was made fifty years ago. In this holy fiftieth anniversary ... you have proven that Italians too have finally been made.

Pascoli's speech caused a furore. It was printed in tens of thousands of copies; *La Tribuna* newspaper added it as a page insert and distributed it to the Italian soldiers fighting in Africa. Pascoli received letters of eulogy from Benedetto Croce and, famously, Gabriele D'Annunzio dedicated his very popular and jingoistic *Canzoni delle gesta d'oltremare* (published in the *Corriere della Sera*) to his poet colleague. The speech was read out in theatres throughout Italy and Pascoli was even sent a bunch of wild-flowers collected in the trenches near Tripoli by some 'humble soldiers'.[57]

In reality the elderly poet had only picked up on a widespread mood and had been able to verbalise not only the nationalist (and in some senses also the Socialist) critique of Italian state and society but had immediately provided a solution to it in a way that would have pleased Giolitti and the impetus behind his 'regime'. As legislation was passed granting universal suffrage, the Italian media celebrated victory in the Libyan war (so very differently from the calamity of Adowa) and congrat-ulated the nation for its brand new and promising colony. The promise was not just for the literate, the educated or the rich. According to Del Boca, where the poetry of D'Annunzio may have jarred, the cheap books of Adriano Salani, the brightly coloured covers of the *Domenica del Corriere* and other cheap illustrated newspapers, the hundreds of thou-sands of postcards celebrating *Tripoli bel suol d'Amore* (Tripoli land of Love] (in the words of a popular song that swept the country) were much more likely to have been read, treasured and believed.[58] According to Giustino Fortunato the peasants of the *latifondi* of the South were discussing how much land they would be given in Africa,[59] and in Sicily in just a few weeks after the war had broken out, more than 10,000 peasants joined the 'Sicilian Cooperative Society for the colonisation of Tripolitania and Cyrenaica'.[60] School text books for children as young as six were singing the praises of Italy's achievements only a year after the conquest.[61]

The 'proletarian nation' may well have (or had perhaps been) stirred. The heady days of conquest were quickly over, in some ways as Turati had hoped, but the long process of subduing the semi-nomadic tribes of Libya's interior was to last until the 1930s, making the hopes of Sicilian peasants and the dreams of Franchetti still just a dream. However, as the great crisis of the First World War loomed, the satisfaction of having at last conquered a worthy colony came to be narrated as the most tangible sign that unification and the survival of the Italian kingdom was about to reap the reward so bitterly sowed over the last half century. A school textbook published in 1916 for Italian eleven-year-olds would have been condoned fully by Benedetto Croce. The conquest of Libya, it concluded after setting pupils a test on Libyan place names, 'is the greatest testimony of the enormous progress our country has made in the fifty years since the foundation of the kingdom'.[62]

Ethiopia 1935–36: 'we are the emigrants of yesteryear'

One of the most potent of the tens of thousands of images to be found in newspapers, textbooks, newsreels and celebratory pamphlets of the Italian conquest of Ethiopia in the mid-1930s shows a maniple of soldiers encamped in Africa carrying a placard with written on it 'we are the emigrants of yesteryear'.[63] No doubt some minor Fascist propagandist had placed the banner in the hands of these now blackshirted colonisers, but the message it carried, as has been shown, was a remarkable summation of the logic of the Italian colonial project as it had emerged in the 1880s. Each 'regime' (Crispi's charismatic and undemocratic nationalism as well as Giolitti's more open and fluid parliamentarianism) had in fact said the same thing. The advent of Fascism in 1922 added little to what had been the major tropes of Italy's previous African dreams. Angelo Del Boca states that the Fascists invented 'absolutely nothing' compared with their Liberal predecessors except that they achieved 'the adherence of the masses to the myth of a place in sun'.[64]

The relationship between 'people and empire' during Fascism requires a more nuanced and accurate unravelling than that of previous 'regimes'. There were no dissenting voices in the 1930s because none could legally be given an airing. Fascism killed debate in the normal sense of the term. Apart from the clandestine press of the exiled political parties, the leaders of which were shocked by what appeared to be the unanimous support granted by the Italian people for Mussolini's renewed war in Ethiopia,[65] the only dissent possible became crime. Richard Bosworth's exploration of 1920s and 30s police archives has highlighted the complexity with which Italians read events and located themselves with respect to what declared itself (and he criticises the historians who may have swallowed the Fascist bait)[66] as a monolithic and 'totalitarian' society. During the war of African conquest the Italian police were 'interested' in cases such as the watermelon seller who stated to his clients that 'you need a big-

6.2 'We are the emigrants of yesteryear'. Photograph depicting Italian troops off to Africa in 1935 as the poor migrants of the past transformed by Fascism into proud and dignified colonists. (Courtesy Giusppe Finaldi from the journal *La Difesa della Razza*, 5 April 1939)

head like the *Duce* to go into a war ... and the Abyssinians are in the right because we are the ones who are breaking into their homes' or even the man who, on returning from Africa, remarked in a café that 'in those sorts of places white men can't survive'.[67] If such innocuous chatter carried a prison sentence then the flag waving, the 'oceanic' crowds and the whistling of the incredibly popular song *Faccetta Nera* (about Italians going to Africa to free a girl with 'a little black face' from slavery) may have been more than a little forced.

The 'totalitarian' onslaught accompanying the launch and prosecution of the Ethiopian campaign in 1935 was overwhelming (Bosworth calls it 'obstreperous'[68]). Gone were the days when popular culture was carried exclusively on the flimsy and easily torn Pennaroli broadsheets, the wood-block prints in Piccinini, the speeches in churches, and the quiet ceremonies remembering the soldiers dying for *Italietta* (a disparaging word referring to the pre-Fascist 'little Italy'). We have now entered the era of cinema, newreel, mass-produced books and newspapers, advertising and the radio. In his seminal analysis of colonial propaganda during Fascism, Adolfo Mignemi argues that the regime knew precisely what it was doing.

[218]

The exceptional effort made by the Regime in terms of the use of the means of propaganda and the uniformity of the State's intervention in the means of communication … in the years 1935–6, points to the centrality of the concept of *consensus factory*.[69]

Mignemi argues that the Fascist regime used all its power as propaganda to ensure that the Ethiopian campaign of 1935–36 had a mass backing; Mussolini effectively 'manufactured consensus' for his colonial goals through directives to the press,[70] the cinema-industry,[71] newsreel-producing companies,[72] as well as launching campaigns for colonial novel-writing,[73] ensuring school-teachers made the war the central issue in teaching over the months of the campaign and much more.

But the idea of a colonialism rammed down Italians' throats, a propaganda bombardment which successfully moulded millions of minds into a single Fascist consensus is as farfetched as Carlo Levi's notion of a completely impervious Italy existing somewhere 'beyond the mountains'. The reality was that Mussolini knew that by pursuing a successful colonial campaign *his* regime would reap all the benefits that his predecessors had hoped would accrue to theirs back in the days of Adowa and Tripoli. It was the same Mussolini who understood as a Socialist in 1911 that a war in Africa would dispel the people from their 'real interests' and make them follow the 'fiction that is the nation' rather than adopting an ideology of class.[74] But it was the regime's shortcomings, its failure to live up to its totalitarian dreams that also fired imperial ambitions. After 1929 the church had become more actively engaged in locating itself as an independent alternative to the regime and Mussolini needed no reminding that he was *Duce* only by the leave of little King Victor Emanuel III. The 'people' themselves, or at least the hundreds of thousands with relatives and *paesani* living now in the USA, Argentina or the many other destinations of Italian migration over the previous half-century, were possibly tempted to relocate their local identities to one that, as Carlo Levi noted, saw New York rather than Rome as its epicentre. The church, the monarchy and these spontaneous 'colonies' attached to (what might become enemy) states that could provide employment and wealth for Italy's masses (at least until the 1930s) tarnished Fascism's exclusive claims to the souls of the people. As has been said, after Italy's successful conquest of Ethiopia the *Duce* took the title 'Founder of the Empire' and it was appended to his name thereafter to the exclusion of all else, suggesting that giving Italy a large colony in Africa was the most tangible sign of how Fascism had indeed successfully harnessed (and served) the Italian 'people'. It was historian Renzo De Felice who, controversially, first saw the Ethiopian War as the moment in which (Fascist) regime and people finally (although not permanently) came together. He wrote,

> the Ethiopian war was Mussolini's political masterpiece and his greatest success because he believed in it profoundly as in probably no other of his political ventures. He believed in it not just instrumentally, as serving his personal prestige ... but intimately as something that corresponded to the raison d'être of his *historical role* because the war assumed for him the value of a *mission* whose aim was to make the (present and future) Nation recognise in his personal *vocation* its own *absolute duty*, and therefore to bring about the identification between *vox ducis* and *vox populi* which until that moment Fascism had been unable to really realise.[75]

Certainly, from the amount of material published in the years that followed the conquest, it would appear that De Felice is right. School textbooks, for example, on the basis of a quantitative analysis I carried out on a sample of almost 1,000 published between 1900 and 1945, show that interest in colonial issues ballooned after 1936. Most history and geography texts for school children dedicated almost 10 per cent of their total number of pages to the Italian Empire; before the mid-1930s the figure had never reached 4 per cent.[76] A series of movies celebrating the conquest was produced by Rome's new Cinecittà studios (some of truly epic proportions),[77] newsreels brimmed with images of Italians in Africa and the 'Founder of the Italian Empire' was constantly depicted as having finally granted that which the Italian people had aspired to for so long. Gargantuan ceremonies were held in Rome celebrating the anniversaries of the proclamation of the empire in October 1936; a huge obelisk was dragged from Axum in Ethiopia, shipped to Italy, and re-assembled with great pomp in 1938 before the massive new Ministry of Colonies (later the World Food Organisation building) in Rome;[78] an imposing colonial exhibition was held in Naples (as its official guide stated, it *had been* through this city that most Italian migrants abandoned their country[79]) in 1940. People fell over themselves to sing the praises of Mussolini having successfully blotted out the shame of Adowa and dedicated poets wrote their usual fantasies.[80] Memoirs of soldiers and workers who went to Africa appear to attest to the fact that this was a popular campaign.[81]

Perhaps the most tangible sign of the 'adherence of the (Italian) masses to myth of the place in the sun' was the very cleverly orchestrated campaign inciting Italian women to donate their gold wedding rings to the regime as part of the regimen of self-reliance spurred by the imposition of economic sanctions on Italy by the League of Nations in 1935. The *Giornata delle Fedi* (Day of Wedding Rings) was held on 18 December of that year and, as the front cover of the popular weekly, the *Domenica del Corriere* put it, was meant to be an 'offering of love and faith by Italian women'[82] to Fascism's colonial politics and therefore a profession of conviction in the legitimacy of the regime itself. That this testament of loyalty was demanded in the face of the condemnation of the democratic powers of the League of Nations (as well as its only Communist member, the Soviet Union), which between them possessed so much of the world's 'living-space', not only revamped the idea of the 'Proletarian Nation' but showed that Fascism was not frightened to challenge the unjust international order for the benefit of the Italian people. Petra Terhoeven has shown that the wedding-ring campaign was no simple directive 'from above' adhered to by the terrified masses of a totalitarian state, but a collective experience whose main drive was not the need to restock Italy's gold reserves in the midst of an expensive colonial war, but 'an end in itself ... a symbolic formula of devotion [to the regime] on the part of a citizenry in fact possessing no power whatsoever'.[83] If the latter was indeed the case then empire was certainly providing, as MacKenzie put it in 1983, 'a national purpose with a high moral content lead[ing] to class conciliation',[84] or in this case, class and gender powerlessness did not hamper consensus. The proportion of Italians who donated their wedding rings 'to the nation' oscillated between 23 per cent in the province of Asti to 90 per cent in the province of Reggio Emilia.[85] While the reasons for which there was a mass, positive response to the regime's demanding of its people such an emotionally charged profession of faith are plural, it is difficult not to be convinced by Terhoeven that the success of the 'Day of Wedding Rings' was anything other than 'a declaration of deep-seated consent for Fascism' and its new empire.[86]

Mussolini had, for a while anyway, gainfully used empire for connecting the Italian people to the state (as restructured by Fascism) in the way that had been envisaged by Liberals before him. However one interprets the propaganda of the late 1930s, there is no question that the successful conquest of Ethiopia was greeted as a confirmation that the Fascist regime was going where previous ones had failed or stalled. According to some historians, by the early 1930s Mussolini's dictatorship itself was in dire need of a revamp. Compromises with the church, the Italian monarchy and the old establishment risked giving the Fascist regime a kind of precocious old age. For all Mussolini's blustering what was passed off as the 'Fascist revolution'[87] had visibly ground to a halt even before the onset of the Great Depression.

With Hitler taking power in 1933 for Italian Fascism the stakes were radically lifted. The 'Night of the Long Knives' in early 1934 and the foreshortening of Mussolini's 'revolution' Hitler seemed in the process of achieving, revealed to many in Italy, and especially to Mussolini himself, just how little Fascism had actually amassed on its CV. It had crushed all opposition to the establishment in the 1920s, it had installed some new

institutions such as the Fascist boy scouts and the Fascist leisure organ-
sation, it had even drained the Pontine marshes and perhaps got the
trains to run on time (no mean feat to be sure) but everybody knew that
Italy was still (more or less) Italy with its diminutive monarch, its old
monuments, its stuttering industrialisation, its English and German
tourists, whose shoes any Italian street kid would have been prepared to
shine for a few lira. Colonialism, or rather, a new Roman Empire came
to the rescue. For historians such as Emilio Gentile,[88] MacGregor Knox[89]
or Davide Rodogno the Italian shift to empire in the mid-1930s was in
fact an

> essential component of a totalitarian project to transform society. The revo-
> lution of 1922 should have founded a 'new civilization', that of Fascism.
> The War in Africa was to provide a new context for Fascism's schemes of
> social engineering. It would drive the renewal of Italian society; it would
> represent the apogee of the myth of national regeneration; and it would be
> the crucible for a new civilization which would give Italy leadership of
> Europe. The colonial war would generate a new kind of humanity bred for
> conquest and domination ... it would accomplish [Fascism's] revolutionary
> endeavour to create a *uomo nuovo* a new Fascist Man.[90]

Yet, taking a broader view, that Italian Fascism went for colonies in the
1930s, was hardly something so striking and so anomalous that it could
only have been connected to a fanatical totalitarian design to recast the
nation in an Orwellian direction. Still, it seems plausible enough to
ascribe the decision to attack Ethiopia to Mussolini's desire to secure his
regime at home vis-à-vis the Italian people. He would be able, in a way
that Liberal Italy had only attained partially, to satisfy the long-frustrated
Italian ambition for a serious Place in the Sun, to avenge Adowa (in
Ethiopia itself rather than in Libya as Giolitti had done) and to thus
secure some really solid credentials for his 'revolution'. What Mussolini
could be sure about in the mid-1930s was that there would be widespread support for a colonial war as long as casualties remained low,
defeats (even minor ones) were avoided (or simply not reported) and the
benefits bestowed by empire on Italy and Italians could be shown to
connect with the 'usual' needs of the Italian people.

The story has a familiar ring about it notwithstanding the ever-present
jutting-jawed bust of Mussolini (carved, for example, by one enterprising
soldier on the mountains of Ethiopia, near Adowa), the blackshirts and
the New Fascist Man; it had been told and retold in the era of Crispi and
Giolitti. The narratives devised in the Liberal period echoed through
Fascism; indeed they were fundamental in delineating what Fascism was
meant to be before the Italian people.

As the crowds celebrated and imagined the benefits Ethiopia or Italian East Africa would bring to them, the Second World War loomed. The Italian Empire was to be one of the first casualties of Mussolini's rash challenging of Britain in 1940. The consensual relationship between people and regime, cemented by the foundation of empire, cooled and then disintegrated as military debacle in Africa, then Europe and then on the peninsula itself followed. The few tens of thousands of settlers who had braved the Libyan deserts or the Ethiopian plateau (still bristling with anti-colonial patriots) were indeed the 'emigrants of yesteryear' but the promises made to them by Fascism (like those of liberalism before) proved hollow. After 1945 the flow of migrants leaving the peninsula returned to the levels of the days of Giolitti and Pascoli; it once again crossed the Atlantic, the Alps and even reached the Antipodes, but, barring a few exceptions, entirely bypassed an Africa where Italian power no longer counted.

The Italian Empire evaporated with Mussolini's passing but not so a strong claim to colonies as a legitimate accoutrement to a modern Italian nation. After 1945 the new republican regime (and all political parties including the Italian Communists) made strenuous efforts to at least retain Libya and Eritrea for the Italian people.[91] It was after all the latter who had had always been considered the receptacle of colonialism's bene-fits bestowed and the new Italian constitution stated that Italy was 'a democratic republic founded on labour'.[92] In 1951, as the final destina-tion of the ex-Italian colonies was discussed at the United Nations, a school textbook (for eleven year olds) in Italy could read:

> until the conclusion of the last war Italy possessed vast tracts of territory in Africa: Libya, Eritrea, Somalia … Their destiny has yet to be definitively decided but Italians are confident that we will be able to bring our labour down there once more.[93]

Conclusion

The construction of the nation in Italy from unification to the end of the Second World War was bound up with a drive to locate the *Patria* [Fatherland] as a Great Power in the international order dominated by the West European states. Throughout this period models of how the state should relate to the 'people' repeatedly (and quite consistently) became linked with colonialism because the latter was seen as providing possible solutions to a succession of obstinate problems that faced Italy's elites in their quest to build an ordered, viable and stable society on their terms. The most pressing dilemma was that the coming together of Italy could never live up to its promise of delivering a satisfied and serene 'people' without the risk of spinning the delicately poised class, economic, regional and cultural equilibrium of the peninsula out of control. As was made patently obvious by the enormous outflow of migrants from the 1880s on, Italy simply lacked the resources and the know-how for every citizen, as a hopeful popular writer and patriot put it in 1886, 'to work for a day when poverty, ignorance, injustice and crime may be banished from your [Italy's] borders and you will be able to live and expand, calm in the majesty of your right and strength'.[94] That day had failed to come in the 1880s, it had failed to come when Italy celebrated its fiftieth anniversary in 1911, and it had yet to materialise after more than a decade of Fascism. The quest for empire was always a message launched candidly at the 'people', to involve them directly in finding a solution to Italy's problems and to unite them, as a common citizenry, with an Italian state dogged by issues of legitimacy. There was no hiding the empire (a vast looting operation not to be shared with the 'people', according to Bernard Porter in the British context), because its very *raison d'être* in the Italian context was as tool of communication between state and 'people'.

Did the 'people' respond? On the whole, and on the basis of much recent research (including my own), it would appear that many did. The cries of 'Long live Menelik' to be heard in the streets in 1896 and beyond were as much about rejecting Crispi and his vision of the Italian nation-state as they were overt anti-colonial statements. It was defeat that made the Sicilian prime minister's efforts come across as humbug. It was to be defeat once again that made Mussolini's imperial posturing seem yet another broken promise. Carlo Levi was glad to see an Italian peasantry impervious to empire and he could therefore peer into the minds of a people untouched by the hex of Fascism. Mussolini, for all his savvy manipulation of Italy's new mass media, had failed to communicate with the people, narrowly defined as they were by this anti-Fascist. Yet the Italian 'people' were also 'the schoolchildren and their teachers, Fascist Scouts, Red Cross ladies, the widows and mothers of Milanese veterans, women of fashion in Florence, grocers, shopkeepers, pensioners, journalists, policemen and government employees in Rome' and they were becoming ever more so. Missionaries and priests, writers, politicians, journalists, film-makers, authors of school textbooks, newsreel film-makers, photographers or the designers of the cover of colour magazines, as well as song-writers and minor poets, to mention just a few of Italy's cultural producers may have spoken to that Italy rather than to Levi's. To these Italians on 'this side of the mountains' empire, or simply the possession of some colonies, was a potent dream that would solve the nation's problems, make Italians (wherever they came from) proud and connect them to the agendas of the state (in its various guises and regimes) interpreted as the legitimate representative of that thing called the 'Italian people'.

Yet this delicate equation had presumed imperial success; apart from the momentary elation of victory in 1912 and 1936, the Italian empire never became a going concern. Italian East Africa was abruptly taken away only five years after it had come into existence and Libya was permanently lost to Italy in 1943, a few short years after its brutal 'pacification'. There had been little time to make something of the rebellious and infertile territories Italy had acquired with so many expectations and the time that there had been had coincided with a crisis in Europe that in the end destroyed the very logic of how state and society in Italy had related to each other ever since Unification. Still, Italy's colonial dreams had in many ways provided a channel of communication between state and people that remained a fundamental if contradictory experience in the long and arduous process of turning peasants into Italians.

Notes

1 C. Levi, *Christ Stopped at Eboli* (Harmondsworth 1984), pp. 130–1.
2 B. Porter, *The Absent-Minded Imperialists: Empire, Society, and Culture in Britain* (Oxford 2004).
3 Ibid., p. 308.
4 See e.g. G. Finaldi, *Italian National Identity in the Scramble for Africa: Italy's African Wars in the Era of Nation-building, 1870–1900* (Bern 2009); N. Labanca, *Oltremare. Storia dell'espansione coloniale italiana* (Bologna 2002), and 'L'Africa italiana', in M. Isnenghi (ed.), *I luoghi della memoria Simboli e miti dell'Italia unita* (Rome-Bari 1996).
5 J. MacKenzie, *Propaganda and Empire* (Manchester 1984), p. 2.
6 R. Battaglia, *La Prima Guerra d'Africa* (Turin 1958), p. 263.
7 A. Del Boca, *Gli Italiani in Africa Orientale I, dall' Unità alla Marcia su Rome* (Milan 1992), p. 299.
8 C. Duggan, *Creare la nazione: vita di Francesco Crispi* (Rome 2000).
9 See for example the very useful J. Davis, 'Remapping Italy's path to the 20th century', *Journal of Modern History*, 66 (1994), pp. 291–320, and R. Bosworth, 'The Italian Novecento and its Historians', *The Historical Journal*, 49 (2006), pp. 317–29.
10 C. Duggan, *The Force of Destiny: A History of Italy since 1796* (Boston 2008), p. 319.
11 See G. Finaldi, 'Culture and imperialism in a "backward" nation? The Prima Guerra d'Africa (1885–1896) in Italian primary schools', *The Journal of Modern Italian Studies*, 8, 3 (January 2003), pp. 374–90.
12 Duggan, *The Force of Destiny*, p. 337.
13 On Franchetti see for example J. Dickie, *Darkest Italy: the Nation and Stereotypes of the Mezzogiorno, 1860–1900* (New York 1999), pp. 64–82, and *Cosa Nostra: A History of the Sicilian Mafia* (New York 2004), pp. 43–54; N. Moe, 'The emergence of the Southern Question in Villari, Franchetti, and Sonnino', in J. Schneider, *Italy's 'Southern question': Orientalism in One Country* (Oxford 1998), pp. 61–71. On Franchetti's colonialism and more see P. Pezzino and A. Tacchini (eds), *Leopoldo e Alice Franchetti e il loro tempo* (Citta di Castello 2002); as well as R. Rainero, *I primi tentativi di colonizzazione agricola e di popolamento dell'Eritrea (1890–95)* (Milan 1961).
14 L. Franchetti and S. Sonnino, *Inchiesta in Sicilia*, Vol. 1 (Florence 1974), p. 232.
15 Ibid., Vol. II, p. 208.

16 The Great Brigandage, as it came to be called, was a full-scale popular revolt against Piedmontese (and Italian) authority which wracked the South of Italy in the 1860s and 70s.

17 L. Franchetti, 'L'Italia e la sua colonia africana', in R. Villari, *Il Sud nella storia d'Italia: antologia della questione meridionale*, Vol. I (Bari 1974), pp. 221–2.

18 See Franchetti's interesting will and testament reprinted in U. Bistoni, *Grandezza e decadenza delle istituzioni Franchetti* (Citta di castello 1997), pp. 3–7.

19 Franchetti, *L'avvenire della colonia eritrea*, p. 22.

20 In P. Rosario, *L'Africa italiane e un propsta dell'onorevole Franchetti* (Bari, 1891), pp. 22–3.

21 Franchetti, preface to O. Pedrazzi, *L'Africa dopo la guerra e l'Italia* (Florence 1917), pp. IV–V.

22 S. Lanaro, *Nazione e Lavoro* (Venice 1988), pp. 20–1.

23 A. Brunialti, *L'Italia e le colonie* (Turin 1896), pp. 343–4. Quoted in N. Labanca, *In marcia verso Adua* (Turin 1993), p. 66.

24 F. Chabod, *Storia della politica estera italiana dal 1870 al 1896. Volume primo: le premesse* (Bari 1951), p. 13.

25 Quoted in C. Dota, 'Il dibattito sul problema coloniale nella stampa socialista (1887–1900)', *Storia Contemporanea*, X (1979), pp. 1047–87, and also in N. Labanca, 'L'Africa italiana', p. 258.

26 On the *Pontremolesi* see G. Martinelli, *Origine e sviluppo dell attivita dei librai pontremolesi* (Pontremoli 1973) and S. Pivato, 'Lettura e istruzione popolare in Emilia Romagna tra Otto e Novecento', in G. Tortorelli (ed.), *L'Editoria italiana tra otto e novecento* (Bologna 1987), pp. 37–8.

27 See the pioneering R. Altick, *The Common Reader: A Social History of the Mass Reading Public, 1800–1900* (Chicago 1957).

28 *L'Ultima battaglia d'Africa* (Fiorenzuola d'Arda 1901).

29 All these titles are gleaned from advertisements in G. Piccinini, *Guerra d'Africa* (Rome 1887–88) or the annual volumes of the *Bollettino delle pubblicazioni italiane* (Florence 1880–1900).

30 Battaglia, *La Prima Guerra*, p. 263.

31 Labanca, *In marcia*, between pp. 172 and 173.

32 Piccinini, *Guerra*, pp. 680–1.

33 See on this also G. Finaldi, 'Italy's Scramble for Africa: from Dogali to Adowa', in J. Dickie and J. Foot (eds), *Disastro!* (New York 2001).

34 (Pieve di Soligo, 1887); poster held at *Avvenimenti (Dogali)* section of the Pubblicazioni Minori area of the National Library of Florence.

35 Labanca, *In marcia*, p. 363.

36 In one 1887 play, for example, Dogali was referred to as the 'Italian Thermopylae'. See M. Frassinesi, *Le termopili italiane. Saati e Dogali. Memoria agli italiani* (Milan 1887).

37 Battaglia, *La Prima Guerra*, pp. 793–807.

38 F. Martini, *Il diario eritreo*, Vol. I (Florence n.d.) p. 159.

39 On the desire that Italy should be a 'Great' power or not be one at all see E. Gentile, *La Grande Italia* (Milan 1997).

40 B. Croce, *Storia D'Italia dal 1871 al 1915* (Bari, Laterza 1928), pp. 271–2.

41 Although a case for the invasion of Libya being the fruit of expanding Italian capitalist interests has certainly been made. See G. Are, *La scoperta dell'imperialismo* (Rome 1985).

42 M. Clark, *Modern Italy, 1871–1995* (London 1984), Chapter 4.

43 S. Romano, *La quarta sponda* (Milan 1977), p. 29.

44 Quoted in F. Perfetti, *Il nazionalismo italiano dalle origini alla fusione col fascismo* (Bologna 1977), p. 175.

45 Quoted in R. Luperini, *La crisi intellettuale nell'età di Giolitti* (Messina 1978), pp. 99–102.

46 Quoted in Clark, *Modern Italy*, p. 137.

47 Quoted in A. Del Boca, *Gli italiani in Libia* (Milan 1993), p. 57.

48 Ibid., pp. 58–9.

49 Quoted in G. Salvemini, *Come siamo andati in Libia e altri scritti dal 1900 al 1915* (Milan 1973), p. 111.
50 The Libyan adventure was supported by such prominent figures of the Italian Left as Angelo Olivetti, Arturo Labriola, Paolo Orano, Ivanoe Bonomi, Roberto Michels and Leonida Bissolati. Most of these Socialist gentlemen would either passively or very openly support Italian intervention in World War I and later Fascism. See Del Boca, *Gli italiani in Libia*, pp. 81–2.
51 B. Mussolini, *La Lotta di Classe* (23 September 1911); quoted in R. De Felice, *Mussolini il rivoluzionario* (Turin 1965), p. 105.
52 Del Boca labels the Italian Socialist Party the 'great loser' of the Libyan war. See *Gli italiani in Libia*, pp. 79–85.
53 Quoted in ibid., pp. 85.
54 G. Ruggio, *Giovanni Pascoli: tutto il racconto della vita tormentata di un grande poeta* (Milan 1998), p. 318.
55 Ibid.
56 G. Pascoli, 'La grande proletaria si è mossa'. Available at http://cronologia.leonardo.it/ storia/a1911f.htm (accessed 5 May 2009). Other quotations from the speech taken from same source.
57 Ruggio, *Giovanni Pascoli*, p. 320.
58 Del Boca, *Gli italiani in Libia*, p. 152.
59 G. Fortunato, *Carteggio 1865–1911* (Rome 1978), p. 369.
60 Del Boca, *Gli italiani in Libia*, p. 153.
61 On this see G. Finaldi, 'La Libia nei manuali scolastici italiani 1911–1960', in N. Labanca and S. Bono (eds), *La Libia nei manuali scolastici italiani 1911–2000* (Rome 2003).
62 G. Moro and E. Oberti, *Storia d'Italia, testo atlante*, Vol. III (Florence 1916), p. 117.
63 This photograph is reproduced in R. De Felice and L. Goglia, *Storia fotografica del fascismo* (Rome 1981).
64 A. Del Boca, *Gli Italiani in Africa Orientale. II. La conquista dell'Impero* (Milan, Mondadori 1992), p. 880.
65 See on this G. Procacci, *Il socialismo internazionale e la guerra d'Etiopia* (Rome 1978).
66 See especially conclusion of R. Bosworth, *Mussolini's Italy: Life under the Dictatorship* (London 2006).
67 Ibid., p. 385. For other cases see esp. pp. 385–95.
68 Ibid., p. 366.
69 Mignemi A. (ed.), *Immagine coordinata per un impero. Etiopia 1935–1936* (Turin 1984), p. 8.
70 V. Castronovo and N. Tranfaglia (eds), *La stampa italiana nell'età fascista* (Rome 1980).
71 G.P. Brunetta, *Storia del cinema italiano: Il cinema del regime 1929–1945* (Rome 1993).
72 C. Carabba, *L'occhio del regime: informazione e propaganda nel cinema del fascismo* (Florence 1979).
73 G. Tommasello, *La letteratura coloniale italiana dalle avanguardie al fascismo* (Palermo 1984).
74 See note 51 above.
75 Quoted in G. Finaldi, *Mussolini and Italian Fascism* (London 2008), p. 77.
76 See on this the data in G. Finaldi, *La Libia nei manuali*, pp. 63–72. The full archive of collected data is available at the Archivio Fotografico Toscano, Prato, Italy.
77 See on this especially G.P. Brunetta and J. Gili (eds), *L'ora d'Africa del cinema italiano: 1911–1989* (Trento 1990) and D. Baratieri, *Memories and Silences Haunted by Fascism: Italian Colonialism 1930s–1960s* (Bern 2010).
78 For a photograph of the ceremony see A. Del Boca and N. Labanca, *L'impero africano del fascismo nelle fotografie dell'Istituto Luce* (Rome 2002), p. 217.
79 G. Dore, 'Ideologia coloniale e senso commune etnografico nella Mostra delle Terre Italiane d'Oltremare', in N. Labanca (ed.), *L'Africa in vetrina, storia di musei e esposizioni coloniali in Italia* (Treviso 1991), p. 49.

80 On these 'poets' see Del Boca, *Gli italiani in Africa Orientale*, Vol. II, pp. 342–50.
81 Ibid., pp. 334–42. On this see especially N. Labanca, *Una Guerra per l'impero. Memorie della campagna d'Etiopia 1935–6* (Bologna 2005).
82 This illustration adorns the cover of A. Del Boca (ed.), *Le guerre coloniali del Fascismo* (Rome 1991).
83 P. Terhoeven, *Oro alla patria. Donne, guerra e propaganda nella giornata della Fede Fascista* (Bologna 2006), p. 308.
84 See note 5 above.
85 See data in Terhoeven, *Oro alla patria*, pp. 310–11.
86 Ibid. p. 306.
87 An exhibition on the 'Fascist Revolution' had been held in Rome in 1932–33 and four million people are meant to have visited it. See J. Schnapp, *Anno X – La mostra della Rivoluzione fascista del 1932* (Pisa 2003).
88 See E. Gentile, *Fascismo di pietra* (Rome 2007), Chapter 7.
89 M. Knox, *Common Destiny, Dictatorship, Foreign Policy and War in Fascist Italy and Nazi Germany* (Cambridge 2000).
90 D. Rodogno, *Fascism's European Empire* (Cambridge 2006), p. 466.
91 See on this issue Baratieri, *Memories and Silences*; also L. Pastorelli, 'Una precoce decolonizzazione. Stampa e ambienti coloniali italiani nel secondo dopoguerra (1945–1949)', *Studi Piacentini*, 28 (2000), pp. 65–95.
92 For the text of the Italian Constitution in English go to http://servat.unibe.ch/icl/it00000_.html (accessed on 19 May 2009).
93 A. Albertoni, *Finestra sul mondo, V elementare* (Florence 1952), p. 197.
94 'Prayer to Italy', in E. De Amicis, *Cuore: The Heart of a Boy* (London 1986), p. 229 (first published in 1886).

AFTERWORD BY MATTHEW G. STANARD

On my way to Perthshire for the symposium that resulted in this book, I stopped in Edinburgh for a day. I had never been to Scotland before, and I thought it would be nice not only to visit the city but also to take a break in between re-reading my colleagues' essays on the trans-Atlantic flight and the intense discussions that lay ahead. I tramped around the city all afternoon: Leith Walk, North Bridge, Kings Stables Road, Salisbury Crags, Parliament, the New and Old Towns. Along the Royal Mile I stopped at St Giles, a church layered in history from the medieval period to the twentieth century. Immediately to my right upon entering was something that roused me from my oblivious sightseeing: a memorial to soldiers killed in an outpost of the erstwhile empire. Of course, I had to take a photograph. As I continued around the building's interior, more photographs followed as the memorials multiplied: to the 93d Sutherland Highlanders who died during the Indian Mutiny; the 92d Gordon Highlanders who died in South Africa and Afghanistan; Royal Scots officers who died during the South African War. After a large monument to the Royal Highlanders, the Black Watch, and the 1882 Egypt campaign, I quit taking photographs because of the sheer surfeit. The cathedral ended my plan to take a break from work: there, in a church in Edinburgh, in summer 2009, I was surrounded by empire.

I was probably more attuned to imperial imagery than most visitors to the cathedral that day, which begs the question as to how metropolitan audiences received and interpreted imperialistic messages, if at all. The authors of this volume are keenly aware of the issue of perception, that is to say the importance of understanding people in the past on their own terms rather than projecting our own sensitivities onto them. The judicious conclusion throughout is that the precise impact of imperialistic messages often has to remain at the level of informed supposition because of the limits to what we can know about what people perceived in the past. But as John MacKenzie points out, the Age of Empire was for Europe a period of rising literacy, cheaper transport, faster communication and mass politics. To believe people of that era remained unmoved by the proliferation of imperialistic messages at the time is to presume a level of absent-mindedness not reflected in the historical record. Moreover, as historians working since the appearance of MacKenzie's seminal *Propaganda and Empire* have shown, many markers of European popular imperialism were unremarkable – literally unremarked on by people at the time – because by the twentieth century they were, like the memorials in St Giles, so commonplace.

Just as one must accept the difficulty of measuring the exact effects of pro-empire messages, so is it important not to equate intended meanings with actual results. As Nicholas Reeves cautions in regard to the well-trod subject of First World War film propaganda, 'the myth of the power of film propaganda was, in reality, incomparably more powerful than the film propaganda itself'.[1] This is not to say that propaganda did not have multiple effects, both intentional and accidental. Take Nazi propaganda. In his autobiography *Five Germanys I Have Known*, Fritz Stern wonders how a hateful and 'filthy' piece of Nazi propaganda on a highway billboard could remain a clear memory to him seven decades later.[2] The question then becomes how best to gauge the results of pro-empire messages and the level of popular enthusiasm, or lack thereof, in different national cases. One way is through comparison, or as Marc Bloch put it, 'there is no true understanding without a certain range of comparison; provided, of course, that that comparison is based upon differing and, at the same time, related realities'.[3] Little comparative work has been done so far despite the now longstanding interest in European colonial cultures among historians.[4] A strength of this volume is its comparative approach, as well as each chapter's unique conclusions about the 'backworkings' of imperialism.[5]

The national cases that have attracted most attention so far are Britain and France, and MacKenzie's and Berny Sèbe's chapters are *tours de force* of the capacious literature that has emerged. Britain was in ways unique, including the significant place of emigration in developing British imperialistic culture and the unspoken yet forceful embrace of empire in advertising. Alternately explicit and implicit to MacKenzie's essay is the persuasive argument that the empire became part and parcel of British culture. Some scholars remain unconvinced of the existence of popular imperialism in Britain or the need to bring the empire into British history, as revealed (to take one example) in the paucity of information on India in biographies of Churchill, considering the centrality of empire to his *Weltanschauung* and India's place in that empire.[6] MacKenzie's chapter confirms that historians can not think about modern British history and culture without thinking about the empire. In the French case, it may be true that smaller groups like the *parti colonial* drove much overseas expansion and that the French never viewed twenty (colonial) servants as compensation for the loss of two daughters (Alsace and Lorraine). But as Sèbe shows, this should not obscure the ubiquity of empire in the lives of French men and women by the mid-twentieth century. Distinct from Britain was the perhaps typically French etatist approach toward cultivating imperialistic sentiment during the inter-war years, which reinforced popular enthusiasm by means of official efforts to drum up support.

Scholars have had much less to say to date about colonial culture in the Netherlands, Belgium, Italy and Germany. As Vincent Kuitenbrouwer explains in the case of modern Dutch imperialism, if one looks beyond outward appearances, the depth, scope and shape of pro-empire senti- ment come into better view. It is tempting to focus on milestones like the South African War or the Aceh War, much as one studying British popular imperialism might narrowly focus on fleeting moments of jingoism. One might also be tempted to concentrate on apparent signs of a *lack* of connections to the East Indies or South Africa, such as the dramatic burning of Dutch-language books by Afrikaners. But beyond such excep- tional moments are important if subtle imperialistic connections and feelings that endured well past the first decade of the twentieth century. The Belgian case is in this way similar: if one looks beyond the obvious – that is, past the palpable horrors of Leopold II and the Congo Free State – one perceives an unexpected level of enthusiasm for empire that not only endured but grew. In the case of Italy, Pep Finaldi makes what is perhaps the most far-reaching re-assessment in the present volume. Whereas historians have pointed to emigration, the search for prestige, and other factors to explain the origins of Italian imperialism, Finaldi turns our attention to the link between imperialism and state authority across political regimes, from Liberal to Fascist Italy. The connections between Italians and their colonies are not merely significant to Italian culture, rather they were at the heart of the empire's genesis (and later expansion) and central to the Italian state's very legitimacy. Bernhard Gissibl does a wonderful job showing how Germany's colonies shaped the metropole profoundly, manifested obviously at *Völkerschauen*, subtly in the sciences (e.g., veterinary medicine), and at unexpected moments such as a textile workers strike. Peculiar to the German case, of course, was the growing imperialistic sentiment without object in the years after 1919. Gissibl is at pains to reveal not only the significance of the local but also the international, highlighting the importance of other empires to Germans, through transnational flows of ideas and people.

The fruitfulness of Gissibl's international perspective reveals the benefits of considering popular imperialism transnationally and compar- atively. Doing so shows that in a surprising number of ways, European states engaged in similar practices and took hold of remarkably comparable ideas and sentiments in regard to their overseas empires. For example, all states made a special effort to instill pro-empire sentiments among young people, and for each the colonies played an important role in the validation of scientific disciplines. Reminiscent of Schumpeter's essay on imperialism's atavistic nature is the striking parallel across countries of monarchy-empire connections, from Victoria (Queen of Britain and Empress of India), to Dutch royals awarding medals to the victors of Lombok, to the close colony-dynasty ties in Belgium from Leopold II to Baudouin.[7] (The exception, of course, was France.) There were analogous views of a larger world in which the culture, language, and people of the nation circulated: a 'greater Netherlands', *la Plus Grande France*, a Greater Britain, and Germany's *Aussiedler*, *Übersiedler* and *Auslandsdeutsche*. All empires played critical if various roles in shaping European nationalisms and legitimising states: Britain's unified Welsh, Scots and English; formal and informal overseas imperialism shaped Dutch nationalism; Italy's colonies helped establish a young state and connected its governments to the people they governed (in Italy); and empires sustained Belgian and French sovereignty during the Second World War. The consensus on empire across governments in Britain and France reveals the depth of imperialistic sentiment in those two countries; in the latter, the empire survived the Popular Front and Third Republic, became a target of intense Vichy and Free French attentions, and was embraced anew by the Fourth Republic.

Considering such similarities, it might be useful to contemplate the possibility of a European colonial culture, that is how imperialism is 'a shared (Western) European experience which in many ways transgresses the particular national outlooks'.[8] To do so is to build on others such as Stefan Berger, who argues that Europe's history more and more will not to be written as a series of parallel national histories but rather as the history of a whole: Europe. 'Notions of national peculiarities and exceptionalism will fade.'[9] This is not to suggest the emergence of sameness because differences can become more intense and complexity more vital as a result of increasing uniformity, as C.A. Bayly has shown.[10] Similarity in practices and ideas may have actually heightened competition among colonising powers as each sought to distinguish itself. This volume shows that there was a great deal of 'othering' by Europeans – not just of Africans and Asians, but of other Europeans. As Gissibl and Kuitenbrouwer demonstrate, the British were objects of admiration, envy and competition in Germany and the Netherlands, and Sèbe points to the Anglophobia that fueled much of France's imperialism. Belgians not only believed they were the best of the colonising powers who had accomplished great things in central Africa where others had failed, they also feared the takeover of the Congo by Western 'others'. In Italy, Fascists viewed the conquest of Ethiopia as a sign that they had achieved success where others had not.

If the contours of French and British colonial cultures are much better known today than two decades ago, there is much to learn about the other cases addressed in this volume, not to mention Japan, Portugal,

Spain and the United States. How such popular imperialisms compare, and how concepts materialised in certain places and circulated transnationally to be appropriated elsewhere, remain issues to be explored further.

Notes

1 Nicholas Reeves, *The Power of Film Propaganda: Myth or Reality?* (London 1999), p. 241.
2 Fritz Stern, *Five Germanys I Have Known* (New York 2006), p. 114. See also Tony Judt, *Postwar: A History of Europe Since 1945* (New York 2005), pp. 804–5.
3 Marc Bloch, *The Historian's Craft*, trans. Peter Putnam (New York 1953), p. 42.
4 An early exception is Thomas August, *The Selling of the Empire: British and French Imperialist Propaganda, 1890–1940* (Westport CT 1985).
5 Herman Lebovics, *Imperialism and the Corruption of Democracies* (Durham NC 2006).
6 John Hickman, 'Orwellian rectification: popular Churchill biographies and the 1943 Bengal famine', *Studies in History*, 24, 2 (2008), pp. 235–43.
7 Joseph Schumpeter, *Imperialism and Social Classes*, trans. Heinz Norden (Oxford 1951).
8 Peo Hansen, 'European integration, European identity and the colonial connection', *European Journal of Social Theory*, 5, 4 (2002), p. 485.
9 Stefan Berger (ed.), *A Companion to Nineteenth-Century Europe, 1789–1914* (Oxford 2006), p. xxv.
10 C.A. Bayly, *The Birth of the Modern World 1780–1914: Global Connections and Comparisons* (Malden MA 2004).

INDEX